T0235176

Communications in Computer and Information Science 717

Commenced Publication in 2007
Founding and Former Series Editors:
Alfredo Cuzzocrea, Dominik Ślęzak, and Xiaokang Yang

Editorial Board

Simone Diniz Junqueira Barbosa
Pontifical Catholic University of Rio de Janeiro (PUC-Rio),
Rio de Janeiro, Brazil
Phoebe Chen
La Trobe University, Melbourne, Australia
Xiaoyong Du
Renmin University of China, Beijing, China
Joaquim Filipe
Polytechnic Institute of Setúbal, Setúbal, Portugal
Orhun Kara
TÜBİTAK BİLGEM and Middle East Technical University, Ankara, Turkey
Igor Kotenko
St. Petersburg Institute for Informatics and Automation of the Russian
Academy of Sciences, St. Petersburg, Russia
Ting Liu
Harbin Institute of Technology (HIT), Harbin, China
Krishna M. Sivalingam
Indian Institute of Technology Madras, Chennai, India
Takashi Washio
Osaka University, Osaka, Japan

More information about this series at http://www.springer.com/series/7899

Gerald Eichler · Christian Erfurth
Günter Fahrnberger (Eds.)

Innovations for Community Services

17th International Conference, I4CS 2017
Darmstadt, Germany, June 26–28, 2017
Proceedings

 Springer

Editors
Gerald Eichler
Telekom Innovation Laboratories
Deutsche Telekom AG
Darmstadt, Hessen
Germany

Günter Fahrnberger
University of Hagen
Hagen
Germany

Christian Erfurth
EAH Jena
Jena
Germany

ISSN 1865-0929 ISSN 1865-0937 (electronic)
Communications in Computer and Information Science
ISBN 978-3-319-60446-6 ISBN 978-3-319-60447-3 (eBook)
DOI 10.1007/978-3-319-60447-3

Library of Congress Control Number: 2017943014

© Springer International Publishing AG 2017
This work is subject to copyright. All rights are reserved by the Publisher, whether the whole or part of the material is concerned, specifically the rights of translation, reprinting, reuse of illustrations, recitation, broadcasting, reproduction on microfilms or in any other physical way, and transmission or information storage and retrieval, electronic adaptation, computer software, or by similar or dissimilar methodology now known or hereafter developed.
The use of general descriptive names, registered names, trademarks, service marks, etc. in this publication does not imply, even in the absence of a specific statement, that such names are exempt from the relevant protective laws and regulations and therefore free for general use.
The publisher, the authors and the editors are safe to assume that the advice and information in this book are believed to be true and accurate at the date of publication. Neither the publisher nor the authors or the editors give a warranty, express or implied, with respect to the material contained herein or for any errors or omissions that may have been made. The publisher remains neutral with regard to jurisdictional claims in published maps and institutional affiliations.

Printed on acid-free paper

This Springer imprint is published by Springer Nature
The registered company is Springer International Publishing AG
The registered company address is: Gewerbestrasse 11, 6330 Cham, Switzerland

Foreword

The International Conference on Innovations for Community Services (I4CS) celebrated its 17th anniversary in 2017. It started as the Workshop on Innovative Internet Community Systems (I2CS) in 2001 and has continued its success story under its revised name I4CS since 2014.

I2CS/I4CS has retained the custom since 2006 that it is organized in German venues on odd years and outside of Germany on even years. In accordance with this tradition, I4CS was held in Germany in 2017. The long-serving Steering Committee chair, Gerald Eichler, offered to arrange I4CS 2017 on the premises of his employer Deutsche Telekom AG in Darmstadt.

The presence of thousands of competing international conferences in the field of computer science every year has coerced the Steering Committee of I2CS/I4CS to act flexibly and, if necessary, to break with traditions in order to remain an appealing hotspot for international scientists, researchers, service providers, and vendors.

I2CS published its first proceedings in the Springer LNCS series (*Lecture Notes in Computer Science*) until 2005, followed by the GI (Gesellschaft für Informatik) and VDI (Verein Deutscher Ingenieure). I4CS commenced with IEEE (Institute of Electrical and Electronics Engineers) before it switched to Springer's CCIS series (*Communications in Computer and Information Science*) in 2016.

Another obvious transformation can be observed in the members of the Steering Committee, and, moreover, the founding members Herwig Unger and Thomas Böhme have left the Technical Program Committee.

Nonetheless, I4CS has maintained its reputation as a high-class C-conference as per the conference portal CORE at http://portal.core.edu.au/conf-ranks/?search=I4CS&by=all.

The proceedings of I4CS 2017 comprise six sections that include 12 full and two short papers out of 31 submissions. This conforms to an acceptance rate of 38.71%.

Interdisciplinary thinking is a key success factor for any community. Hence, I4CS 2017 spanned a plurality of topics, grouped into three areas: "Technology," "Applications," and "Socialization."

Technology: Distributed Architectures and Frameworks

- Infrastructure and models for community services
- Data structures and management in community systems
- Community self-organization in ad hoc environments
- Search, information retrieval, and distributed ontology
- Smart world models and big data analytics

Applications: Communities on the Move

- Social networks and open collaboration
- User-generated content for business and social life
- Recommender solutions and context awareness
- Augmented reality and location-based gaming
- Purity in Web and mobile applications

Socialization: Ambient Work and Living

- eHealth challenges and ambient-assisted living
- Intelligent transport systems and connected vehicles
- Smart energy and home control
- Internet of Things and cyber physical systems
- Security, identity, and privacy protection

Many thanks to the 22 members of the Technical Program Committee (TPC) for their valuable reviews and to Gerald Eichler for this year's organization and, therefore, the continuation of I4CS!

Apart from the Best Paper Award based on the reviews of the TPC and the Best Presentation Award chosen by evaluation of all conference participants, the Young Scientist Award, which was newly introduced in 2014, will be given again.

The 18th I4CS will take place in the middle of 2018, but its venue has not been decided yet. Hence, please regularly check the permanent conference URL http://www. i4cs-conference.org/ for more details! Applications of prospective TPC members and potential conference hosts are welcome at request@i4cs-conference.org.

June 2017   Günter Fahrnberger

Preface

Since 1997 Darmstadt (a town of about 140,000 inhabitants in Southern Hessia) has been known as the first City of Science in Germany. One fifth of the population are students of the Darmstadt Technical University (TUD), the University of Applied Sciences Darmstadt (h_da), and of other private colleges. Many scientific institutes, e.g., several Fraunhofer Society research institutes (FhG) or the Helmholtz Society for Heavy Ion Research (GSI), have their home here on the eastern edge of the Rhine Valley. The European Space Agency (ESA), the European Space Operations Control (ESOC), and the European Organization for the Exploitation of Meteorological Satellites (EUMETSAT) are Germany's hot spots for space and satellite missions.

Nevertheless, many research and innovation activities of Deutsche Telekom are concentrated in Darmstadt. The former Research and Technology Centre (FTZ) created many new innovative departments. Since 2016, these activities have been driven by the new board area Technology and Innovation (VTI). As a logical consequence, the 17th International Conference on Innovations for Community Services (I4CS 2017) was given the promising motto "Technology Inspires Innovation."

Many thanks to our former colleagues of the Telekom Innovation Laboratories (T-Labs) for hosting the 17th I4CS. The conference venue, the so-called Freiraum, creates an excellent environment for knowledge exchange among scientists, students, vendors, SMEs, and operators.

We are proud to continue the close corporation with Springer's CCIS series for publication. After a long period of publishing proceedings after the event, the I4CS Steering Committee decided to go back to publishing proceedings before the event, which allows all participants to receive their personal copy with the conference pack. I would like to thank Günter Fahrnberger, T-Mobile Austria, and Christian Erfurth, University of Applied Sciences Jena, who did a great job as proceedings chair and program chair, respectively.

June 2017

Gerald Eichler

Organization

Program Committee

Marwane Ayaida	University of Reims, France
Gilbert Babin	HEC Montréal, Canada
Ernesto William De Luca	Georg Eckert Institute – Leibniz Institute for International Textbook Research, Germany
Gerald Eichler	Telekom Innovation Laboratories, Germany
Christian Erfurth	EAH Jena, Germany
Günter Fahrnberger	University of Hagen, North Rhine-Westphalia, Germany
Hacene Fouchal	University of Reims Champagne-Ardenne, France
Michal Hodon	University of Zilina, Slovakia
Philippe Hunel	University of Antilles-Guyane
Peter Kropf	University of Neuchâtel, Switzerland
Ulrike Lechner	Universität der Bundeswehr München, Germany
Karl-Heinz Lüke	Ostfalia University of Applied Sciences, Germany
Raja Natarajan	TIFR, India
Frank Phillipson	TNO, The Netherlands
Davy Preuveneers	K.U. Leuven, Belgium
Srini Ramaswamy	ABB Inc., USA
Wilhelm Rossak	Friedrich Schiller University of Jena, Germany
Joerg Roth	Nuremberg Institute of Technology, Germany
Volkmar Schau	Friedrich Schiller University of Jena, Germany
Julian Szymanski	Gdansk University of Technology, Poland
Leendert W.M. Wienhofen	SINTEF, Norway
Ouadoudi Zytoune	Ibn Tofail University, Kénitra, Morocco

Additional Reviewers

Gros-Desormeaux, Harry
Späthe, Steffen

Contents

Infrastructure Planning

Energy Management

Spatial Guidance [Short Papers]

Data Analytics

Extracting Wikipedia Data to Enrich Spatial Information

Jörg Roth[✉]

Faculty of Computer Science,
Nuremberg Institute of Technology, Nuremberg, Germany
Joerg.Roth@th-nuernberg.de

Abstract. Freely available geo data allow a developer to create new types of remarkable services related to the user's location. Even though current geo data sources have a high coverage and quality, they do not contain all information required by new services. This is because geo data sources usually focus on object geometries and object types. Important information is often missing. As an example: city entries mainly contain the city name and border, but not the name of mayor, amount of taxes, year of foundation, number of districts etc. These data are available in online encyclopediae such as Wikipedia, but there is no obvious approach to relate both sources. Our objective was thus to create an automatic import from Wikipedia articles that describe geo objects and extract all relevant data. To extract processible values we are able to identify property types such dates, money values, powers, heights, sizes etc. This makes it possible to use these data for further computation, e.g. to search for maxima, build averages and sums or to create comparative conditions in queries.

Keywords: Geo data · Encyclopedic data · Data fusion

1 Introduction

Geo data form the foundation for different kinds of new services. Many innovative services have a relation to locations and are able to identify a user's position, display a map of friends or compute driving distances. Often, location-based services are sub-components of social services or community services.

Open Street Map (*OSM*) is a great source for geo data and enables such services. In contrast to closed geo services such as Google Maps, Open Street Map applications cannot only use pre-defined services to display maps – developers are able to create arbitrary new services as they are able to access the underlying structured geo data. All geometric information (in particular their vector representation) and non-geometric information (e.g. names, types, properties and relations to other objects) are available per object. A service developer can load the freely available geo data and import it into own formats appropriate for the respective service.

The geo data itself, however, still is incomplete for some services. This is because OSM data historically was mainly intended for map rendering. Even though contributors can assign properties to every object, many objects mainly contain a name, a type, and geometry.

© Springer International Publishing AG 2017
G. Eichler et al. (Eds.): I4CS 2017, CCIS 717, pp. 3–17, 2017.
DOI: 10.1007/978-3-319-60447-3_1

Other sources may fill this gap. As the counterpart of OSM for non-geographic data we may consider Wikipedia: an online encyclopedia and similar to OSM organized as a community project. Many objects appear in both databases, especially entries about cities, regions and countries, but also about touristic sights. Our main approach was to identify these data to enrich our geo database. We pursued the following goals:

- We want to integrate the short description of geo objects that appear in Wikipedia into our geo object database.
- We want to take over object properties from Wikipedia to our database. If these properties have numerical characteristics, we want to transfer the value and unit in a processible representation. In particular, all numerical values are mapped to a comparable format that, e.g. abstracts from the physical unit stated the Wikipedia article (e.g. miles vs. km).
- We want to index all Wikipedia texts that are related to geo objects by a text search index. Thus, we can use these words in search queries to find objects.

It was in particular not a goal to take vector geometries from Wikipedia. Even though for some objects such information is available in Wikipedia articles, we rely on the original OSM source. As a major objective, all these goals must be achieved by autonomous mechanisms that work without any user intervention. All potential decisions must be formulated as a-priori rules. Once started, the processing of many million geo objects must run in a batch manner.

In this paper, we present an import mechanism of encyclopedic data to a geo database inside the HomeRun project.

2   Related Work

We first distinguish *knowledge* from *data*. This distinction is not obvious. We here consider *knowledge* as collection of higher-level structures about an object, e.g. triples of *subject–predicate–object*. In contrast, *data* are plain values in e.g. columns of a database table. This means, extracting data follows a more traditional approach of storing objects in a table-oriented manner. Many projects that deal with Wikipedia as source try to extract *knowledge*. YAGO2 [6], e.g., is an ontology-driven project that extracts many million triples from Wikipedia, also spatial information. In contrast [1] takes OSM as source and transfers geo object information to a knowledge database. Even though a knowledge-based approach is more general and flexible, it also has to deal with the problem to understand value/unit pairs in a processible manner. In this paper, we only discuss the import of *data* that, however, can be stored in knowledge database in later stages.

Our approach deals with two data sources – geo data on the one hand and encyclopaedic facts on the other hand. Combining these data can be executed in two directions: starting from a geo object we look up the corresponding encyclopedia entry or starting from an encyclopedia entry we may look up the corresponding geo object. As our goal was to enrich an existing geo database we pursued the first direction. The geo data source Open Street Map already has a formalized structure [3]. The most important issue is: how we make use of encyclopedic data from Wikipedia to enrich existing geo data. This especially means: is there an additional usage scenario for Wikipedia articles besides presenting articles to people.

Former research deals with similar questions. We can identify two major directions: access and semantic analyses. Different former work addresses the problem of *accessing* articles [7, 21]. For a longer time, the only programmatic way was to import so called Wikipedia *dumps*. They contain all articles in the *Wikitext* format [2] that forms the basis for rendering articles in HTML. The articles themselves are structured in XML, whereas also information about the articles are stored, e.g., a classification and information about creation and modifications. The goal of access platforms was to get an API to load the deep structure of articles, sections, paragraphs and links to other articles.

Once access to articles is established, the next goal was to conduct a semantic analysis. Thus, some platforms perform basic pre-computing to simplify such analyses. E.g. the platform presented in [20] derives a list of triples (*noun-phrase relation noun-phrase*) for every article. The main goal: classify articles and detect relations between articles and the respective concepts they describe. Some approaches focus on *relatedness* between concepts and try to answer questions such as 'How related are *Cat* and *Dog*?'. This is answered using text mining or analysing links between articles [7]. In [21] further natural language processing (*NLP*) techniques are incorporated. Further work use Wikipedia meta data, in particular the article classification and links between articles to detect semantic relatedness [4, 9, 10]. In [18] the authors suggest new types of meta data (typed links and attributes) that should be contributed by article authors to support a semantic analysis.

Even though several existing work deals with automatic analyses of Wikipedia articles, they mainly either focus on the technical access or to create relations between concepts. Incorporating content into other data repositories is not intended. To try to access certain properties of entities described in Wikipedia articles and to assign these values to (geo) objects is a new approach.

3 Incorporating Wikipedia Entries to Geo Objects

The *HomeRun* project [11] has a long tradition to deal with geo data. HomeRun is a platform for low-cost development of location-based services (also small scale services). It provides a set of basic services, e.g. import of geo data from public sources, map rendering and route planning. HomeRun also supports mobile devices to execute applications, even running 'offline', i.e. with all geo data stored on the device.

The main data source currently is Open Street Map, even though the HomeRun import chain also was able to take geo data from other geo data sources, e.g. from land survey offices. Merging data with different sources already is an important topic, as some information is missing or does not have the desired quality. E.g.:

- The OSM positions are only stored in 2D without height information, i.e. only represent a projection on the Earth's surface. Our import thus adds elevation information from NASA [8].
- For redundancy reasons, borders of cities, regions, states etc. are in OSM represented as an unordered collection of lines (so-called *relations*). If a border is incomplete, it is not possible to reconstruct a ring. Thus, we additionally load borders from another source [5], if borders cannot properly be generated from OSM.

As a next step, we want to add a further source: Wikipedia. This, however, differs in many aspects from existing work: first, information is not geometric as our other sources. Second and more important: the content is primarily intended to be read by users and it is not prepared for further automatic processing.

However, some existing features are encouraging:

- There is a special tag in the OSM object structure that indicates the URL to the corresponding Wikipedia article, if available. Thus, it is not required to 'guess' a link to an article, e.g. using the object's name.
- Even though an article is like a book or book chapter structured for human readers, there are some parts that in principle can automatically be read (Fig. 1). Foremost: for many types of articles there is an *infobox* that indicates important properties as pairs of keys and values.

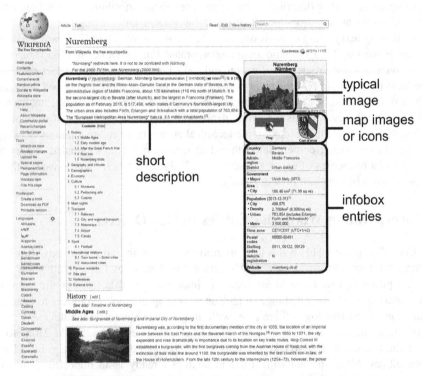

Fig. 1. Example Wikipedia article and important entries to import

- Moreover: there is a common understanding in the community, which properties are expected for a special type of article – e.g. for cities we have properties such as *Country*, *Area*, *Population* and *Population Density*.
- A typical article contains a short description of the specified object. Also, this short description can be found in the article structure.

We thus have a good chance to automatically read certain content. Our goal was to pre-process content as much as possible. E.g. if a certain property indicates a numerical value, we want to be able to use this value for computations and statistical analyses later. Thus, our mechanism must be able to understand different number formats including physical or other units. Only if numerical interpretation fails, we take the original text, but then further computation is disabled.

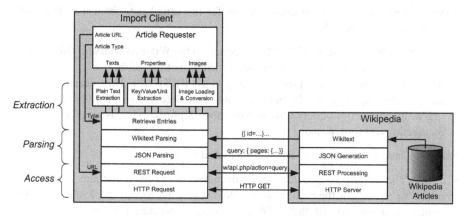

Fig. 2. Stack to access Wikipedia articles

For text mining among our geo data, we additionally add the article's plain text to our symbio-spatial search engine [16]. This engine allows to formulate complex queries that contain texts, addresses, object types but also spatial relations (e.g. *nearby a lake*). Textual queries currently only use object names and addresses, but we now are able to extend it to index entire articles. As some of these words may not represent the actual object, search words from articles get lower priorities compared to object names – however they significantly improve the search experience.

3.1   Retrieving Articles and Entries

Figure 2 shows the execution stack to get articles and article entries. The approach is based on the Wikipedia REST API [19] to get the raw articles' format in Wikitext. This API also allows writing back edited articles. Thus, it is possible to develop an own authoring environment to read, edit and write Wikipedia articles without the need to use the Web-based editing facilities offered by Wikipedia. However, for our approach, we only need to read articles from Wikipedia.

It would also be possible to load Wikipedia articles directly using HTTP with the respective URL that is, e.g., a result of a browser search. As all URLs are built in a straight-forward manner, it is very easy to generate the respective HTTP request. E.g. to get the HTML-formed article for the city of Nuremberg, the URL is https://en.wikipedia.org/wiki/Nuremberg.

However, the result is formed in HTML, thus underwent an additional step. As HTML pages both contain the page structure as well as layout definitions, it is more difficult to get the original article structure. Thus, we decided to use the REST API that provides the basic article definition. Another benefit: the API allows reading only a certain section of an article. Thus, entire processing can focus on interesting parts of the article rather then the entire text. We divide the steps to get desired article entries as follows (Fig. 2):

Access: These layers are responsible to transfer the actual data from the Wikipedia server to the requesting client:

- *HTTP*: The basis forms an HTTP GET request to the Wikipedia server. This request is always answered, even if a requested article is not available.
- *REST*: The request is structured according to the REST API. This means, the URL encodes the requested article, but also some parameters, e.g. https://en.wikipedia. org/w/api.php?action=query&titles=Nuremberg&prop=revisions&rvprop=content &rvsection=0&format=json.

Parsing: These layers read the actual content and structure:

- *JSON*: The lower layer provides JSON decoding of results. It contains information about the success of the request. If the request was not successful, JSON variables contain a description of the problem. In case of success the variable `query:` `pages` contains the requested article section.
- *Wikitext*: The article structure is then parsed using a Wikitext parser. This is because of two reasons: first, we need to know the structure to find interesting parts of the article, e.g. the infobox or the short description. As these parts are not explicitly indicated in the article document, we need to detect them using structural information. Second: we need the structure to produce plain texts or to extract property values in a later stage.

Extraction: The upper layers access entries inside the article and convert them to the required format:

- *Retrieve Entries*: Once we know a list of requested entries, we try to detect them in the article structure. The type of article passed from the Article Requester helps this component to identify significant entries.
- The loaded entries now undergo a final step that depends on the entry types. Currently we support plain text, images and pairs of key values with units.

The result entries are now ready to be stored in the geo object's data. In our case of the HomeRun database, geo objects refer to entries in a properties table that holds all non-geometric characteristics. Until now, this table only contains properties expressed by object tags in Open Street Map. Now additional properties of Wikipedia are stored there.

3.2   Retrieving and Processing Entries

Once the content and structure is parsed, we try to identify interesting entries in the article. As Wikipedia stores a plenty of different articles with different structures, this is not trivial. The problem is, even if the layout is obvious for human readers, it is not obvious for a program to identify, e.g. the short description or infobox. Some examples of misleading document structures:

- The short description is not necessarily the first text in the article. Sometimes, e.g., there is a text declaring an article is a redirect from another article.
- Sometimes the first descriptive text section is about which other articles have a similar topic. Such a text contains a lot of links to other articles that are meaningless in plain texts stored in our database.
- An infobox is usually stored as Wikitext table. However, also the table of content or some images may appear as table.

As a result, we applied a heuristic approach to identify certain entries in the article. In this approach we formulate a set of rules that have to be fulfilled in order to get the right entry in the structure tree. Some examples:

- The short description is a text (not table) that does not contain any file download link, image or table. In addition some texts must not appear in the description, e.g. '*For other uses...see...*'.
- The infobox is either the first, second or last table of the first section with two columns and a set of expected property keywords in the first column (e.g. *State, Population, Postal codes*).

Wikipedia authors make use of so-called *templates*. Templates are building blocks of Wikitext fragments that provide a basic structuring and layout. To ensure a similar look of articles, Wikipedia makes heavily use of templates for, e.g. tables of contents, disambiguation references, maps etc. The Wikipedia API reflects the usage of templates with two modes to get articles: the requester can either load an article still with templates or can load an article where all templates are replaced by their respective Wikitext fragments. The latter case is called *expanded mode*. Even though, templates would simplify to find important entries in the article, we decided to use the expanded mode, because we do not have access to the underlying template definitions and they may change without prior notice.

Once appropriate entries are detected, a type-dependent conversion is applied. For plain text entries, all Wikitext tags are removed. As it is also possible for an article author to embed HTML into Wikitext, we also have to consider HTML tags. If tags enclose references, they have to be removed. Formatting tags are removed at all. Finally, a conversion of character sets is applied to get the plain text in the desired encoding.

If the desired entry is an image, the image is loaded – usually the embedded images are represented by an URL and not embedded in Wikitext. In addition, images undergo a technical transformation regarding size, resolution and image format, to meet the requirements for the later usage (e.g. for a smart phone app or for map rendering).

3.3   Properties of Key/Value/Unit

Original geo objects imported from Open Street Map already contain properties. Even though Open Street Map allows assigning arbitrary property tags to characterize geo objects, they typically are used to

- define an object type (e.g. lake, highway, tree);
- define object names (for different purposes);
- control rendering of maps (e.g. tell if an object should not be painted at all);
- provide information for route planning (e.g. speed limits);
- provide additional information to the object's geometry;
- offer additional information about the object, e.g. opening hours, type of restaurant, parking prices.

Very often, information of the latter case is missing. This is because Open Street Map mainly is used to draw maps and maybe to support route planning – the origin of Open Street Map was to collect information about *streets*. This is also one reason why classification of geo objects from Open Street Map is very difficult [14].

Wikipedia on the other hand provides a lot of additional information, not stored in Open Street Map, e.g. population, important people, object classification, organisation, history, usage or costs. Even though the actual object geometry is exactly defined by OSM, additional geometric information can be read from Wikipedia, e.g. volumes or surface areas of barrier lakes.

The respective information may be spread over an article, thus not within reach for automatic processing. Fortunately, infoboxes as shown in Fig. 3 indicate the most important properties in tables of keys and values.

A major goal is not only to copy the pairs of key/value from the table, but to process values in such a way to enable further processing. This means:

- Keys must be mapped to a representation that allows to check for equality.
- Numbers must be transferred from their textual representation to native numbers.
- Units must be recognized and all properties of the same kind have to be mapped to the same unit in order to be comparable and to create sums of property values. E.g., units are converted between Imperial and metric units (e.g. miles to km), but also scaled to the same basic unit, e.g. m^2 to km^2.

We want to fulfil these goals, because we want to support queries such as: 'What is the average capacity of barrier lakes in Bavaria?', or 'What were the average building costs of Universities in Germany built between 1950 and 1960?', or 'What is the sum of power in Megawatts of all power plants in the North of Germany?'.

These goals are surprisingly hard to achieve, because also infoboxes are primarily intended to be read be people, not programs. Some problems, we have to face:

- Equal keys have different representations regarding upper/lower case, abbreviations or the usage of hyphens.
- Different meanings of keys may have the same texts. E.g. the German 'Land' may mean 'Country' or 'Federal State' in different articles.
- Some infoboxes are nested or have section headings. Here, a certain key is meaningless without the knowledge of the section heading. E.g. for universities, we may not only have 'employees', but also 'academic' and 'non-academic' employees. Thus, the key 'academic' solely is misleading if we do not take into account the section heading.

Gottleuba Dam	
Country	Germany
Location	Sächsische Schweiz-Osterzgebirge, Saxony
Coordinates	50°50'04"N 13°55'51"E
Construction began	1965
Opening date	1976

Dam and spillways	
Impounds	Gottleuba
Height	53.2 m (174.5 ft)
Length	327 m (1,073 ft)
Width (crest)	7 m (23 ft)
Dam volume	270,000 m³ (9,500,000 cu ft)
Spillway capacity	176 m³/s (6,215 cu ft/s)
Reservoir	
Total capacity	14.02 hm³ (11,370 acre-ft)
Catchment area	35.3 km² (13.6 sq mi)
Surface area	660,000 m² (7,104,181 sq ft)
Power station	
Type	Conventional
Installed capacity	53 KW

Fig. 3. Example of a Wikipedia infobox

- Even for numeric values, there exist several ways for textual representations. E.g. we can use blanks or ',' to separate thousands, or we can use scientific representation such as $3.5.10^6$. Small numbers can be written as words, e.g. *'none'*, *'zero'* or *'one'*.
- There exist words or letters that modify the value, e.g. 'million', or 'mio.'. Some letters, e.g. k or M are considered to be part of the physical unit, but sometimes lead to confusion. E.g. km^2 obviously does not mean thousand m^2 but $(km)^2$. The problem is even worse, as authors faulty write, e.g. 'K' instead of 'k', or m2 instead of m^2.
- Even for a certain unit, there exist multiple spellings. E.g. for monetary costs, we have '€', 'Euro', 'Eur.', and 'EUR' only for €-values.

There may be textual supplements behind the value, e.g. *'measured 2005'* or *'see below'*. We have to detect and remove these additions to get the raw unit. However, this is not trivial, as most physical units also contain letters, similar to the additional words.

To control and structure the recognition of values and units, we provide a table of keys and their values/units. Table 1 shows some of them, but the table is by far not complete. We detected 348 different keywords and assigned rules to understand the values. Besides the physical units for keys, we have lists of all spellings (and typical misspellings) of units, a list of words for value multipliers and patterns for additional texts. Moreover we have a list of typical textual expressions that actually indicate a number, e.g. *'uninhabited'* for *'Population: 0'*.

Table 1. Wikipedia properties (selection)

Property	Restrictions, variations	Numb/unit
Height, depth, elevation	Min, max, height above valley bottom, height difference, depth of reservoirs	m
Area	...of city, countries, regions	km^2
Area	...of barrier lakes, estates, parks, places	m^2
Length, width	...of barrier lakes, buildings	m
Volume, capacity	...of barrier lakes, reservoirs	m^3
Volume per time	Spillway capacity, rate of flow	m^3/s
Slice Plane, radius, circumference	...of pipes, tunnels	m^2, m resp.
Date	Start, stop of commencement, extended, start of operation, idle since, closed, demolition	date
Costs	Budget, sales, building costs	€
Building type	...of castles, walls, ruins, new buildings	–
Power	...of power plants, transformers, power storages	MW
People	Architect, builder, planer	–
Government, administration	Mayor, vice, district administrator, chair, director	–
Name	Official name, local name	–
Affiliation	State, country, region, district, city, quarter, municipality	–
Number of parts	Number of quarters, number of regions	integer
Population	...of city, region, country	integer
Density of population	...of city, region, country	$1/km^2$
People counts	Number of e.g. visitors, employees, members	integer
Address	Town hall, administration, head office	–
Keys	Official keys such as NUTS, LOCODE, AGS, IBNR, BIC	resp. format
Vehicle registration	First letters of licence plates	resp. format
Dialing codes	First digits of telephone numbers	resp. format

4 Evaluation and Sample Scenarios

4.1 Evaluation of Results

We fully implemented and integrated the approach in our HomeRun tool chain. During the import of OSM data a lot of pre-processing is performed [12] and the original data is enriched. This is required, as original OSM data has several drawbacks regarding geometry representation, route planning and classification of objects. This is an ideal point to query Wikipedia articles for geo objects.

OSM offers its data in compressed XML files – so called *planet* files. There exist sub files for continents, countries and regions. The following analysis is based on the file *Germany* from two time stamps: Nov. 2015 (1) and Jan. 2017 (2). Table 2 shows basic numbers.

Table 2. Wikipedia import statistics (OSM file Germany)

Category	Count (1)	Count (2)
Geo object statistics		
OSM objects in the file	43407661	50864433
OSM objects with Wikipedia link	71040	83169
Ratio	0.164%	0.164%
Success/Failures		
Successfully processed	56041	64781
Success ratio	78.9%	77.9%
Failed GET/JSON indicated error	3804	4178
Failed parsing Wikitext	11195	14210
Infobox properties		
Infobox properties (total count)	383266	430917
Infobox properties with value or unit error	1203	1447
Error ratio	0.31%	0.36%
Avg. infobox properties per geo object	6.84	6.65

A first observation: even tough the amount of total geo objects increased, the ratio of geo objects with Wikipedia entry remains nearly the same. It is considerably low with 0.164%. One explanation: most of the geo objects with a reference are areas with an administrative border such as cities, regions or counties. But these types of objects only represent a very small amount of geo objects in the OSM database (only 0.05%).

From the amount of geo objects with a Wikipedia link, some references could not successfully be processed, due to technical errors:

- Some accesses produce low-level errors related to HTTP GET or the JSON result does not contain a Wikipedia article. Usually the reason for this was an outdated URL in the OSM entry. Sometimes, the original page was replaced by a hub page to represent the different meanings of a term.
- A high amount of errors is a result of parsing the Wikitext content. This was because either the sources were malformed, or the Wikitext parser was not able to successfully parse the structure. Note that Wikitext may contain embedded HTML, thus can be very complex – actually the Wikitext parser must also contain an HTML parser to get the entire structure tree. The amount of parsing can be reduced using another (esp. more tolerant) parser.

The last section in Table 2 shows statistics about infobox properties. The amount of read failures is very low (0.31%). Most of them are a result of unrecognized additional texts in the value descriptions. Most of them cannot easily be solved by automatic mechanisms, as they significantly affect the interpretation of values. Some examples:

- Texts such as '*in summertime*' or '*only department...*' limit the value to certain times, locations or impose other limitations. As a result, the value cannot be used *as is*.
- Some texts indicate ranges or open intervals, e.g. '*more than*' or '*$value_1 - value_2$*'. As the distribution of values inside these intervals is not given, we cannot express this property by a single value.

The second reason for failures were typos in units (e.g. m^2 instead of m^3 for volumes). In principle, most of the problems with properties and values cannot easily be solved in the current workflow and format for Wikipedia articles, as they conflict the major goal of Wikipedia: to provide a human-readable article that may contain additional values and properties that again are interpreted by people.

Table 3 shows the distribution of Wikipedia articles to geo object types. Our classification of geo objects is a so-called *strong classification* [14] in contrast to the *weak classification* of the original OSM source.

As stated above, most geo objects with a corresponding Wikipedia article are regions with an administrative border e.g., cities. The second type of objects are those with a touristic or historic meaning such as castles, museums, monuments or touristic sights. The third type are objects related to traffic and transportation, e.g. railway stations, canals, routes or roads.

If we look at the degree of objects of a certain type that are covered by Wikipedia articles, only cities have a sufficient coverage (95.8%). For other object types the coverage is too low, for e.g., a detailed statistical analysis. However, for certain objects, an application can benefit from the additional Wikipedia entries.

Table 3. Distribution of Wikipedia articles to Geo object types (file *Germany*, Jan. 2017)

Geo object type	Objects with Wikipedia article	Total number of objects	Ratio (%)	Geo object type	Objects with Wikipedia article	Total number of objects	Ratio (%)
City	11053	11543	95.8	Canal	402	12268	3.3
County	400	557	71.8	Chur. Instit.	1179	37640	3.1
Parish	980	1413	69.4	Chapel	208	7708	2.698
Provinc. Town	1492	2410	61.9	Tower	224	8560	2.617
Castle	1483	4356	34.0	Bike Route	223	10181	2.190
District	3100	9934	31.2	Hike Route	318	20351	1.563
Suburb	1567	8913	17.6	River	4425	383797	1.153
Museum	793	6928	11.4	School (basic & sec.)	435	38121	1.141
Railway Station	731	6986	10.5	Rail Track (demount.)	303	26593	1.139
Village	7587	80879	9.4	Park	371	32873	1.129
Theater	211	2358	8.9	Graveyard	350	33290	1.051
Church	1404	18733	7.5	Wayside Cross	311	34990	0.889
Protected Landscape	283	3910	7.2	Rail Track	768	104773	0.733
Archeol. Site	486	7171	6.8	Highway	326	46007	0.709
Touristic Site	3041	52217	5.8	Pedestr. Area	265	38398	0.690
Historic. Site	1874	45999	4.1	Fed. Highway	883	153621	0.575
Monument	413	10267	4.0	Industr. Area	235	43508	0.540
Route	500	13520	3.7	Lake	1083	217195	0.499
Mountain	772	22081	3.5	Bridge	948	278986	0.340

4.2 Sample Scenarios

The imported entries are incorporated into the HomeRun database format and reside side-by-side with entries originated by Open Street Map. All HomeRun services take the required data from the HomeRun database in their respective data representation. Whereas the map rendering service *dorenda* [13] operates on the HomeRun SQL database, the route planning service *donavio* [15] first transfers the road network in an own format, specialized for high-performance graph algorithms.

The original SQL database now allows executing queries on entries from Wikipedia. E.g. if we want to get the power facility with the highest output power, we simply enter:

```
select d_id from domain_properties
where p_id=10411 and double_value=
   (select max(double_value)
     from domain_properties where p_id=10411)
```

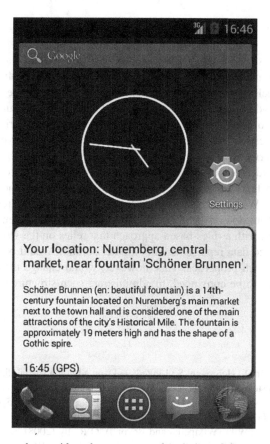

Fig. 4. Smart phone widget that presents a description of the current location

In this query, the property ID 10411 represents the Wikipedia infobox entry *'power plant capacity in Megawatts'*. The result d_id of this query is the geo object's ID. With this, it is possible to query everything known from this object e.g., its name, geometry, or further properties. As another example, we query universities with more than 40000 students:

```
select d_id from domain_properties
where p_id=11519 and int_value>40000
```

Here, the property ID 11519 represents *'number of enrolled students'*. Note that such queries are only possible, since the respective entries are taken from Wikipedia – these properties currently are not available in OSM.

As another example, we extended our *HomeRun Reverse Geocoding* framework [17]. It provides a purely textual description of the current location hat may, e.g. be read aloud by text-to-speech services of a smart phone for blind people. In the older version, it only provides a small text that summarizes city, address, nearby places or important sights. With our new approach, we are able also to print the short description from Wikipedia of the most important geo object in the nearer area (Fig. 4).

5   Conclusions

In this paper we presented an approach to import data from Wikipedia to enrich our geo data inside the HomeRun project. The import mechanism was fully established and integrated to HomeRun's import tool chain. The general results are encouraging: we now get a lot of additional properties as processible value with unit, currently not available in the geo data source. In addition, we get a short description and typical images of the corresponding object. We can use these entries for different types of applications and services.

It causes considerable efforts to get processible properties from texts. This is because Wikipedia texts are not intended for this type of usage. The problem is very similar to semantic Web approaches: if sources are primarily prepared to be rendered for users, it is difficult to convert them into machine readable content afterwards. We solved this problem with a rules-based approach that relies on the *strong classification* of the HomeRun geo data representation. Another solution would be to extend article structures to store such properties. This, however, would change the overall goal and article authors have to be convinced, to administrate such structures.

References

1. Auer, S., Lehmann, J., Hellmann, S.: LinkedGeoData: adding a spatial dimension to the web of data. In: Bernstein, A., Karger, D.R., Heath, T., Feigenbaum, L., Maynard, D., Motta, E., Thirunarayan, K. (eds.) ISWC 2009. LNCS, vol. 5823, pp. 731–746. Springer, Heidelberg (2009). doi:10.1007/978-3-642-04930-9_46
2. Barrett, D.J.: MediaWiki (Wikipedia and Beyond), O'Reilly (2008)
3. Bennett, J.: OpenStreetMap. Packt Publishing, Birmingham (2010)

4. Gabrilovich, E., Markovitch, S.: Computing semantic relatedness using Wikipedia-based explicit semantic analysis. In: Proceedings of the 20th International Joint Conference on Artificial Intelligence (IJCAI 2007), Hyderabad, India, 6–12 January 2007, pp. 1606–1611 (2007)

5. Global Administrative Areas. http://gadm.org/

6. Hoffart, J., Suchanek, F.M., Berberich, K., Weikum, G.: YAGO2: a spatially and temporally enhanced knowledge base from Wikipedia. Artif. Intell. **194**, 28–61 (2013)

7. Milne, D., Witten, I.H.: An open-source toolkit for mining Wikipedia. Artif. Intell. **194** (2013), 222–239 (2013). Elsevier

8. NASA: Advanced Spaceborne Thermal Emission and Reflection Radiometer (ASTER). http://asterweb.jpl.nasa.gov/

9. Ponzetto, S.P., Strube, M.: Deriving a large scale taxonomy from Wikipedia. In: AAAI 2007 Proceedings of the 22nd National Conference on Artificial Intelligence - Volume 2, 22–26 July 2007, Vancouver, British Columbia, pp. 1440–1445 (2007)

10. Prato, A., Ronchetti, M.: Using Wikipedia as a reference for extracting semantic information from a text. In: Third International Conference on Advances in Semantic Processing, SEMAPRO 2009, 11–16 October 2009, Sliema, Malta, pp. 56–61 (2009)

11. Roth, J.: Die HomeRun-Plattform für ortsbezogene Dienste außerhalb des Massenmarktes. In: Zipf, A., Lanig, S., Bauer, M. (eds.) 6. GI/ITG KuVS Workshop Location Based Services and Applications, Heidelberger Geographische Bausteine Heft 18, 2010 (2010). (in German)

12. Roth, J.: Übernahme von Geodatenbeständen aus Open Street Map und Bereitstellung einer effizienten Zugriffsmöglichkeit für ortsbezogene Dienste, Praxis der Informationsverarbeitung und Kommunikation (PIK), vol. 13, no. 4 (2010). (in German)

13. Roth, J.: Combining symbolic and spatial exploratory search – the homerun explorer. In: Innovative Internet Computing Systems (I2CS), Hagen, 19–21 June 2013, Fortschritt-Berichte VDI, Reihe, vol. 10, no. 826, pp. 94–108 (2013)

14. Roth, J.: From weak to strong geo object classification. In: Schau, V., Eichler, G., Roth, J. (eds.) Proceedings of the 10th Workshop Location-Based Application and Services (LBAS) 16–17 September 2013, University of Jena, Germany, Logos Verlag Berlin, pp. 3–12 (2014)

15. Roth, J.: Predicting route targets based on optimality considerations. In: International Conference on Innovations for Community Services (I4CS), Reims (France) 4–6 June 2014, pp. 61–68. IEEE Xplore (2015)

16. Roth, J.: Fast spatio-symbolic searching in huge geo databases. In: Proceedings of the 11th Workshop Location-Based application and Services (LBAS), 18–19 September 2014, Telekom Innovation Laboratories, Darmstadt, Germany, Logos Verlag (2015)

17. Roth, J.: Generating meaningful location descriptions. In: International Conference on Innovations for Community Services (I4CS), 8–10 July 2015, Nuremberg (Germany), pp. 30–37. IEEE Xplore (2015)

18. Völkel, M., Krötzsch, M., Vrandecic, D., Haller, H., Studer, R.: Semantic Wikipedia. In: Proceedings of the 15th International Conference on World Wide Web (WWW 2006), 23–26 May 2006, Edinburgh, Scotland, pp. 585–594 (2006)

19. Wikipedia 2017: MediaWiki action API. https://www.mediawiki.org/wiki/API:Main_page/en

20. Wu, F., Weld, D.S.: Open information extraction using Wikipedia. In: Proceedings of the 48th Annual Meeting of the Association for Computational Linguistics, Uppsala, Sweden, 11–16 July 2010, pp. 118–127 (2010)

21. Zesch, T., Müller, C., Gurevych, I.: Extracting lexical semantic knowledge from Wikipedia and Wiktionary. In: Proceedings of the Sixth International Conference on Language Resources and Evaluation (LREC 2008), 28–30 May 2008, Marrakech, Morocco (2008)

Towards the Automatic Sentiment Analysis of German News and Forum Documents

Andreas Lommatzsch[✉], Florian Bütow, Danuta Ploch, and Sahin Albayrak

Technische Universität Berlin, FG AOT, Ernst-Reuter-Platz 7,
10587 Berlin, Germany
{andreas.lommatzsch,danuta.ploch,sahin.albayrak}@dai-labor.de,
florian.buetow@campus.tu-berlin.de
http://www.aot.tu-berlin.de/

Abstract. The fully automated sentiment analysis on large text collections is an important task in many applications scenarios. The sentiment analysis is a challenging task due to the domain-specific language style and the variety of sentiment indicators. The basis for learning powerful sentiment classifiers are annotated datasets, but for many domains and especially with non-English texts hardly any datasets exist. In order to support the development of sentiment classifiers, we have created two corpora: The first corpus is build based on German news articles. Although news articles should be objective, they often excite subjective emotions. The second corpus consists of annotated messages from a German telecommunication forum. In this paper we describe the process of creating the corpora and discuss our approach for tracing sentiment values, defining clear rules for assigning sentiments scores. Given the corpora we train classifiers that yields good classification results and establish valuable baselines for sentiment analysis. We compare the learned classification strategies and discuss how the approaches can be transferred to new scenarios.

1 Introduction

With the growing amount of textual content on the internet, the fast and efficient processing of new information is crucial in many application scenarios. Advanced machine learning approaches have been applied to address this issue. An important research topic is the automated sentiment analysis of texts. For example, press relations departments need text-mining algorithms for monitoring how institutions or companies are perceived in the media; customer relation departments need to know how the products and services offered by a company are perceived. Moreover, sentiment analysis can be used for determining engaging topics and mining the relevance of terms. Most sentiment analysis approaches use supervised machine learning algorithms or expert-defined lexicons.

The automated sentiment analysis is a challenging task due to the fact that sentiment can be expressed in several different ways and the used vocabulary highly depends on the specific scenario. Typically, the definition for positive

© Springer International Publishing AG 2017
G. Eichler et al. (Eds.): I4CS 2017, CCIS 717, pp. 18–33, 2017.
DOI: 10.1007/978-3-319-60447-3_2

and negative sentiments must consider the intentions of the authors as well as the expectations of the audience ("readers"). In this paper we explain in two different scenarios how to create suitable corpora ("datasets") enabling supervised machine learning approaches for the task of sentiment analysis based on labeled datasets. The paper describes the process of creating the corpora and the scenario-dependent criteria for annotating the texts. Subsequently, the properties of the created corpora as well as different baseline classification algorithms are discussed.

The analyzed application scenarios are as follows: First, we explain our corpus tailored for the automatic sentiment analysis of German news articles. Our dataset consists of sentences randomly extracted from German news articles and their corresponding sentiment annotations. The scenario has been defined with respect to the requirements of a press-relation department.

The second part describes the creation of a corpora consisting of messages of a German discussion forum that focuses on telecommunication related devices and services. The automated sentiment analysis has the goal to detect discontented users. The sentiment classifier enables customer relation departments to act more quickly and to improve user satisfaction.

The remaining paper is structured as follows. In Sect. 2, we discuss the challenges in creating corpora for the automated sentiment analysis and explain the scenario-specific requirements. In Sect. 3 we analyze existing corpora and their characteristics. Section 4 describes the creation of the German News corpus in detail. The section discusses the statistics and the experiences in building a classifier based on the created corpus. Section 5 describes the creation of the forum corpus in detail and explains the performance of the learned classifiers. Finally, we present a conclusion in Sect. 6 and discuss ideas for further improving the sentiment classifiers.

2   Corpus Requirements

In order to learn a sentiment classifier for texts, an appropriate dataset is required. When selecting or creating a dataset, the following aspects must be considered:

- How well do the corpus elements correspond with the content of the use case with respect to natural language and domain?
- On which layer of abstraction should the text be annotated for the use case (e.g. phrase-layer, sentence-layer, paragraph-layer, or document-layer)?
- Do the annotation values match the objectives of the scenario (e.g. positive & negative or positive & neutral & negative)?
- Which definition of a sentiment and polarity should the corpus follow?

In this paper we analyze two scenarios:

(1) We discuss the task of learning a sentiment classifier tailored to the needs of a press relationship department of major German university. The classifier should support news articles from various sources. The sentiment classification of news articles is especially challenging because news articles tend to be objective

and avoid strong emotional words. This makes the classification of news articles more difficult compared to the analysis of colloquial language used in tweets or product reviews.

(2) We discuss the task of learning a sentiment classifier tailored to analysis of the discussion boards of a big German telecommunication company. The main challenge in the scenario is that almost all messages are related to problems or questions; but users may describe problems in a friendly, objective style. Thus, the definition of the sentiment in this scenario is focused on the style and does not consider the described problem. Additional challenges consist in the colloquial language and a big number of spelling mistakes characteristic for user-generated content.

Analyzing the specific properties of both scenarios, we find that requirements with respect to sentiment analysis differ a lot.

(1) News articles are typically longer texts reporting about an event or a specific incident ("news"). The automated sentiment analysis should not only classify complete articles, but also support the exploration of subjective "hotspots" in texts. This requires a sentiment analysis of single sentences and a corpus annotated on this layer that enables us to apply supervised methods. Simply annotating whether a sentence is either neutral or subjective is insufficient because the polarity (positive or negative) of a piece of text is essential for tracking trends in the perception of topics and named entities in the media. Therefore, we propose creating a corpus with three sentiment labels: positive, negative and neutral. We favor a sentiment definition that also considers the discussed topics and that allows human annotators to imply world knowledge during the annotation process. The sentiment annotations should reflect how the topics are perceived in the society in general in order to be able to annotate topic polarity within apparently objective sentences.

(2) Messages in discussion forums tend to come in letter-like forms with salutation and closing. The main part consists of the problem description and a personal judgment. The sentiment is sometimes explicitly (e.g. "I am upset about the answer") or indirectly expressed by rhetorical questions ("do I have to wait for a year for getting a response?"). In order to understand the sentiment, the context is important. That is why the sentiment analysis cannot be done on word level or sentence level in this scenario. The sentiment analysis should consider the complete message having a focus on the intention of the user, giving only a low weight to (often very formal) opening and closing (flowering) phrases. In order to enable the comparison of the created corpus based on forum messages with the German news corpus, we annotate the forum corpus with the same three sentiment labels: POSITIVE, NEGATIVE and NEUTRAL. Since the forum focuses on the questions and problems reported by users, we expect a small number of positive messages; but we want to use an annotation scheme similar to the German news dataset.

Both analyzed scenarios have specific challenges and requirements highly depending on the domain and the use case. Before we present the process of creating the corpora in detail, we review existing research and discuss how this work is related to the state of the art.

3   Analysis of Available Corpora

A requirement for learning sentiment classifiers are adequate corpora. In order to apply supervised machine learning approaches the corpus must provide texts annotated with a sentiment label ("class label"). Machine Learning approaches analyze the texts and extract patterns characteristic for the classes.

Corpora developed for sentiment classification highly depend on the language and the specific application scenario. There are very few freely distributed sentiment analysis corpora created from German texts.

German News Corpus. Two popular German corpora for sentiment analysis are the PRESSRELATIONS dataset [10] and the MLSA corpus [5]. The PRESS-RELATIONS dataset focuses on articles regarding German political parties, making it more suitable in sentiment classification for politics. It contains 617 news articles with 1,521 annotated statements using numeric sentiment scores between −1 and 1. The statements are usually between one and four sentences long [10].

The MLSA corpus covers a wide spectrum of topics and uses a multi-layered approach. It consists of 270 sentences, each of them annotated on the layers: sentences (layer 1), words and phrases (layer 2) and events and expressions (layer 3). Each layer has been annotated by multiple annotators, whose annotations were then combined into inter-annotator agreement measures. The sentiment definition used by MLSA is a reasonable basis for annotating objective journalistic texts, since they consider topic polarity within objective sentences.

Corpora for the Sentiment Analysis of Forum Messages. Forums allow users to discuss all types of questions. User-generated content tends to be emotional; thus forum messages are an interesting source for sentiment analysis. Ali et al. [1] analyze positive and negative opinions in a health-related forum. They annotated 607 posts using three classes (POSITIVE, NEGATIVE, and NEUTRAL). Based on the annotated corpus, lexicon-based features as well as rules-based features have been derived. The research shows that classification precision depends on the class. Domain-optimized classifiers outperform baseline algorithms such as Naive Bayes or Support Vector Machine (SVM).

Bosco et al. [3] investigate sentiments and irony in online political discussions. The research discusses how to develop corpora for mining and analyzing opinions and sentiments in social media.

Boland et al. [6] created a German text corpus for sentiment analysis that contains sentence-wise annotations of product reviews from six categories including "Mobile", "Tablet" and "Smartphone" that all are marked as positive, negative, mixed (positive and negative) or neutral. Still, the domain differs from our scenario. Although users write their opinion about technical devices, they do not report concrete problems with them and do not ask questions. The aim of reviews is rather to assess the overall performance of the products, and in contrast to a forum message, a review is more informative and less personal.

All presented datasets do not completely fulfill the requirements of our scenarios in terms of domain and size. That is the reason for us to create new datasets tailored for learning classifiers. The corpora are optimized for the analysis of sentiments in German news and forum texts. Nevertheless, we take the characteristics of existing datasets into account as basis for creating new datasets.

4 Creating the German News Corpus

We analyze the scenario of analyzing the sentiment of German news articles. In order to apply a machine learning approach a corpus is needed matching the specific requirements of the scenario. Since the analysis of already existing corpora has shown, that no suitable dataset for our scenario exists, we create a new corpus. We identify the following necessary steps for the annotation process which include:

- Deciding on a sentiment definition and formulating detailed annotator instructions.
- Choosing a range of possible annotation values.
- Deciding on a document source, the corpus alignment, and the classification target domains.
- Annotating the documents based on one or multiple annotator scores.

In the following paragraphs we present our sentiment definition and describe the corpus creation procedure. Finally we give a short overview of the created corpus. To avoid discrepancies between our corpus and the target classification domain, we use news articles that were previously crawled by a press review software for university-related news in German.

4.1 Sentiment Definition and Annotation Procedure

We annotate all dataset items using a 3-value scale, distinguishing between negative, neutral and positive sentences. This annotation scheme enables us to learn a classifier separating both neutral vs. polar as well as positive vs. negative sentences. This is important because the identification of polar text in journalistic articles is an especially challenging task. For the exact definition when to assign what sentiment label, we applied the categorization presented in the MLSA corpus paper [5]. Clematide et al. discern subjective and objective texts. The authors note that objectively written texts may also contain sentiments, giving the example of a sentence that talks about rising unemployment. According to the paper the sentence is negative, since a rising unemployment is normally considered as negative by readers [5].

Figure 1 shows the steps of the annotation process. We annotate randomly selected sentences from news articles. This ensures that neutral and polar sentences are annotated to result in a realistic term distribution. The occurrence of subjective and objective as well as neutral and polar sentences is the basis for learning good classifiers in the news domain. In general, polar sentences are hard to find in news articles, if only subjective statements are considered. However,

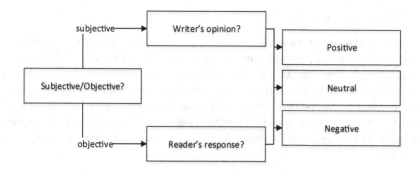

Fig. 1. The annotation procedure considers the writer's as well as the reader's viewpoints.

an institution or company often mentioned in sentences with negative topics (such as strikes or quality problems) is perceived negatively and might get a bad reputation. Even though, the sentences might be objective, a polarity in the perceived sentiments is interesting to find. Therefore, this should be reflected in the annotated corpus. Our sentiment definition relies on the polarity of the topic for the average reader, if the author writes in an objective style. There is another dimension to it, being the cultural or political background and personal opinions of a reader [5], which differ from person to person. For simplicity we assume there is a general consensus for many concepts and topics about their polarity.

In the first phase of the annotation, the sentences are classified by three expert annotators who all work on a separate subset of the extracted documents. After this initial phase, one of the annotators reviews the whole corpus to ensure consistency and to increase quality within the corpus. Apart from the already mentioned challenges, several discoveries were addressed in the review process.

Depending on the algorithms used for classification, a specific problem arises when annotating. Pang et al. identified sentences that mostly comprise positive words but are actually negative or vice versa [7]. Humans understand these sentences easily but they are difficult to handle by bag-of-words approaches. Such sentences may be unsuitable for optimizing the classifier for a particular scenario. In order to create a strongly tailored corpus, sentences from the text source may have to be excluded. In our case, we re-evaluated the corpus and deleted the corresponding sentences.

After the first phase of the annotation process the corpus contained only a relatively small fraction of polar sentences, because news articles are usually objective. In order to slightly attenuate the strong bias and to give the classifier additional data to judge polar sentences, additional polar sentences were added in a second annotation phase.

4.2   Corpus Statistics

The result of the annotation procedure is a corpus having a class distribution heavily leaning towards neutral sentences (see Fig. 2). With 2,369 sentences, it is also much larger than the MLSA corpus [5] and provides a source for a domain that is rarely covered by German corpora. Since the bias in the sentiment scores is created by the bias in the crawled texts, it is an interesting question whether this is actually useful for very specific classification models. From the large number of sentences it can be inferred that this bias applies to the domain of the texts as a whole.

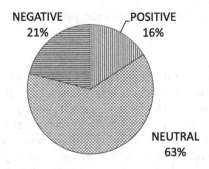

Fig. 2. German news corpus class distribution

4.3   Learning and Evaluating Sentiment Classifiers

Based on the created corpus we learn a classifier and evaluate the classifier using cross-validation.

Setup. We use the Weka machine learning framework [11] to learn a classifier based on our dataset. We choose the Multinomial Naive Bayes classifier and evaluate our model applying 10-fold cross-validation. In order to calculate the feature vectors for the sentences we use bigrams, single word tokens, a customized stop words list and the German snowball stemmer.

Results. We evaluate the classifiers using 10-fold cross-validation on the corpus. In order to get a better understanding of the performance of the Multinomial Naive Bayes classifier, we compare the strategy with a ZEROR classifier ("baseline"). ZEROR classifies every item as the class with the highest number of items in the training set. Since the neutral sentences form the majority of the sentences with 63.3%, we conduct further tests with a smaller subset of the corpus. We consider only a sample of neutral sentences to compensate for the imbalance compared to positive sentences; a class proportion of 2.5:1 is used. This does not mean the model should necessarily be created from a subset of the corpus, but it shows the effect of the bias towards the dominant class in the corpus on the evaluation results.

Table 1. Baseline comparison complete corpus [4]

	Multinomial NB			ZeroR (Baseline)		
	Negative	Neutral	Positive	Negative	Neutral	Positive
Precision	67.7%	76.3%	74.1%	-	63.3%	-
Recall	51.5%	90.3%	43.2%	0.0%	100.0%	0.0%
Accuracy	74.8%			63.3%		

Table 2. Baseline comparison 2.5:1 corpus [4]

	Multinomial NB			ZeroR (Baseline)		
	Negative	Neutral	Positive	Negative	Neutral	Positive
Precision	71.0%	70.0%	73.0%	-	52.0%	-
Recall	60.4%	85.8%	45.9%	0.0%	100.0%	0.0%
Accuracy	70.6%			52.0%		

The evaluation results (Table 1) show that baseline ZEROR classifier reaches an overall accuracy of 63.3%. This can be explained by the bias towards neutral sentences in the dataset. The Multinomial Naive Bayes classifier considerably outperforms the baseline and provides good classification results. After balancing the classes in the dataset (reducing the number of neutral sentences in the corpus), the ZEROR baseline drops (see Table 2). The classification accuracy of the Multinomial Naive Bayes drops slightly; the change is much smaller than the changes observed for the ZEROR classifier. Another interesting change is the improved recall of the polar classes with Multinomial Naive Bayes, especially of the negative class. In general, the recall of negative sentences is higher than the recall of positive sentences, with and without balancing. Possible reasons for this are the slightly smaller number of the positive instances in the corpus and the higher variance in the positive sentences.

4.4 Classifier Comparisons and Discussion

The analyzed scenario and the domain-specific bias have a big influence on the learned classifiers and the observed classification accuracy.

Optimizing the Corpus and the Learning Procedure. The use of the full corpus provides the best results in terms of accuracy. This shows that a bias has a positive influence on the overall accuracy when the same bias exists in the documents to be classified. This can be explained by the fact that the Multinomial Naive Bayes and other classifiers are more likely to classify towards that bias. If the recall of the less prominent classes is too small, one has to consider alleviating this bias. For future work, we plan analyzing whether this still applies when balancing is completely done by annotating new documents for the smaller classes instead of removing parts of the most prominent class from the corpus.

Renni et al. consider a bias based in the training set a problem in the traditional Naive Bayes classification [9]. Different applications may have different requirements in terms of recall and precision of each individual class. Thus, the bias may help improving the classification accuracy by integrating domain specific knowledge. In order to profit from the bias, the training data must be taken from the same domain or source as the test data to ensure the matching class distribution.

It could be argued that models performing well on the test set should be able to classify any sentence correctly with a good probability. Still, in our tests the overall accuracy dropped when cutting away larger parts of the instances assigned to the neutral class. This suggests that it makes sense to use a bias in the sentiment classification. Excluding sentences from the corpus would reduce the total corpus size and would require additionally annotated sentences for the smaller classes. It should also be noted that there can be other reasons to apply a bias not discussed here, one example being that certain decisions are especially costly.

Comparison with Existing Corpora. In a 3-fold cross validation with a corpus consisting of positive and negative movie reviews, Pang et al. achieved up to 81.5% classification accuracy [7]. While our results are slightly lower, we argue that there are several factors in our setup that pose new challenges [4]. Pang et al. only consider 2 classes (positive and negative reviews) in their evaluation [7]. We also consider the news domain to be at least as difficult to classify as movie reviews by the nature of the texts. News articles contain much less easily identifiable strong words that state opinions than reviews. Our sentiment definition that takes an author's sentiment as well as the reader reaction into account may also lead to more complicated classification scenarios and therefore lower accuracy. Another difference between our setups is that their results cannot be traced back to specific hotspots in a document, since Pang et al. do not split documents to the sentence level [7]. Lastly, it has to be noted that the corpus can be used with more sophisticated classification algorithms and feature selection to improve the accuracy while still relying on the same data.

5   Creating the German Forum Corpus

In addition to the corpus based on news document, we created a corpus consisting of messages extracted from a German discussion forum focused on telecommunication topics. The forum is mainly used by persons who have problems with the telecommunication services or questions related to devices offered by a major German telecommunication company.

The sentiment analysis in the telecommunication forum is important for improving the customer satisfaction and for the efficient detection of problems with devices and services. In contrast to the news articles created by professional journalists, the messages in the forum are created by "regular" users. Thus, the analyzed messages are characterized by informal language and (partially) explicit sentiment statements.

5.1 Criteria for Labeling the Corpus

In the analyzed scenario, users typically describe concrete problems and ask other users for support or suggestions. The messages in the forum are often written in a personal, emotional style. Thus, the messages related to unpleasant problems may contain an explicit sentiment statement. Like news articles also forum messages may express sentiments implicitly. Apparently objective messages (like "Do I have to wait for a year for getting a response?") show well the intention of the writer when including common sense for the interpretation of the message. For the creation of the Forum corpus we take both into consideration, explicit and implicit sentiments and use a three-level annotation scale:

1. We annotate messages as POSITVE if users want to say thanks to friendly employers or praise the good service quality (e.g. increased free data volume).
2. Messages are labeled as NEUTRAL if users ask questions in an objective way (e.g. "How do I block a specific telephone number"). This means, that the fact-focused description of a problem is labeled as NEUTRAL even though the message is related to a problem.
3. We label messages as NEGATIVE, if users complain about products or services in an emotional way. Indicators for a negative sentiment are the use of emotional words, the frequent use of exclamation marks and sentences explicitly containing a negative sentiment (e.g. "I am very angry").

The sentiment annotation considers the overall sentiment of a message. This means that salutation and complimentary close have only a very low influence on the sentiment, since even angry users may try to ensure a minimum level of politeness.

5.2 Forum and Corpus Statistics

The created corpus consists of 1,000 messages crawled from the telecommunication forum in December 2016 and January 2017. The analyzed forum is organized in threads each typically starting with a question or a problem description. The subsequent messages in the thread are comments from users and employees of the company typically providing advice or hints for tackling the described problem. Since the main use case in the analyzed scenario is the detection of arising problems, we only analyze the first message of each thread. Posts having a negative sentiment often result in "vulgar", fruitless discussion. The automatic sentiment analysis enables the fast intervention and is the basis for improving the customer satisfaction.

In contrast to the German news corpus, we annotate the forum corpus on the message level. This is due to the observation, that typically several sentences are needed for deriving the sentiment. The messages in the dataset typically consist of 2–6 sentences (∅5 sentences) having in average 71 words. The properties of the annotated messages are shown in Table 3.

The distribution of the assigned annotations in the dataset is imbalanced. Figure 3 shows that 84% of the messages are annotated as NEUTRAL. This means

Table 3. The table lists the text message characteristics of the German Forum dataset.

Text message property	Average	Median
Number of sentences	5.4	4
Number of words	70.8	49
Number of words excluding stop words	51.9	42
Number of distinct stems (excluding stop words)	32.4	25

that the majority of analyzed forum messages are formulated in a non-emotional style. Only 1% of the messages are annotated as POSITIVE. This very small number can be explained by the fact that we only analyzed the first message of each forum thread: Only very few users start a new thread for compliment the forum employers.

Fifteen percent of the analyzed messages have a negative sentiment. The number of messages in a negative sentiment is rather small with respect to the total number of messages. This shows that the majority of users describes questions in an objective way without negative emotions.

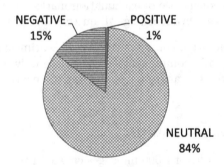

Fig. 3. The class distribution in the Forum corpus

5.3 Sentiment Classification and Evaluation

We analyze different classification approaches and evaluate the classifiers based on the created corpus. At first we test classifiers based on expert-defined rules. Subsequently, we train a Multi-Nominal Naive Bayes classifier using the Weka machine learning framework.

Classification Based on Expert-Defined Rules. We analyze static, rule-based approaches tailored to the specific characteristics of the application scenario. The rules are expert-defined and not explicitly trained on the corpus.

Punctuation Mark-Based Classifier. For automatically classifying the text in the corpus, we start with a **punctuation mark-based approach**. The idea behind the approach is that emotional and (in particular) angry people extensively use exclamation marks and sequences of questions marks. Thus, the numbers of "emotional" punctuation marks seems to be a promising indicator for identifying messages in a negative sentiment.

Due to the small number of positive messages in the created corpus, the defined classifier only considers the classes NEUTRAL and NEGATIVE. The classifier extracts all sequences of exclamation marks and questions marks. All sequences containing at least one exclamation mark are counted and weighted by the length of the sequence. In order to compute a score, the weights are summed up. If the score is above a threshold the message is classified as NEGATIVE; otherwise as NEUTRAL. We use the threshold 2 maximizing the F1 score for the class NEGATIVE.

The classification performance is presented in Table 4. The results show that sequences of exclamation marks are valuable indicators for detecting angry users; the classifier has a reasonable precision. The low recall shows that exclamation marks are only used in a small fraction of the negatively labeled messages. Overall, the exclamation mark-based classifier can be an initial starting point for the sentiment classification. In order to improve the classification accuracy it should be combined with alternative approaches.

Term-Based Classifier. In addition to the punctuation-based classification approach, we implement a classifier based expert-defined terms ("keywords") and phrases. Therefor a set of 45 emotional words and phrases (indicating a negative sentiment) have been defined. The classifier assigns the label NEGATIVE if at least one of the words or phrases has been used in a message[1].

The classification accuracy is shown in Table 4. Overall, the classification precision is good and outperforms the punctuation mark-based classifier. Analyzing the reasons for the measured performance, we have to keep in mind, that the classifier is highly optimized for the scenario; thus the classifier tends to overfit the dataset. Moreover, the classifier relies on the occurrence of single words resulting in volatile classification results.

Nevertheless, the results show that the term-based approach tailored to the vocabulary of the specific scenario reaches a high classification accuracy.

SentiWS-Based Classifier. In order to compare the term-based approach with existing approaches, we use the SentiWS corpus [8] for building a classifier. The SentiWS corpus provides 1,650 positive entries and 1,818 negative entries. Each entry consists of a weight and the related surface forms. We classify the forum messages by computing the average sentiments score of the words (part of the SentiWS corpus). Messages having a score above a threshold (0) are classified as NEUTRAL; messages having a score below the threshold are classified

---

[1] Keyword/phase set: abgespeist, abzocken, ärgere, ärgerlich, arsch, beschwerde, blöd, desaster, die nase voll, dumm, dümmer, enttäuscht, ex-kunde, frechheit, frustriert, grottig, hinhalten, hohn, idiot, kann doch nicht so schwer sein, katastrophe, minderwertigste, nervt, nicht kapiert, opfer, rausnehmen, reklamiert, schämen, schnauze, scheiss, schlimmer, schuld, teufel, unfassbar, unzufrieden, verärgert, vergebens, versagt, verschlimmbesserung, verschonen, verschont, vertrösten, verzweifeln, wird mir schlecht.

as negative. The threshold 0 maximizes the F1 score for the class NEGATIVE. Due to the very small number of messages labeled as POSITIVE, we implement the classifier so that only the labels neutral and negative are predicted.

The evaluation results show a lower performance of the classifier (with respect to both accuracy and recall of negative messages) compared with the other classifiers (cf. Table 4). Reasons for the low performance are that the SentiWS corpus does not match the specific properties of the forum. Moreover, the users in the forum often use polite salutations even if the message has a negative sentiment. Averaging the sentiment scores over the complete message does not seem to be an adequate approach in the forum scenario.

Table 4. Comparison of the different static classifiers

	Keyword-based		Punctuation mark-based		SentiWS-based	
	Negative	Neutral	Negative	Neutral	Negative	Neutral
Precision	62.7%	96.1%	50.0%	87.6%	21.6%	87.5%
Recall	62.7%	97.0%	27.2%	94.5%	50.3%	67.4%
Accuracy	93.7%		84.6%		64.9%	

Classification Applying Machine Learning. We use the Weka machine learning framework [11] to learn a classifier based on our dataset. We choose the Multi-nominal Naive Bayes classifier and evaluate our model applying 10-fold cross-validation. In order to calculate the feature vectors we use single word tokens, a default German stop word set[2] and the German snowball stemmer.

Results. The results (cf. Table 5) have been achieved using 10-fold cross-validation on the corpus. The Naive Bayes Classifier performs only slightly better than the baseline recommender (ZEROR). This shows that single words are only weak features for predicting the sentiment. We analyze the terms that have the highest impact in the learned classifier. The terms having the highest weight for identifying messages labeled as NEGATIVE are: "hotline", "wait", "week", and "long". This indicates that messages with a negative sentiment are often related to long response times (users must wait for weeks) and to problems with the hotline.

Nevertheless, the sentiment detection is challenging. Most messages are written in an objective style. Even messages labeled as NEGATIVE often contain a neutral problem description. Thus, the analysis on message level might not give enough weight to the emotional sentences. An annotation on sentence level could address this issue.

Another challenge in the analyzed dataset is the strong bias towards messages labeled as NEUTRAL. Due to the limited size of the dataset, the number of training samples for the rare classes (POSITIVE, NEGATIVE) is rather small. In order to address this issue, we will extend the corpus with additional messages.

---

[2] c.f. https://lucene.apache.org/core/6_2_0/analyzers-common.

Table 5. Comparison of the classification strategies learned on the Forum corpus evaluated using 10-fold cross-validation.

	Multinominal Naive Bayes			ZeroR (Baseline)		
	Negative	Neutral	Positive	Negative	Neutral	Positive
Precision	60.3%	91.0%	33.3%	-	63.3%	-
Recall	49.7%	94.3%	12.5%	0.0%	100.0%	0.0%
Accuracy	87.1%			84.5%		

5.4 Discussion

The comparison of the different classification approaches shows that the sentiment classification is a challenging task. Overall, the term-based classifiers performed best. Due to the specific characteristics of the scenario, the term-based classifiers must be optimized to the analyzed use-case. Classifiers build based on documents from other domains (e.g. the SentiWS classifier) show a significantly lower accuracy.

The presented German sentiment forum dataset has a strong bias towards NEUTRAL messages. The number of messages having a positive sentiment is so small that not sufficient training examples exist for learning rules how to identify positive messages.

Overall, the most messages in the analyzed forum are written in a polite, objective style. The automatic detection of messages having a NEGATIVE sentiment is hard. Since the dataset is labeled on message layer, the extraction of the discriminating terms and phrases is an additional challenge. Due to the specific vocabulary and user habits in the forum, classifiers must be optimized. In the analyzed use case the detection of upset, annoyed users is one important task (measured based on the recall for the class NEGATIVE). The analyzed classifiers show, that keyword-based algorithms are a promising starting point for further improvements.

As future work, increasing the corpus size, additional text analysis methods as well as more complex classification algorithms (based on artificial neural networks or deep learning approaches) should be researched. In addition, the combination of different classifiers is a promising an approach. Since negative sentiments can be expressed in several different ways, an ensemble of classifiers, each analyzing one specific aspect, should be able to reach a significantly higher accuracy than a single classifier.

6 Conclusion and Future Work

In this paper we presented the creation of two new corpora tailored to the sentiment analysis of German news articles as well as German forum messages. We discussed the relevant challenges and solutions when creating a dataset for learning a sentiment classifier. In addition, we explained the characteristics of our datasets and showed how to learn powerful classifiers based on the datasets. Since sentiment analysis corpora for languages other than English are very rare, this provides new opportunities to increase the classification quality in the domains at hand. We have discussed the challenges that occur and have considered solutions and open questions to be answered in the future. We use the created corpus to classify documents with good results. Many papers focus on tweaking classification algorithms and feature selection, but we consider the corpus creation to be an important step as well. Sentiment definition and bias can have a significant impact on the classification. The created datasets show that there is often a strong bias towards one class. A strong bias makes the interpretation of accuracy values difficult due to the fact that classifiers always predicting the most dominant ("most popular") class reach a high accuracy.

One interesting topic for the future research is the cost-sensitive learning. The consideration of costs could counteract the bias inherent in the datasets. We argue that there is no strict necessity to remove a bias since it can be useful if the target domain exhibits it as well, or if the use case demands it. Another related research topic would be the consideration of a specific machine learning approach when creating a corpus. Considering our examination of the MLSA corpus, enhancements in the form of inter-annotator agreements could also be applied in the future to further improve the annotation quality. Finally, the most important results of our work are the corpora itself as one of the few German sentiment analysis datasets. They can be used as a starting point to improve classification by focusing on the algorithms instead, or as a basis for bigger corpora.

Another interesting research question is how sentiment classifiers learned for a specific domain can be transferred to other domains. Our analysis shows that classifiers optimized for one application scenario often perform poorly when using these models in new use cases. Balahur et al. state that the sentiment of news articles is a unique domain with special needs [2]. They propose that for news sentiment analysis, the source, the target and different perspectives on an article (reader interpretation, author intention) should be considered. As we use Multi-nominal Naive Bayes, identifying source, target and different perspectives would be possible for the annotators but would not make a difference for the algorithm. When working with more sophisticated algorithms and feature selection methods, going back to these observations may help in further improving sentiment analysis.

Acknowledgment. This work was supported in part by the German Federal Ministry of Education and Research (BMBF) under the grant number 01IS16046.

References

1. Ali, T., Schramm, D., Sokolova, M., Inkpen, D.: Can I hear you? Sentiment analysis on medical forums. In: Proceedings of the International Joint Conference on Natural Language Processing 2013, pp. 667–673. ACL (2013)

2. Balahur, A., Steinberger, R.: Rethinking sentiment analysis in the news: from theory to practice and back. In: Proceeding of WOMSA, vol. 9 (2009)
3. Bosco, C., Patti, V., Bolioli, A.: Developing corpora for sentiment analysis: the case of irony and Senti-TUT. IEEE Intell. Syst. **28**(2), 55–63 (2013)
4. Bütow, F., Schultze, F., Strauch, L., Ploch, D., Lommatzsch, A.: Sentiment analysis with machine learning algorithms on German news articles. Project report, Berlin Institute of Technology, AOT (2015). http://www.dai-labor.de/publikationen/ 1052
5. Clematide, S., Gindl, S., Klenner, M., Petrakis, S., Remus, R., Ruppenhofer, J., Waltinger, U., Wiegand, M.: MLSA-A multi-layered reference corpus for German sentiment analysis. In: LREC, pp. 3551–3556 (2012)
6. Boland, K., Wira-Alam, A., Messerschmidt, R.: Creating an annotated corpus for sentiment analysis of German product reviews. Monograph, GESIS - Leibniz-Institut für Sozialwissenschaften (2013). http://www.ssoar.info/ssoar/bitstream/ handle/document/33939/ssoar-2013-boland_et_al-Creating_an_Annotated_Corpus_ for.pdf
7. Pang, B., Lee, L., Vaithyanathan, S.: Thumbs up? Sentiment classification using machine learning techniques. In: Proceedings of the ACL-02 Conference on Empirical Methods in Natural Language Processing, vol. 10, pp. 79–86. Association for Computational Linguistics (2002)
8. Remus, R., Quasthoff, U., Heyer, G.: SentiWS - a publicly available German-language resource for sentiment analysis. In: Chair, N.C.C., Choukri, K., Maegaard, B., Mariani, J., Odijk, J., Piperidis, S., Rosner, M., Tapias, D. (eds.) Proceedings of the Seventh International Conference on Language Resources and Evaluation (LREC 2010). European Language Resources Association (ELRA), Valletta, Malta (2010)
9. Rennie, J.D., Shih, L., Teevan, J., Karger, D.R.: Tackling the poor assumptions of naive Bayes text classifiers. In: Proceedings of the Twentieth International Conference on Machine Learning (ICML-2003), vol. 3, pp. 616–623 (2003)
10. Scholz, T., Conrad, S., Hillekamps, L.: Opinion mining on a German corpus of a media response analysis. In: Sojka, P., Horák, A., Kopeček, I., Pala, K. (eds.) TSD 2012. LNCS, vol. 7499, pp. 39–46. Springer, Heidelberg (2012). doi:10.1007/ 978-3-642-32790-2_4
11. University of Waikato: Weka 3 - Data Mining with Open Source Machine Learning Software in Java. http://www.cs.waikato.ac.nz/ml/weka

Concept of Observer to Detect Special Cases in a Multidimensional Dataset

Michel Herbin[(⊠)], Didier Gillard, and Laurent Hussenet

CReSTIC, Université de Reims Champagne-Ardenne, Institut of Technology, IUT,
Chaussée du Port, 51000 Chalons-en-champagne, France
{Michel.Herbin,Didier.Gillard,Laurent.Hussenet}@univ-reims.fr
http://crestic.univ-reims.fr

Abstract. In a dataset, the special cases are data that appears to be inconsistent with the neighborhoods of data. The special cases are warnings that usually require specific processing in social networks, medical applications or complex processes. This paper proposes to use the observer's paradigm to detect special cases in a multidimensional data space. Thus the observations allow to define the neighborhoods of data. Then we propose a rareness index for each data. The special cases have the highest values of rareness index. Experimental results show the ability of the method to detect these special cases. We conclude this paper with a brief discussion.

Keywords: Case-Based reasoning · Special cases · outliers · Curse of dimensionality

1 Introduction

At I4CS 2016, we use the concept of observer as a new paradigm to select the prototypes of a dataset [1]. In this paper, we deepen the concept of observer and we complete the previous communication. We propose a new method to detect the special cases in a multidimensional data set.

In [1], the prototypes are defined as the leaders in a network of data i.e. the data that is often prefered. In this paper, the special cases define the mirror image of the prototypes i.e. the cases that are rarely prefered. The detection of the special cases is generally restricted only to the outliers. The classical methods assume some patterns or statistical model of data distribution [2] and the outliers are often excluded of the analysis of the data set. In this paper we consider that each data require its own processing and the special cases are not excluded from the data analysis. Thus we propose a case-based approach to analyze the data set. But contrary to case-based reasoning methods [3] we want to effectively detect the special cases because these cases are warnings which require specific processing in social networks, medical applications or complex processes.

The prototypes are generic cases that are defined by their ability to sum up or to aggregate data. They are in the middle of the other data. For instance,

© Springer International Publishing AG 2017
G. Eichler et al. (Eds.): I4CS 2017, CCIS 717, pp. 34–44, 2017.
DOI: 10.1007/978-3-319-60447-3_3

when data represents the sensors of a wireless network, the prototypes could be used as base stations for managing the network (see a simulation of prototype detection in [5]). They also could be considered as leaders in a social network or typical cases in a medical application. On the contrary, the special cases are defined by their ability to be rare or lonely among the other data. Special case is data that appears to be inconsistent with its own neighborhood [4]. In this paper, we define neighborhoods of each data and we propose a rareness index for evaluating each data. The special cases are at the top of the rareness values.

In the next section of this paper, we define the concepts of observers and observations in a multidimensional dataset. With the approach we propose for detecting special cases, each data is an observer of the dataset. An observation consists in ranking the other data in respect with the observer. The ranking consists in a scan of the data set to rank data. But because of the dimensionality, the scan is not trivial. The dimensionality and the heterogeneousness of data complexity the determination of a scan because of the curse of dimensionality. After proposing the observations of the dataset, we define the neighborhoods of data and we compute a rareness index of data. The rareness index is based on observations (i.e. rankings) of the dataset. The special cases have the highest values of rareness. The experimental results are proposed in various circonstences and we conclude with a brief discussion.

2   Rareness and Observations

2.1   Observers and Observations

Let Ω be a set of n data defined by: $\Omega = \{X_1, X_2, X_3, \ldots X_n\}$. The indices $1, 2, 3, \ldots n$ give the canonical order of data. This is the order in which the data is provided. We define an observation of Ω by any order that we use when ranking data. If we use the canonical order, then the observation is $(1, 2, 3, \ldots n)$. If we use a ranking function called $rank$ in Ω, let $rank(X_i)$ be the rank of X_i. The ranks lie between 1 and n. The observation of Ω is defined by:

$$obs = (rank(X_1),\ rank(X_2),\ rank(X_3),\ \ldots\ rank(X_n))$$

For instance, if the $rank$ function is the increasing order using a data set defined by three real values: $\Omega = \{8, 19, 4\}$ with $X_1 = 8$, $X_2 = 19$ and $X_3 = 4$, then the observation is $(2, 3, 1)$ while the canonical observation remains $(1, 2, 3)$. Note that the $rank$ function is not trivial when the dimension of the data space is higher than three. When the dimension is equal to two or three (2D or 3D), there are some algorithms for defining the scan of data [6]. But as soon as the dimension exceeds three, such scannings become complex and are of little use.

The ranking and therefore the observation are obtained by comparing the data. Before we describe the comparisons in multidimensional space, we deal the ranks in case of equality between data or in case of impossibility of comparing data. In case of equality, the data is ranked using the canonical order as a second key for ranking. When the comparison is impossible or not defined, the data is ranked at the end of the ranking using again the canonical order.

In the following, we describe the observations that we use in this communication. When p is the dimension of the data space, each data is characterized using p attributes: $a_1, a_2, a_3, \ldots a_p$. Thus the data X_i is considered as a vector defined by:

$$X_i = (a_1(X_i), a_2(X_i), a_3(X_i), \ldots a_p(X_i))$$

To determine an observation of Ω (i.e. to rank data), a classical way consists in using a metric or a pseudo-metric in the data space. Unfortunately, such a metric or a pseudo-metric has generally no meaning when the dimension of data space increases. This phenomenon is known as the curse of dimensionality. In spite of lot of works for breaking the curse of dimensionality, the use of a pseudo-metric remains most often irrelevant when the dimension increases [7,8].

In this paper we will not rank data in the whole space in dimension p. We propose to rank data using each attribute separately. Then we obtain p rankings of Ω. Moreover we will not combine these rankings to obtain a single ranking because such a combination is not fully relevant (see social choice theory and Arrow's impossibility theorem [9]). The p rankings give p observations of Ω. Let us detail these rankings i.e. these observations.

Each observation depends on the observer we use in the data space. In this paper, each data of Ω is an observer. We have n observers of Ω. Let X_i be an observer with $1 \le i \le n$. When using each attribute separately, each observer gives p observations of Ω because we have p attributes. Let a_j be an attribute with $1 \le j \le p$. The observer X_i can rank data using the deviation between the attribute value of X_i and the attribute value of the other data. If the attribute a_j is numeric, the deviation between X_i and X_k is equal to: $|a_j(X_k) - a_j(X_i)|$. We can rank these deviations in an increasing order to obtain the observation from X_i for the attribute a_j. The rank of X_k among the deviations from X_i for the attribute a_j is denoted $rank^j_{X_i}(X_k)$. Thus the observation from X_i for the attribute a_j is defined by:

$$obs^j_{X_i} = (rank^j_{X_i}(X_1), \ rank^j_{X_i}(X_2), \ rank^j_{X_i}(X_3), \ \ldots \ rank^j_{X_i}(X_n))$$

To sum up we have n observers and each observer gives p observations of Ω.

2.2 Neighborhoods and Rareness

The data X_i is considered as a special case when X_i is different from its neighbors. In other words, X_i is observed by its neighbors and X_i is a special case when the rank of X_i is high for its neighbors. Let X_k be a neighbor of X_i, $rank_{X_k}(X_i)$ is the rank of X_i observed by X_k. This rank is defined through the index of rareness we propose in this paper. Because each observer gives one observation for each attribute, then we have p indices of rareness for each observer. In the following we combine these indices to obtain a global rareness index of X_i within Ω.

Neighborhoods. First let us define the neighborhoods of X_i. Again, the curse of dimensionality makes difficult to define a neighborhood of data. Indeed, the topology becomes particularly complex when the dimension of the data set increases. The classical definition of a neighborhood with the nearest neighbors assumes that a metric or a pseudo-metric is meaningful. Unfortunately the classical metrics have no meaning in high dimensional data set. Therefore the concept of neighborhood becomes questionable when the dimension increases [7]. In this paper, we propose to circumvent this difficulty by define several neighborhoods of X_i. The neighborhoods are defined for each attribute separately. Because we have p attributes, we define p neighborhoods of X_i.

The neighborhood of X_i for the attribute a_l with $1 \leq l \leq p$ is obtained using the classical α nearest neighbors of X_i for the values of a_l. In the following, we explain how we select the value of α between 2 and n. Therefore the neighborhood of X_i for the attribute a_l is defined by:

$$N_{X_i}^l = \{X_k \in \Omega \text{ with } rank_{X_i}^l(X_k) \leq \alpha\}. \tag{1}$$

Each data X_i has p neighborhoods and each neighborhood has the same number of neighbors (i.e. the number α).

Indices of Rareness. The rareness of X_i is defined through the observation of X_i by its neighbors. Let X_k be a neighbor of X_i. X_k is also an observer of Ω. $rank_{X_k}^j(X_i)$ is used as basis for indicating the rareness of X_i for the attribute a_j. The higher $rank_{X_k}^j(X_i)$ is, the more special (i.e. the rarer) the case X_i is when X_k observes X_i. Because the neighborhoods are defined using the α nearest neighbors of X_i, we consider that the $rank_{X_k}^j(X_i)$ have no meaning when they are greater than α. Thus we trunc the ranks to α in the neighborhood of X_i. In this paper the rareness index of X_i observed by its neighbor X_k with the attribute a_j is a number between 0 and 1 which is defined by:

$$rareness_{X_k}^j(X_i) = \frac{min(rank_{X_k}^j(X_i), \alpha)}{\alpha} \tag{2}$$

Let us consider the set of the observers X_k of X_i within a neighborhood of X_i. For each neighborhood $N_{X_i}^l$ of X_i, the mean of rareness indices from X_k defines the global rareness index of X_i for this neighborhood with the attribute a_j. The rareness of X_i within the neighborhood $N_{X_i}^l$ for the attribute a_j is defined by:

$$rareness_{N_{X_i}^l}^j(X_i) = \frac{\displaystyle\sum_{\substack{X_k \in N_{X_i}^l}}^{k \neq i} rareness_{X_k}^j(X_i)}{\alpha - 1}. \tag{3}$$

Thus each neighborhood $N_{X_i}^l$ gives p rareness indices, one for each attribute a_j with $1 \leq j \leq p$,

Within a neighborhood $N_{X_i}^l$, we select among the p rareness indices the one that has the highest value. Thus the rareness of X_i within the neighborhood $N_{X_i}^l$ is defined by:

$$rareness_{N^l_{X_i}}(X_i) = \max_{1 \le j \le p} rareness^j_{N^l_{X_i}}(X_i). \tag{4}$$

This index is obtained for the attribute that makes X_i the rarest (i.e. the more special).

Because we have p neighborhoods of X_i, we define the global rareness of X_i as the one which makes X_i the rarest. The global rareness of X_i is defined by:

$$rareness(X_i) = \max_{1 \le l \le p} rareness_{N^l_{X_i}}(X_i). \tag{5}$$

This approach makes it possible to indicate both the neighborhood and the attribute for which X_i is the rarest.

When the global rareness of each data is computed, we can give the top of the rareness data i.e. the top of the special cases.

Size of the Neighborhoods. In this paper, we define the neighborhoods of X_i using the α nearest neighbors of X_i. Such neighborhoods depend on the value of α and α lie between 2 and n. The smallest value of α is 2 and the biggest one is n. Let us study the values of the rareness indice when α increases from 2 to n.

If α is equal to 2, the neighborhoods of X_i are defined with only two nearest neighbors. In this case, each neighborhood has only one neighbor X_k which is distinct from X_i. Keeping the two nearest neighbors, the rank $rank^j_{X_i}(X_k)$ is always equal to 2. Let us recall that each neighborhood is defined using X_i as an observer. But when we change the observer, the rank $rank^j_{X_k}(X_i)$ using X_k as an observer is seldom equal to 2. Some of these ranks are greater than 2 when $1 \le j \le n$. Then the rareness of X_i becomes equal to one because of the truncation of the rank with α (see Eq. 2). Because the rareness indice has the maximum value (i.e. one) for each data, the number of data with the highest rareness is equal to n.

On the contrary, the number of data with the highest rareness value is equal to zero when α is equal to n. Indeed, if X_k is one of the n nearest neighbor of X_i, X_k belongs to a neighborhood of X_i when α is equal to n and the rank $rank^j_{X_k}(X_i)$ is lesser than n except in one case out of n. Thus the rareness of X_i is lesser than one (see Eq. 3).

In this paper, the special cases are data at the top of rareness values in Ω. When rareness value of a data is equal to one, we assume that this data is always a special case. For each value of α between 2 and n, we compute the number of these assumed spacial cases with a rareness value equal to one. This number of data with a rareness value equal to one decreases from n to zero when α increases from 2 to n. If we search the top-x of special cases in Ω, we propose to select the smallest value of α that gives a number of assumed special cases lesser than x.

3   Experimental Results

3.1   Toy Example

Let us explain the workflow using a toy example. We simulate five data $(n = 5)$ in dimension two with: $\Omega = \{$A, B, C, D, E$\}$ (see Table 1). We are in a 2D data space where the two attributes are called x and y.

Table 1. Toy example with five observers: A, B, C, D and E, and two attributes: x and y.

Observers			Observations	
X	x	y	obs_X^x	obs_X^y
A	2	5	(1, 2, 3, 4, 5)	(1, 3, 4, 5, 2)
B	6	4	(5, 1, 2, 3, 4)	(2, 1, 3, 5, 4)
C	7	3	(5, 2, 1, 3, 4)	(3, 2, 1, 5, 4)
D	8	8	(5, 4, 2, 1, 3)	(2, 4, 5, 1, 3)
E	9	5	(5, 4, 3, 2, 1)	(2, 3, 4, 5, 1)

Let us explain the procedure we use to compute the observations. Let B be the observer of Ω we consider. Using the attribute x, we have:

$$|x(A) - x(B)| = 4,$$
$$|x(B) - x(B)| = 0,$$
$$|x(C) - x(B)| = 1,$$
$$|x(D) - x(B)| = 2,$$
$$|x(E) - x(B)| = 3.$$

Thus we obtain:

$$rank_B^x(A) = 5,$$
$$rank_B^x(B) = 1,$$
$$rank_B^x(C) = 2,$$
$$rank_B^x(D) = 3,$$
$$rank_B^x(E) = 4.$$

Therefore we have:

$obs_B^x = (5, 1, 2, 3, 4).$

With the attribute y, we obtain:

$obs_B^y = (2, 1, 3, 5, 4).$

Now let us explain the computation of rareness indices. In dimension two, we define two neighborhoods of each data with the attributes x and y. When $\alpha = 4$, each neighborhood has four neighbors. The two neighborhoods of B are: $N_B^x = \{B, C, D, E\}$ and $N_B^y = \{A, B, C, E\}$. First we consider the attribute x. We compute the rareness indices in the neighborhood N_B^x. The ranks of B in this neighborhood (see $obs_X^x(B)$ in Table 1) are:

$$rank_B^x(B) = 1,$$
$$rank_C^x(B) = 2,$$
$$rank_D^x(B) = 4,$$
$$rank_E^x(B) = 4.$$

The rareness of B is defined by each neighbor (see Eq. 2) with:

$$rareness_B^x(B) = 1/4,$$
$$rareness_C^x(B) = 2/4,$$
$$rareness_D^x(B) = 4/4,$$
$$rareness_E^x(B) = 4/4.$$

Then the rareness of B in N_B^x for the attribute x (see Eq. 3) is equal to:

$$rareness_{N_B^x}^x(B) = 10/12.$$

With the same process for the attribute y, we obtain:

$$rareness_{N_B^x}^y(B) = 9/12.$$

Taking into account the two attributes x and y, the rareness in N_B^x (see Eq. 4) is defined by:

$$rareness_{N_B^x}(B) = 10/12.$$

Using the same computation method, we obtain in N_B^y:

$$rareness_{N_B^y}(B) = 8/12.$$

Then the global rareness of B (see Eq. 5) is equal to:

$$rareness(B) = 10/12.$$

Using this approach with $\alpha = 4$, the rareness of each data is computed:

$$rareness(A) = 1,$$
$$rareness(B) = 0.8333,$$
$$rareness(C) = 0.9167,$$
$$rareness(D) = 1,$$
$$rareness(E) = 1.$$

Note that three observers have a rareness value equal to one when $\alpha = 4$.

We can compute the rareness of each data using values of α between 2 and 5. When α increases, the number of data with a rareness value equal to one decreases (see an example of decreasing this number in function of α in Fig. 3). For each value of α, we compute the number of data with a rareness value equal to one. When $\alpha = 4$, this number is equal to three. When $\alpha = 5$, this number is equal to two (see Fig. 1). The selection of α is based on this number of data with a rareness value equal to one. If we search for three special cases, we increase α from 2 until this number becomes lesser than three. This result is obtained when $\alpha = 5$. The three special cases are A, C and D. Figure 1 gives the three special cases with bold points in right. Figure 1 displays also the rareness index of each data obtained when $\alpha = 5$. Note that C and E have the same rareness value, only the canonical order allows to separate C and E.

3.2   Complex Topology and Special Cases

In this experiment, we simulate a dataset with 500 data ($n = 500$). Each data has six attributes ($p = 6$). The attributes 1, 2, 3, 4, 5 and 6 of 496 data has

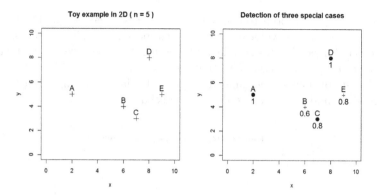

Fig. 1. Toy example in 2D space with $\Omega = \{A, B, C, D, E\}$ in right. In left, rareness values of data and detection of three special cases (A, D, C) using five nearest neighbors ($\alpha = 5$).

randomly uniformly and independently distributed in areas that we delimited by red rectangles (see Fig. 2). Four special data are simulated. They are called A, B, C and D. A is outside the distribution only for the attribute 1, A is in the distribution for the five other attributes. B is outside the distribution only for the attribute 2, B is in the distribution for the other attributes. C and D are outside when we consider both the attributes 3 and 4, otherwise C and D are in the distribution. All data are in the distribution of the attributes 5 and 6.

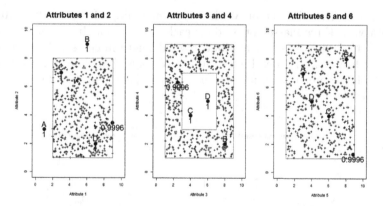

Fig. 2. Complex topology and detection of 5 special cases (space in dimension 6 with $n = 500$). (Color figure online)

We propose to automatically detect five special cases and we expect that A, B, C and D are detected. with the method we describe previously. First we select the value of α. When α increases from 2 to 500, the number of data with a rareness value equal to one decreases (see Fig. 3). We choose α when this number is lesser than five because five is the number of special cases we search.

We obtain $\alpha = 74$. Therefore the neighborhoods of each data have 74 neighbors. Because we have 6 attributes, we have six neighborhoods for each data.

We use these neighborhoods to compute the rareness of each data. The five data with the highest rareness value are proposed as special cases. The rareness values of the detected special cases is indicated (see Fig. 2). The cases A, B, C and D are detected as special cases. Note that we can change the seed for generating data with distributions in the same areas [11]. The dataset changes but we again obtain A, B, C and D in the five detected special cases.

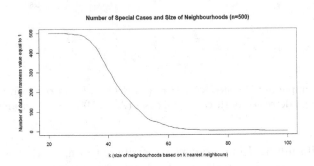

Fig. 3. Selection of α for k-nearest-neighbors: α (i.e. k) in function of the number of data with a value of rareness index equal to one.

3.3   Iris Dataset and Special Cases

The classical *IRIS* dataset of Machine Learning Repository of UCI [10] has 150 data with three classes of 50 data each: Iris Setosa, Iris Versicolour, Iris Virginica. Each data has four attributes: sepal length in cm, sepal width in cm, petal length in cm, and petal width in cm. We add four data taken randomly inside the hypercube containing the iris dataset. These data are called A, B, C and D (see Fig. 4).

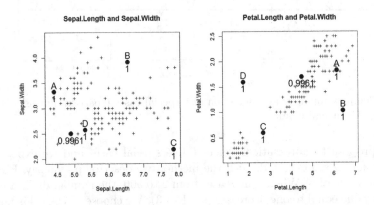

Fig. 4. *IRIS* dataset in dimension 4 and four random data A, B, C and D ($n = 154$). A, B, C and D are detected when we search five special cases.

When we search five special cases, we choose $\alpha = 56$. Thus we use neighborhoods with 56 nearest neighbors. A, B, C and D are detected as special cases (see Fig. 4). Note that such data is not detected when it lies in the middle of one iris distribution: Iris Setosa, Iris Versicolour or Iris Virginica.

4 Discussion and Conclusion

The experimental results show the ability to detect automatically the cases that are inconsistent with their neighborhoods, including outliers. The method does not need for statistical properties of data distributions, it does not need for a model or clusters of data. The results are obtained even in a multidimensionnal space with complex topology (see the example in Sect. 3.2). The method we propose has some drawbacks. The results are less convincing when data are very dispersed in the data space, for example in a high dimensional space. Moreover, the computation cost is proportional to the dimension p of the data space.

The method is programmed in language R with shinyapps (see the code in [11]). The method is based on neighborhoods defined through the α nearest neighbors. The detection of the special cases at the top of rareness values is fast when the parameter α is estimated. The computational cost is mainly due to the estimation of α.

In social network, the detection of the special cases can be important in a community. These cases can be interpreted as signs of either a weak belonging to the community or the emergence of a new trend in this community. The future work consist to explore these hypotheses. The method we propose could give the attributes and the neighborhoods that lead to the special cases. That could help to explain the difference between an alarm which requires a specific processing and an outlier which is only an error or a noise.

References

1. Herbin, M., Gillard, D., Hussenet, L.: Using data as observers: a new paradigm for prototypes selection. In: Fahrnberger, G., Eichler, G., Erfurth, C. (eds.) I4CS 2016. CCIS, vol. 648, pp. 39–46. Springer, Cham (2016). doi:10.1007/978-3-319-49466-1_3
2. Zhang, Y., Meratnia, N., Havinga, P.: Outlier detection techniques for wireless sensor networks: a survey. IEEE Commun. Surv. Tutorials **12**(2), 159–170 (2010)
3. Gundersen, O.E., Sormo, F., Aamodt, A., Skalle, P.: A real-time decision support system for high cost oil-well drilling operations. AI Mag. **34**(1), 21 (2012)
4. Shekhar, S., Lu, C.-T., Zhang, P.: Detecting graph-based spatial outliers. Intell. Data Anal. **6**(5), 451–468 (2002)
5. Herbin, M.: Selection of prototypes in 2D dataset with sub-sampling (2016). https://michelherbin.shinyapps.io/essaishiny/
6. Wang, J., Shan, J.: Space filling curve based point clouds index. In: Proceedings of the 8th International Conference on GeoComputation, pp. 551–562 (2005)

7. Houle, M.E., Kriegel, H.-P., Kröger, P., Schubert, E., Zimek, A.: Can shared-neighbor distances defeat the curse of dimensionality? In: Gertz, M., Ludäscher, B. (eds.) SSDBM 2010. LNCS, vol. 6187, pp. 482–500. Springer, Heidelberg (2010). doi:10.1007/978-3-642-13818-8_34

8. Jain, A.K., Duin, R.P.W., Mao, J.: Statistical pattern recognition: a review. IEEE Trans. Pattern Anal. Mach. Intell. **22**(1), 4–37 (2000)

9. List, C.: Social choice theory (2013). https://stanford.library.sydney.edu.au/archives/win2013/entries/social-choice/

10. Bache, K., Lichman, M.: UCI Machine learning repository. University of California, Irvine, School of Information and Computer Sciences (2013). http://archive.ics.uci.edu/ml

11. Herbin, M.: Code in R, Figures for I4CS (2017). https://michelherbin.shinyapps.io/i4csfigures/

Cooperative Networks

An Extended Tester for Cooperative Intelligent Transport Systems

Hacène Fouchal[(✉)], Geoffrey Wilhelm, Emilien Bourdy,
and Marwane Ayaida

CReSTIC, Université de Reims Champagne-Ardenne,
51687 Reims, Cedex 2, France
{hacene.fouchal,geoffrey.wilhelm,emilien.bourdy,
marwane.ayaida}@univ-reims.fr

Abstract. C-ITS (Cooperative Intelligent Transport System) equipments are usually validated using testing procedures. The ETSI organism provides a set of test suites to check the conformance of communication protocoles implemented on these equipments. An adapted interface (denoted Upper Tester) has to be developed on any equipment which requires to be tested.

In order to provide validated C-ITS equipments, the need to check the correctness of all functional parts becomes of high interest. One of the main functional part of a C-ITS equipment is to trigger automatically specific events when some conditions are satisfied. In order to test these event triggering conditions, we may emulate the environment (with its sensors) with an appropriate interface (denoted extended upper-tester).

Moreover, a C-ITS equipment is expected to achieve manual events, such as opening a salt container in case of recovering slippery roads. Its execution could trigger conditions to send some appropriate messages as slippery roads ahead. For this purpose, we designed an extended Upper Tester from the one introduced by ETSI. Its aim is to manage the manual and the automatic triggering conditions and to test the results of these events.

In this paper, we present this extended set of tests and their implementation in a real deployment project (SCOOP@F) of a complete C-ITS architecture.

Keywords: C-ITS · Validation · Formal testing · Networking · TTCN-3 · Evaluation

1 Introduction

Connected vehicles is one of the attractive issue nowadays either from industry development point of view or from research point of view. This issue has allowed the rapid growth of C-ITS (Cooperative-Intelligent Transport Systems). These systems use mainly V2X communications which could be Vehicle-to-Vehicle communications (V2V) or Vehicle-to-Infrastructure communications (V2I). Vehicles

© Springer International Publishing AG 2017
G. Eichler et al. (Eds.): I4CS 2017, CCIS 717, pp. 47–55, 2017.
DOI: 10.1007/978-3-319-60447-3_4

are equipped with On -Board Units (OBU) to handle the collection of informations from various sensors on vehicles and take care of information. The "I" part is usually managed by road operators. The infrastructure is a set of Road Side Units (RSUs) and C-ITS Central server which are in charge of collecting events from vehicles and sending precise and real-time informations to vehicles. Since the industry (in particular, car manufacturers) are highly interested to this issue, standards have to be agreed. Based on the mandate M451 from the European Commission, the European Telecommunications Standards Institute (ETSI) [1] has defined basic specifications for communication protocols which have to be implemented by RSUs and OBUs in order guarantee interoperability of equipments. All involved communication protocols have been described. The lower parts consider mainly ITS-G5 (based on the MAC protocol IEEE 802.11p). The upper layers are network layer (with geo-networking), the transport layer (with Basic Transport Layer (BTP)) and facilities layer (a kind of application layer for adapted messages to be handled by equipments).

Similar specifications have been defined in the USA. The US department of transportation is very active for rapid deployment of connected vehicles in the USA. Recently a merger of European standards with US standards is on-going in order to have common standards for car manufacturers. Real experimentations have started on 2012 after some research experimentation projects. The field is still new and C-ITS deployment is not simple. A higher coverage of infrastructure networks requires the installation of a large number of RSUs by road operators. This task has a very cost and the direct benefit is not easy to measure. In many countries different business models have been proposed and are still in a preliminary step. We notice also that car manufacturers and providers are developing thousand cars equipped with OBUs and have to be ready around 2020 to be on open roads for extensive validation.

In the background of this issue, a complete, secure and robust validation process has to be developed. Since vehicles are involved in injuries and deaths accidents, then connected vehicles have to be validated carefully befere industrial deployment.

This paper aims to present our proposed extended tester of ITS equipments which considers the triggering conditions of automatic events and the analysis of exchanged messages between C-ITS equipments.

The paper is organised as follows. Section 2 discusses the C-ITS general environment. Section 3 gives an overview of some related works. Section 4 details our extended tester. Then, Sect. 5 gives a conclusion and some hints about future works.

2   C-ITS Environment

We briefly explain the main components used in C-ITS and the validation processes.

2.1   C-ITS Components on the C-ITS Stations

A complete usual C-ITS is composed of different ITS-Stations:

- V-ITS-S: This component is a mobile station which could be a user vehicle or a road operator vehicle. It is also denoted OBU, for On-Board Unit.
- R-ITS-S: This component is a road side unit which could be used either for I2V or V2I communications. It is also denoted RSU, for Road Side Unit.
- C-ITS-S: This component is the central station of a road operator which is in charge of collecting data and which could be considered as the interface between road managers and users.

2.2   Common Layers

In this section, we recall the main used layers over RSUs and OBUs.

The upper layers respect the following standard protocols:

- Physical layer: It is based on an OFDM modulation principle and used the bandwidth of 10 MHz reaching a data rate of 6 Mb/s.
- MAC Layer: It is based on the 802.11p access layer. It is quite similar to a common WiFi considering priorities [2].
- GeoNetworking: The GeoNetworking protocol [3] is a network layer protocol. It uses geographical positions to forward packets. The main principle of this protocol is to forward packets using a broadcasting method. However for some cases, unicast forwarding is used.
- BTP: The Basic Transport Protocol (BTP) [4] is an intermediate layer between the facilities layer and the networking layer. It allows each ITS component to use a service provided by the geo-networking layer.
- Facilities layer: The facilities layer is a set of ITS objects. A facility is a component that provides functions, information or services to ITS applications. It exchanges data with lower layers and with management and security entities of the ITS stations.

  Among all the proposed protocols, we can cite the most used ones:
  - Cooperative Awareness Messages (CAMs) [5] provide the vehicle's presence information, positions as well as basic status of communicating ITS stations to neighboring ITS stations that are located within a single hop distance.
  - Decentralized Environmental Notification Messages (DENMs) [6] are mainly used by the Cooperative Road Hazard Warning (RHW) [7] application in order to alert road users when detecting events.
- Application layer is related to all applications implemented on an ITS component. We can cite the following known as Day-One C-ITS list from the EC:
  - In-vehicle signaling: it shows driving dynamic information as GPS position, speed, etc.
  - Data collection: it is executed by road operators with vehicle's data, road event, data launched by a driver (animal on the road, etc.) or automatic data launched by a car (emergency brake, warning lights,...), etc.

- Road hazard signaling, unexpected and dangerous events: alerts described by an European directive (temporary slippery road, pedestrian on the road, reduced visibility,...), etc.
- Information about road traffic: traffic lights, expected journey time, alternative routes, etc.
- Relay parkings and multimodal system: location and availability of relay parkings, public transportation scheduling, etc.

3   Related Works

In this section, we will describe some related works on validation of C-ITS such as [8–10]. All these works have focused on testing C-ITS components.

In [8], a testing methodology is proposed. This study handles systems implementing intersection related Vehicle-2-X applications as systems under test. The stimulation of the system under test is based on input streams and the evaluation is based on output streams. In addition, results of a proof of concept using the Audi travolution system are presented.

[9] focusses on conformance, interoperability and network integration testing. The proposed approach is based on the RM-ODP model to generate conformance points and on the use of the UML formalism to specify the test system. The TTCN-3 language is used to write the test cases.

In [10], the author presents a methodology to develop test tools for road safety telematic systems. In this study, the key design considerations and the architectural approach able to build test tools. Their purpose is to be are able to cope with the foreseen communication technology evolution. The eCall use case is handled with details.

In [11], presents CAM rate analysis. In fact, it measures the received rate of CAM messages and shows that it can be high even when the vehicle density is low. For this purpose, they simulate road traffic in typical highway scenarios and measure sent CAM rates. They have introduced the notion of relative channel load and they have presented a new approximative channel model to determine a vehicle's message reception probability. This model has been used to simulate a vehicle's received CAM rates and they have proposed a simple approximation formula.

[12] gives an overview on how research on vehicular communication evolved in Europe and, especially, in Germany. They describe the German field operational test simTD. The project simTD was the first field operational test to evaluate the effectiveness and benefits of applications based on vehicular communication in a setup that is representative for a realistic deployment environment. It is, therefore, the next necessary step to prepare for an informed deployment decision of cooperative systems.

Most of these test tools use test cases derived from test purposes proposed by system designers. In general, It would be much more efficient to have automatic test sequences generation as it has been done in our previous works [13–15].

3.1   ETSI Methodology

The ETSI has proposed a methodology for conformance testing and interoperability testing for all standard protocols used on C-ITS (and many other protocols as well). This methodology is gathered in a set of documents where one could find:

- A general methodology containing all the standardised procedures.
- A set of test purposes (vital properties) to be verified on each defined protocol layer.
- A set of test adapters to be implemented in order to be able to run all defined test cases.
- A set of test cases to be executed on each SUT (System Under Test).

All these testing procedures are "black box" procedures.

Each component will be tested in line with the process presented in the Fig. 1. On one hand, we have the tester composed of two elements: a computer equipped with a TTCN compiler software and a G5 gateway customised to forward all 802.11p messages received by the wireless interface on the other interface (Ethernet, here). This allows the computer to analyse the G5 flow in order to execute the tests. The tester is linked to the system under test by an ethernet connection. Thanks to these two links (G5 gateway and ethernet link), we can execute automatically all test cases provided by the standard.

An equipment could be tested if it integrates an Upper Tester which will stimulate a System Under Test (SUT) with some events and then checks how the component will react to these stimuli. A provider has then to develop the Upper Tester for only testing purposes.

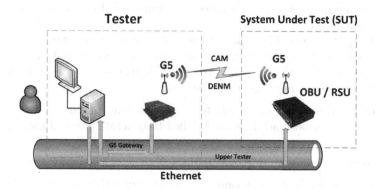

Fig. 1. Conformance tests architecture

4   Extended Tester

Our tester extension deals with testing the triggering conditions and their consequences (which are mainly the generated messages with their correct parameters). On a V-ITS-S, DENM messages are triggered respecting some conditions of the vehicle [6] and their environment (sensors of the vehicle which could be connected to the vehicle engine or to the vehicle sensors or to the vehicle parts). A set of test cases have been derived from the specification of these triggering conditions. In order to achieve these test cases, we either need to have a connection to a CAN Bus emulator or to implement an adapted upper tester on each component to be able to receive primitives emulating car environment events. Such tests will allow us to ensure that the same understanding of the interpretation of these conditions and their impacts.

4.1 Extended Upper Tester Primitives

In order to emulate vehicle sensors and external events, a set of primitives have been specified, they can be split into 5 groups:

- Security vehicle parts: These primitives are dedicated to change values on security sensors such as ABS, acceleration, braking pressure, friction coefficient, parking brake status, steering wheel angles, gear level position, etc. With such primitives, the tester is able to switch on the ABS or to change the gear level.
- Engine parameters: These primitives are in charge of notifying troubles on the engine such as a lack of power, the battery status, etc. We can emulate some troubles on the engine, for instance low incoming oil level.
- Passenger components parameters: These primitives take care of the vehicle's components used by the passengers in the vehicle such as doors, seats, belts, etc. These primitives allow the tester to emulate door unlocking required in case of crashes.
- External parameters: These primitives fix the values of some external (to the vehicle) parameters as lane number, rain fall level, front wash status, front wiper status, etc.
- Internal parameters: These primitives deal with some internal parameters as airbag status, etc. We can emulate some situations related to the internal part of the vehicle as airbag which is triggered. It may express a crash situation and an emergency message has to be sent.

All these primitives help testers to check in a finer manner the reaction of vehicles when specific conditions are fulfilled to generate adapted messages.

4.2 Testing of Triggering Conditions

The car2car consortium has proposed common triggering conditions for some usual events. Some of these conditions have been adopted by the ETSI standards and are defined in [6]. An OBU should absolutely embed the handling of these conditions. In order to test if an OBU implements properly these triggering conditions, we have derived adapted test cases to cover expected faults of an OBU.

To better understand the testing of the triggering conditions, we will explain in detail one example of them. We have chosen the "Emergency Braking" use case. The triggering conditions of this use case are mainly:

1. Warning lights are switched on
2. Braking deceleration is greater than 4 m/s^2

The Test Purpose (TP) related to this use case is presented on Fig. 2 which is extracted from our testing toolbox. When we execute the related test case of this test purpose, two primitives are used. Each primitive aims to fix one parameter on the OBU. The first one is used to switch on the warning lights and the second one is used to fix the braking deceleration to 5 m/s^2 for example. After sending these stimuli to the SUT, we expect to receive a DENM message to alert for Emergency Braking, This DENM message will have fixed values for some fields as:

- CauseCode set to 99
- SubCauseCode set to 1
- InformationQuality set to 1
- ValidityDuration set to 2
- RelevantTrafficDirection set to 0
- RelevanceDistance set to 3

In order to check the conformance of the OBU, it must transmit a DENM with all these fields correctly filled. For this reason, the purpose of the test case consists of verifying that the DENM (received by the G5 Bridge and forwarded to the Tester) should match with the template already defined in the test case with the parameters defined previously. If the DENM matchs the template, the test case has a success verdict. Otherwise, it fails.

```
1113
1114        /**
1115         *
1116         * @desc Check that the emergency braking use case is set with information quality set to 1
1117         * <pre>
1118         * Pics Selection: PICS_SCOOP_UEV_TRIGGERING
1119         * Initial conditions:
1120         *     with {
1121         *         the IUT being in the "initial state"
1122         *     }
1123         * Expected behaviour:
1124         *     ensure that {
1125         *         when {
1126         *             warning lights are triggered
1127         *             + braking value > 4 m/s²
1128         *         }
1129         *         then {
1130         *             The IUT sends a denm containing
1131         *             CauseCode set to 99
1132         *             SubCauseCode set to 1
1133         *             InformationQuality set to 1
1134         *             ValidityDuration set to 2
1135         *             RelevanceTrafficDirection set 0
1136         *             RelevanceDistance set to 3
1137         *         }
1138         *     }
1139         * </pre>
1140         */
1141        testcase TC_SCOOP_DENM_UEV_D10_AUTO_Q1() runs on ItsScoop system ItsScoopSystem {
1142
1143            f_SCOOP_DENM_UEV_D10_AUTO_Q1();
1144
1145        }
```

Fig. 2. Test purpose of emergency braking

Many other test cases have been developed to the different triggering conditions in order to verify the way of the implementation of these triggering conditions. This allows us to qualify the way of the implementation of the triggering conditions on the OBU. For some triggering conditions, more than one test case is required.

5   Conclusion and Future Works

The paper has described an extension of test cases to be used in order to test C-ITS components. This extension covers mainly how the triggering conditions are handled by OBUs of vehicles. This verification is very important before any real deployment. In fact, handling properly triggering conditions means that vehicles will send the right message at the right moment with the correct value parameters.

This proposal is a first step of getting standardised test cases about triggering conditions. Our set of primitives could help providers of OBU software to prepare their equipment for laboratory testing which is mainly achieved thanks to the Upper Tester.

As a future work, we intend to integrate all these test cases in a complete framework in order to test all parts of an ITS equipment.

Acknowledgement. This work is partially supported by the EC SCOOP project (INEA/CEF/TRAN/ 2014/1042281).

We thank Christine Tissot and Alexander Froetscher for their fruitful comments.

References

1. European Telecommunications Standards Institute (ETSI). http://www.etsi.org
2. IEEE Draft Standard for Amendment to Standard [for] Information Technology-Telecommunications and information exchange between systems-Local and Metropolitan networks-Specific requirements-Part II: Wireless LAN Medium Access Control (MAC) and Physical Layer (PHY) specifications-Amendment 6: Wireless Access in VehicularEnvironments, in IEEE Std P802.11p/D11.0 April 2010, pp. 1–35, 15, June 2010
3. Intelligent Transport Systems (ITS); Vehicular Communications; GeoNetworking; Part 4: Geographical addressing and forwarding for point-to-point and point-to-multipoint communications; Sub-part 1: Media-Independent Functionality. ETSI EN 302 636-4-1 V1.2.1, July 2014
4. Intelligent Transport Systems (ITS); Vehicular Communications; GeoNetworking; Part 5: Transport Protocols; Sub-part 1: Basic Transport Protocol. ETSI EN 302 636-5-1 V1.2.1, August 2014
5. Intelligent Transport Systems (ITS); Vehicular Communications; Basic Set of Applications; Part 2: Specification of Cooperative Awareness Basic Service. ETSI EN 302 637–2 v. 1.3.2, November 2014
6. Intelligent Transport Systems (ITS); Vehicular Communications; Basic Set of Applications; Part 3: Specifications of Decentralized Environmental Notification Basic Service. ETSI EN 302 637–3 V1.2.2, November 2014

7. Intelligent Transport Systems (ITS); V2X Applications; Part 1: Road Hazard Signalling (RHS) application requirements specification ETSI TS 101 539–1 V1.1.1, August 2013
8. Roglinger, S.: A methodology for testing intersection related Vehicle-2-X applications. Comput. Netw. **55**(14), 3154–3168 (2011). doi:10.1016/j.comnet.2011.06.014. ISSN: 1389–1286
9. Banos, J., Cardenas, C., Perez, C.: Testing of wireless heterogeneous networks. In: MELECON 2006 - 2006 IEEE Mediterranean Electrotechnical Conference, Malaga, p. 679, doi:10.1109/MELCON.2006.1653190
10. Polglase, J.B., Angelat, C.C., Ortega, A.P.: Tools, test, for road safety telematic systems. In: IEEE 65th Vehicular Technology Conference - VTC2007-Spring, pp. 2560–2564, Dublin (2007). doi:10.1109/VETECS.2007.527
11. Breu, J., Brakemeier, A., Menth, M.: Analysis of cooperative awareness message rates in VANETs. In: 13th International Conference on ITS Telecommunications, Tampere, Finland, November 2013
12. Weis, C.: V2X communication in europe? From research projects towards standardization and field testing of vehicle communication technology. Comput. Netw. **55**(14), 3103–3119 (2011)
13. Fouchal, H., Petitjean, E., Salva, S.: Testing timed systems with timed purposes. In: 7th International Workshop on Real-Time Computing and Applications Symposium (RTCSA 2000). IEEE Computer Society 2000, Cheju Island, South Korea, pp. 166-171, December 2000. ISBN: 0-7695-0930-4
14. Salva, S., Petitjean, E., Fouchal, H.: A simple approach to testing timed systems. FATES01 (Formal Approaches for Testing Software), a satellite workshop of CONCUR, Aalborg, Denmark, August 2001
15. El-Fakih, K., Yevtushenko, N., Fouchal, H.: Testing timed finite state machines with guaranteed fault coverage. In: Núñez, M., Baker, P., Merayo, M.G. (eds.) FATES/TestCom -2009. LNCS, vol. 5826, pp. 66–80. Springer, Heidelberg (2009). doi:10.1007/978-3-642-05031-2_5. ISBN 978-3-642-05030-5

dSDiVN: A Distributed Software-Defined Networking Architecture for Infrastructure-Less Vehicular Networks

Ahmed Alioua[1](✉), Sidi-Mohammed Senouci[2],
and Samira Moussaoui[1]

[1] Computer Science Department, USTHB University, Algiers, Algeria
{aalioua, smoussaoui}@usthb.dz
[2] DRIVE Labs, University of Burgundy, Nevers, France
Sidi-Mohammed.Senouci@u-bourgogne.fr

Abstract. In the last few years, the emerging network architecture paradigm of Software-Defined Networking (SDN), has become one of the most important technology to manage large scale networks such as Vehicular Ad-hoc Networks (VANETs). Recently, several works have shown interest in the use of SDN paradigm in VANETs. SDN brings flexibility, scalability and management facility to current VANETs. However, almost all of proposed Software-Defined VANET (SDVN) architectures are infrastructure-based. This paper will focus on how to enable SDN in infrastructure-less vehicular environments. For this aim, we propose a novel distributed SDN-based architecture for uncovered infrastructure-less vehicular scenarios. It is a scalable cluster-based architecture with distributed mobile controllers and a reliable fallback recovery mechanism based on self-organized clustering and failure anticipation.

Keywords: Vehicular Ad-hoc networks · Infrastructure-less zones · Software-Defined networking · Distributed control · Mobile controllers · Clustering

1 Introduction

Actually, people spend more and more time in transportation, whether in personnel vehicles or public transport. Thus, vehicles have become an important part of peoples travel experience. In this context, Intelligent Transportation System (ITS) and more specially Vehicular Ad-hoc Networks (VANETs) have attracted in the last past decade lots of interests for the purpose of improving travelling safety, comfort and efficiency via enabling communication between vehicles in an infrastructure-less vehicle-to-vehicle (V2V) mode and/or between vehicles and infrastructure in an infrastructure-based vehicle-to-infrastructure (V2I) mode.

Nowadays, VANET architectures suffer from scalability issues since it is very difficult to deploy services in a large-scale, dense and dynamic topology [1]. These architectures are rigid, difficult to manage and suffer from a lack of flexibility and adaptability in control. Hence, it is hard to choose the adequate solution to use, according to the actual context, because of the diversity of deployment environments and the large

© Springer International Publishing AG 2017
G. Eichler et al. (Eds.): I4CS 2017, CCIS 717, pp. 56–67, 2017.
DOI: 10.1007/978-3-319-60447-3_5

panoply of solutions that are generally adapted only in a certain context and particular situation. These constraints limit system functionality, slow down creativity and often lead to under-exploitation of network resources. Therefore, current VANET architectures cannot efficiently deal with these increasing challenges and the need of a new flexible and scalable VANET architecture become an absolute requirement.

In the last few years, the emerging network architecture paradigm of Software-Defined Networking (SDN) has become one of the most important technologies to manage large scale networks. SDN has been proposed as an attractive and promising paradigm to address the previous VANET architecture challenges. SDN is mainly based on a physical separation between control plane (network management features) and data plane (data forwarding features) and a logically centralized control and intelligence in a software controller. Other remaining equipment becomes simple data transmitter \ receiver with minimal intelligence. OpenFlow [2] is the most used standard for communication between the control plane and data plane. OpenFlow defines two types of network equipment, the controller that centralizes the network intelligence and vSwitchs that ensure only data forwarding. The controller handles the vSwitchs via installing flow entries in flow tables.

Given the growing popularity of SDN, researchers are increasingly exploring the possibility of integrating SDN in VANETs. Recently, some works have shown interest in the use of the SDN paradigm in VANETs and propose Software-Defined Vehicular Network (SDVN) architectures [1, 3–15]. These works have shown that SDN can be used to bring flexibility, scalability and programmability to VANETs, exploit the available network resources more efficiently and introduce new services in current vehicular networks. However, almost all of the proposed SDVN architectures are infrastructure-based and generally propose to host the controller somewhere on the fixed infrastructure of vehicular networks. Unfortunately, the total coverage of fixed infrastructure is not yet reached in current VANET systems. Therefore, uncovered infrastructure-less VANET zones already exist and they must be taken into consideration in the design of future SDVN architectures.

In this paper, we propose a novel distributed cluster-based architecture to enable SDN in infrastructure-less VANET environments with mobile controllers and an efficient fallback recovery mechanism based on self-organized clustering and failure anticipation. Integrating SDN in such uncovered areas is much more difficult given the dynamic sparse topology, the absence of the infrastructure support, and the vehicles' autonomous nature. To the best of our knowledge, this is the first work that integrates SDN in infrastructure-less VANET environments.

Our key contributions can be summarized as follows:

- We propose a new distributed scalable SDN-based architecture for infrastructure-less VANET,
- We present a novel kind of mobile multi-controllers, installed close to mobile vehicles to ensure a reasonable end-to-end delay and better support delay-sensitive-services,
- We furnish an efficient fallback recovery mechanism based on self-organized clustering and controller failure anticipation.

The rest of this paper is organized as follows. First, we provide an overview of existing related SDVN architectures in Sect. 2. In Sect. 3, the proposed distributed SDN-based infrastructure-less VANET architecture is presented and the fallback recovery mechanism is described. Section 4 brings two possible use-cases for the proposed architecture. Based on experimental evaluations, we demonstrate in Sect. 5 the reliability and the efficiency of our proposition. Finally, the conclusion is drawn in Sect. 6.

2 Related Work

Since the first work proposed in 2014 by Ku et al. [1] that explores how to integrate SDN in VANET scenarios, researchers investigated more and more how to benefit from SDN advantages to improve the performance of current VANET architectures. Recently, some SDVN works [1, 3–10] propose SDN-based architecture with the use of one controller generally hosted somewhere on the fixed infrastructure to handle the entire network. However, this assumption seems clearly impracticable in such dynamic, dense and large networks. In fact, this generates a high end-to-end delay especially when the distance between vehicles and controller is too large, which makes this solution not suitable for most delay-sensitive services. There is also a high risk of controller bottleneck and control overhead in case of a huge number of vehicle requests. Given these limitations, authors in [11–15] propose to use multiple controllers instead of a single controller and each controller handles a part of the network. The use of multiple distributed controllers can achieve scalability and reliability even in dense and heavy data loads. Much better, some of the previous works [5, 12–14] propose to install controllers (all or some) in the edge of the network, the closest as possible to vehicles to guarantee a reasonable end-to-end delay and satisfy the delay-sensitive application requirements. Furthermore, the fully centralized control of SDN presents a serious risk of reliability and security if the controller is unreachable especially if the system control is based on one unique controller, even worse with the intermittent and unstable nature of wireless connections. For this aim, works in [1, 3, 9, 12, 14] propose to use a fallback recovery mechanism as a backup solution if the controller is inaccessible.

Almost all proposed SDVN architectures are infrastructure-based and then host their controllers somewhere on the fixed infrastructure and no alternative was proposed for infrastructure-less zones, when the fixed infrastructure is totally absent or the coverage is not available. If we admit that the total and full coverage of fixed infrastructure is not yet reached in VANET system even with the integration of new emerging heterogeneous technologies as cellular technologies. For example inside tunnels when the coverage is not reachable and some rural areas where the fixed infrastructure is totally absent either because the deployment is very difficult, costly or not profitable. Thus, uncovered infrastructure-less VANET areas still exist and must be taken into consideration in the design of future SDVN architectures. We propose in the next section a distributed cluster-based SDN architecture for infrastructure-less VANET scenarios with multiple mobile controllers.

3 Proposed Architecture

In this section, we present our novel distributed multi-hop SDN-based architecture for infrastructure-less VANETs that uses only V2V communications via IEEE 802.11p, called *distributed Software-Defined infrastructure-less Vehicular Network (dSDiVN)*. dSDiVN uses the emerging concept of SDN to introduce flexibility, facility and scalability to the network. However, as it is well known, SDN relies on a centralized control for network management, which seems impracticable in large scale networks such as VANETs. Thus, dSDiVN proposes to combine SDN with clustering technique to partition the network and assign for each partition a dedicated controller. Hence, dSDiVN is based on a logically centralized, but physically distributed multi-hop control plane, which can benefit from the scalability and reliability of the distributed architecture while preserving the simplicity of the centralized management. dSDiVN uses multiple mobile controllers that interact each other and work together to get a global view of the network state. Partitioning the network makes it more stable, smaller and less dynamic for a vehicle, and can reduce overhead and latency.

The dSDiVN architecture is detailed below.

3.1 dSDiVN System Architecture

dSDiVN is based on a combination of two emerging network paradigms: SDN and clustering. Indeed, the control logic in clustering technique when the cluster head centralizes the cluster intelligence and the cluster members have a minimal intelligence, is very similar to that used by SDN paradigm. In this context, dSDiVN involves to: *(i)* organizing and partitioning the network according to certain criteria in partitions (*i.e.*, segments) using the clustering technique, *(ii)* grouping vehicles that are situated in the same geographic area (*i.e.*, segment) and which have similar characteristics (position, velocity, direction, etc.) at the same virtual group (i.e., cluster), *(iii)* choosing a leader (*i.e.*, cluster head) for each partition, *(iv)* deploying a local controller on each partition leader (*i.e.*, cluster head), and *(v)* connecting the adjacent controllers to build a back-haul for network control and enforce global policies. By partitioning the network and using distributed controllers, dSDiVN can better deal with scalability, handles easily increasing load, introduces efficiently specific new services to a particular cluster and effectively offers more reliability.

For cluster's management and maintenance, dSDiVN adopts and adapts the clustering algorithm in [16] based on CGP [17], which is a distributed multi-hop geographic clustering algorithm. As shown in Fig. 1, the uncovered road is divided into equal size segments of 150 m each (half of IEEE 802.11p coverage area) to ensure that adjacent controllers on cluster heads always be reachable to each other. Each segment represents a virtual cluster (called *Software-Defined domain, SD-domain*), that regroups all mobile vehicles (called *Software-Defined mobile vehicle, SD-vehicle*) which roll in the same direction and are situated in the same SD-domain. The elected cluster head (called *SD-domain head, SD-DH*) will be the SD-vehicle that has the longest time to life in the SD-domain (*i.e.*, the longest SD-domain travel time) to minimize the cluster maintenance overhead. Upon elected, each SD-vehicle domain head enables its local mobile controller and starts managing a backup candidate list in order to anticipate its potential failure and prepare the recovery controller. The identifier of the best candidate (*i.e.,* recovery controller) is sent periodically to all cluster members (called *SD-domain members, SD-DM*) via flow rules and stored in the flow table. For that, we propose to add a novel field to the flow table entry for storing the identifier. A replication of local mobile controller knowledge base is compressed and backed-up periodically on the recovery controller to allow fast service resume if the controller failed. Adjacent local mobile controllers are connected with each other via IEEE 802.11p to build a control backhaul for dSDiVN, see Fig. 1.

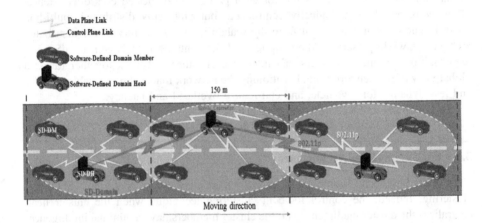

Fig. 1. dSDiVN System architecture.

Each local mobile controller maintains a local view of the network state of its SD-domain. A global view of the network state can be obtained by exchanging the local view of adjacent controllers. The local mobile controller is considered in control as a master of its SD-domain members where it collects data from the multiple members (slaves), and equivalent to its mobile neighbor controllers where all the controllers collaborate to get a global view of the entire network.

3.2   dSDiVN SDN Architecture

dSDiVN is based on the three layers of SDN architecture, as illustrated in Fig. 2:

(1) **Data plane layer**: It consists of all SD-vehicle SD-domain members that only perform collection and forwarding of data information,
(2) **Control plane layer**: It consists of all local mobile controllers deployed on the SD-vehicle SD-domain heads that centralize the network control,
(3) **Service and application layer**: It contains all the services and applications such as routing, security and QoS services. To minimize the cost of installing new services, the service is initially installed in one controller and after that communicated hop by hop to the adjacent controllers,

(4) **Communication interfaces**: OpenFlow is an IP-oriented protocol and there is not a no-IP version compatible with safety VANET application features. Also, there are no standardized SDN interfaces for directly integrating SDN into VANETs. Therefore, we propose to use: *(i)* a customized version of OpenFlow protocol adapted to V2V communications as southbound API to communicate between the control plane and the data plane and, *(ii)* a customized interface as northbound API to communicate between the control plane and applications [9].

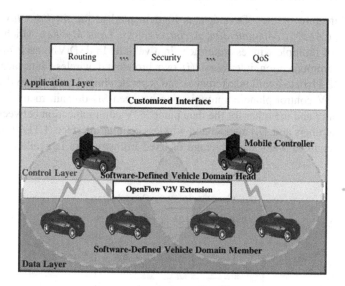

Fig. 2. dSDiVN 3-tier SDN architecture.

In dSDiVN, all SDN components are implemented on the unique hardware component, *i.e.,* the wireless mobile vehicle that the internal architecture is detailed below.

3.3 Software-Defined Wireless Mobile Vehicle

A software-defined wireless mobile vehicle (SD-vehicle) is a traditional vehicle with an additional SDN module which consists of hardware and software resources that allow SDN to function on the mobile vehicle. From the hardware side, it consists of a computing and storage unit that offers the SDN platform to install different services (to limit hardware modification, it is preferable to reuse, if possible, the available resources of the OBUs - on board units). From the software side, it consists of basic SDN components: SDN operating system, virtual machines on the hypervisor, network services, etc. Moreover, dSDiVN defines two main software SDN components, as illustrated in Fig. 3:

(1) *The local mobile controller (simplified mobile controller)*: It is initially in standby mode and it is enabled when the hosting SD-vehicle is selected as an SD-domain head. It is known as mobile because it is implemented on a mobile vehicle and can migrate from an SD-domain head to another, when it hosting SD-vehicle leave an

SD-domain. The mobile controller centralizes the intelligence and controls all the vehicles of its SD-domain. To the best of our knowledge, we are the first that propose a mobile controller in an SDVN architecture.

(2) *The monitoring and collection agent*: it ensures data forwarding and monitoring of SD-vehicle parameters (*e.g.,* position, velocity, direction, etc.). This monitored information is periodically communicated to the mobile controller. The local monitoring and collect agent receives and executes control directives from its mobile controller via flow rule entries installed in its flow table.

The architecture of the SD-vehicle is implemented at the *facilities layer* of the standard *ISO CALM (Communication Architecture for Land Mobile)*, which assumes the existence of multiple wireless interfaces in a vehicle. In dSDiVN, each SD-vehicle has several communication interfaces: *(i)* two broadband wireless interfaces DSRC (*i.e.,* IEEE 802.11p), to avoid interferences and separate control traffic from data traffic: one for the V2V control plane communication between SD-domain members and the mobile controller and the other for the data plane V2V communication between vehicle SD-domain members and, *(ii)* a wideband wireless cellular interface (LTE/4G), initially disabled and enabled when the coverage of fixed infrastructure is available, as illustrated in Fig. 3.

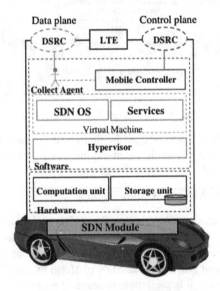

Fig. 3. Internal architecture of software-defined mobile vehicle.

The fallback recovery mechanism of dSDiVN is presented below.

3.4 Fallback Recovery Mechanism

In a fully centralized architecture such as the one that adopts SDN, all system reliability relies on the central controller. Therefore, it is necessary to envisage a back recovery mechanism if this central controller is unreachable [1]. In [1, 14], authors propose to switch to traditional VANET routing when the connection with the controller is lost. This may increase the complexity of software and hardware design [12]. In [9], authors use trajectory prediction to pre-install entries in the flow table that can be used for a short period of time when the controller fails but this initiative does not envisage any solution if the controller failure lasts after the end of the entry. In [12], two types of hierarchical controllers are used, and if the high-level controller fails, the low-level controllers take over to ensure service continuity but no solution is envisaged if one of the low-level controllers failed.

Our architecture is based on a cluster-based distributed multi-hop control system. As fallback recovery mechanism, we simply propose to profit from the self-organized clustering technique, permanently anticipating the possible failure of each controller and prepare in advance the recovery scenario. Thus, if a mobile controller fails, the pre-prepared recovery controller (see Sect. 3.1) will take over to ensure the service continuity. When the SD-vehicles are aware of the controller failure, they will start to send their requests directly to the recovery controller using the beforehand pre-installed identifier as prevention recovery solution, see Sect. 3.1. The recovery controller when enabled, use the knowledge base replication to immediately start to respond the SD-vehicle requests.

Some possible use-cases of dSDiVN are presented in the next section.

4   dSDiVN Use Cases

In this section we present two possible use-cases of our dSDiVN architecture:

- *SDN-assisted efficient data collection and dissemination*: the data collected at each SD-vehicle level are not useful individually. However, the aggregation of all data of a geographical area allows having a vision on the network state. By separating the data plane from the control plane, mobile controllers can centralize the collection of data from various sensors installed on SD-vehicles, each in its SD-domain. Unlike traditional networks, mobile controllers can handle the collected data in a more informed way to extract useful information and improve the system decision. Also, by collaborating with each other, mobile controllers can build a global view of current network state and can choose the most optimal path to disseminate/route this extracted information.
- *SDN-assisted VANET safety applications*: dSDiVN uses only V2 V based IEEE 802.11p communications, which are more suitable for safety applications. Moreover, mobile controllers based on the information observed of current traffic conditions can collaborate each other to: *(i)* ensure better persistence and availability of emergency alert messages by accurately defining the danger zone extent (size) and the duration of the emergency alert, *(ii)* choose the fastest path to disseminate the alert message, and *(iii)* treat the emergency traffic with more priority in reservation of specific frequencies and channels over the remaining normal traffic.

5 Numerical Results

In this section, we describe our simulation configuration, metrics and results. The simulation model is built based on the system architecture described in Sect. 3.1, and it is implemented using the network simulator NS3 [18] and the traffic simulator SUMO [19]. The aim of the simulations is to evaluate the reliability of the fallback recovery mechanism and the effect of controller distance on flow rule installation time.

For simulation, we consider an infrastructure-less VANET scenario where the network is deployed in 1000×1000 m area (a cell of Manhattan Grid). The road is divided into equal segments of 150 m each, see Fig. 1. Node density is 200 nodes. Each vehicle has IEEE 802.11p based interface with a transmission range up to 300 m and a velocity between 10 and 30 m/s. The simulation time is 120 s and the packet generation rate is 5 packets/s. The performance metrics we used are:

- *Flow rule installation time*: it represents the elapsed time since an SD-vehicle requests the controller for a new flow rule and the time when the flow rule is installed in the SD-vehicle flow table,
- *Packet delivery ratio*: is the ratio of packets successfully received to the total sent.

5.1 Controller Failure

In this evaluation, we study how dSDiVN with the proposed fallback recovery mechanism (multi-controllers cluster-based with failure anticipation and recovery controller pre-preparation) reacts to the controller failure. We focus on one cluster and we simulate a controller failure of 5 s at the 61st s. Afterwards, we compare the dSDiVN fallback recovery mechanism (we simplified dSDiVN) with that of self-organized cluster-based of dSDiVN without fallback recovery (we simplified self-organized) and with works [3–8, 10], that use one controller without fallback recovery mechanism (we simplified no-back-recovery) according to the packet delivery ratio. The comparison results are illustrated in Fig. 4.

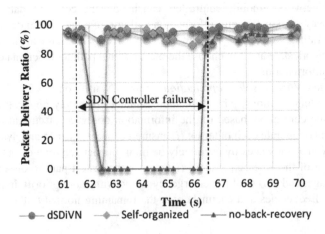

Fig. 4. Controller failure.

As illustrated in Fig. 4, we can see that just when the controller fails, the packet delivery ratio in no-fall-recovery starts to decrease dramatically and it still drops until the controller resumes the service. For the case of self-organized, the delivery radio drops for a short time, which represents the time until the reelection of a new SD-domain head and the synchronization with the newly elected controller; after that, the system resumes a good delivery ratio. This behavior can be justified by the fact that in the SDVN solution, the reliability of the system resides on one central controller and as soon as the controller fails, it stops installing flow rules in flow tables; therefore, the service is interrupted. Much more resistant, the packet delivery ratio in dSDiVN undergoes a very slight effect, thanks to the efficient preventive fallback recovery mechanism based on distributed multi-controllers, self-organized clustering and failure anticipation. When the controller fails, SD-vehicles can directly synchronize and direct their requests to the pre-selected recovery controller using the pre-installed identifier, see Sect. 3.1.

This evaluation demonstrates the reliability and the efficiency of our fallback recovery mechanism and confirms the result in [1]: the use of a fallback recovery mechanism is primordial when operating the centralized SDN-based control in VANET especially when the system control lies on one central controller, more worst with the intermittent wireless link nature.

5.2 Effect of Controller Distance on Flow Rule Installation Time

In this evaluation, we aim to study the effect of controller distance, which represents the physical distance between the controller and SD-vehicles, on the flow rule installation time. Thus, we use a simple scenario when an SD-vehicle sends a request to its controller and we have varied the distance between the SD-vehicle and the controller for different request packet sizes.

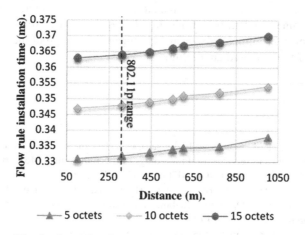

Fig. 5. Controller distance vs. flow rule installation time.

Figure 5 shows that flow rule installation time increases with the increase of the distance between the controller and the SD-vehicle and even with the increase of packet size. This evaluation is performed in a cell of Manhattan Grid with 1000 m using LTE communication. However, the result can be generalized for large scale scenarios in infrastructure-based areas. In this case, the result can be too worst and the system cannot ensure a packet delivery ratio that satisfies the requirements of delay-sensitive services especially when the distance reaches hundreds of kilometers.

From this evaluation, we can conclude that the controller should be installed the closet as possible to vehicles to guarantee the suitable flow rule installation time of delay-sensitive services and react rapidly to real-time events.

In our architecture, the controllers are installed on the SD-domain head vehicles (the farthest distance of a controller is 150 m) and communicate with forwarding vehicles via V2V and IEEE 802.11p (more adequate to satisfy safety service requirements), which allows dSDiVN to ensure a good and adequate flow rule installation time and a better support of delay-sensitive services and real-time events.

6 Conclusion

In this paper, we propose dSDiVN, distributed Software-Defined infrastructure-less Vehicular Network, a novel distributed multi-hop SDN-based clustered architecture for infrastructure-less vehicular networks with mobile multi-controllers and a reliable fallback recovery mechanism. Our dSDiVN bridges the gap of no SDN-based architecture in infrastructure-less VANET zones. Numerical results demonstrate that the reliability of our fallback recovery mechanism and the negative effect that represents the far distance of controller on the flow rule installation time which is the main requirement of the VANET safety applications.

The sparse network topology that results in partitioning of the network rests an open challenge in front of integrating SDN in infrastructure-less VANET areas. As short-term perspective of this work, we plan to extend our architecture to deal with the network partitioning problem by introducing drones to connect isolated mobile controllers, as we plan to do more advanced experimentations to proof the feasibility and the efficiency of the proposed architecture.

References

1. Ku, I., Lu, Y., Gerla, M., Gomes, R. L., Ongaro, F., Cerqueira, E.: Towards software-defined vanet: Architecture and services. In: Proceedings of the 13th Annual Mediterranean Ad Hoc Networking Workshop (MED-HOC-NET), pp. 103–110 (2014)
2. McKeown, N., Anderson, T., Balakrishnan, H., Parulkar, G., Peterson, L., Rexford, J., Shenker, S., Turner, J.: Openflow: enabling innovation in campus networks. SIGCOMM Comput. Commun. **38**(2), 69–74 (2008)
3. Khan, U., Ratha, B.K.: Time series prediction QoS routing in software defined vehicular ad-hoc network. In: The Proceeding of International Conference on Man and Machine Interfacing (MAMI), pp. 1–6 (2015)
4. Li, H., Dong, M., Ota, K.: Control plane optimization in software-defined vehicular ad hoc networks. IEEE Trans. Veh. Technol. **65**, 7895–7904 (2016)

5. Wang, X., Wang, C., Zhang, J., Zhou, M., Jiang, C.: Improved rule installation for real-time query service in software-defined internet of vehicles. IEEE Trans. Intell. Transp. Syst. **18**, 225–235 (2017)
6. Luo, G., Jia, S., Liu, Z., Zhu, K., Zhang, L.: sdnMAC: a software defined networking based MAC protocol in VANETs. In: The Proceeding of the 24th IEEE/ACM International Symposium on Quality of Service (IWQoS), pp. 1–2 (2016)
7. Liu, Y.C., Chen, C., Chakraborty, S.: A software defined network architecture for geobroadcast in vanets. In: The Proceeding of IEEE International Conference on Communications (ICC), pp. 6559–6564 (2015)
8. Zhu, M., Cao, J., Pang, D., He, Z., Xu, M.: SDN-based routing for efficient message propagation in vanet. In: The Proceeding of WASA, pp. 788–797 (2015)
9. He, Z., Cao, J., Liu, X.: SDVN: enabling rapid network innovation for heterogeneous vehicular communication. IEEE Netw. **30**(4), 10–15 (2016)
10. Chang, Y.-C., Chen, J.-L., Ma, Y.-W., Chiu, P.-S.: Vehicular cloud serving systems with software-defined networking. In: Hsu, C.-H., Xia, F., Liu, X., Wang, S. (eds.) IOV 2015. LNCS, vol. 9502, pp. 58–67. Springer, Cham (2015). doi:10.1007/978-3-319-27293-1_6
11. Huang, X., Kang, J., Yu, R., Wu, M., Zhang, Y., Gjessing, S.: A hierarchical pseudonyms management approach for software-defined vehicular networks. In: The Proceeding of the 83rd Vehicular Technology Conference (VTC Spring), pp. 1–5 (2016)
12. Kazmi, A., Khan, M.A., Akram, M.U.: Devanet: decentralized software-defined vanet architecture. In: The Proceeding of IEEE International Conference on Cloud Engineering Workshop (IC2EW), pp. 42–47 (2016)
13. Zheng, Q., Zheng, K., Zhang, H., Leung, V.C.M.: Delay-optimal virtualized radio resource scheduling in software-defined vehicular networks via stochastic learning. IEEE Trans. Veh. Technol. **65**, 7857–7867 (2016)
14. Truong, N.B., Lee, G.M., Ghamri-Doudane, Y.: Software defined networking-based vehicular adhoc network with fog computing. In: The Proceeding of IFIP/IEEE International Symposium on Integrated Network Management (IM), pp. 1202–1207 (2015)
15. Salahuddin, M.A., Al-Fuqaha, A., Guizani, M.: Software-defined networking for rsu clouds in support of the internet of vehicles. IEEE Internet Things J. **2**, 133–144 (2015)
16. Remy, G., Cherif, M., Senouci, S.M., Jan, F., Gourhant, Y.: Lte4v2x-collection, dissemination and multi-hop forwarding. In: The Proceeding of IEEE ICC 2012, pp. 10–15 (2012)
17. Salhi, M.O.C.I., Senouci, S.M.: A new architecture for data collection in vehicular networks. In: 2009 IEEE International Conference on Communications, pp. 1–6 (2009)
18. Network simulator 3 (ns-3). http://www.nsnam.org/
19. Simulation of urban mobility (sumo). http://sumo-sim.org/

Optimization Algorithms

On a Fog Computing Platform Built on ARM Architectures by Docker Container Technology

Andreas Eiermann, Mathias Renner, Marcel Großmann,
and Udo R. Krieger[✉]

Fakultät WIAI, Otto-Friedrich-Universität,
An der Weberei 5, 96047 Bamberg, Germany
udo.krieger@ieee.org

Abstract. Fog computing constitutes currently a challenging effort to establish the concepts and services of cloud computing at the edge of converging wireless networks and wired high-speed backbones. We discuss the concepts of our fog computing platform HCL-BaFog. It is built on top of Hypriot Cluster Lab (HCL) which has been developed by the Hypriot Pirate Crew in recent years based on single board computers with an ARM architecture. It uses LINUX container technology as underlying open source platform that has been established by means of the rapidly evolving framework Docker. We present the design principles of our fog computing platform and discuss its different software components. To create clusters of fog cells subject to high-availability requirements and to provide failsafe data processing, we further summarize some performance results on the integration of the orchestration tools Docker Swarm Mode and Kubernetes on HCL and draw some conclusions regarding their suitability for fog computing.

Keywords: Fog computing · Hypriot Cluster Lab · ARM architecture · Container virtualization · Docker Swarm Mode · Kubernetes · High-availability

1 Introduction

In recent years cloud computing has established the versatile technical basis to deploy very rapidly new services and customer applications as effective, easily manageable, low cost entities by means of distributed data centers and software virtualization. The underlying service architectures such as platform as a service (PaaS), storage as a service (StaaS), or infrastructure as a service (IaaS) use virtual machines as foundation for effective service provisioning and modern communication infrastructures on top of powerful physical servers and software-defined networks.

Software virtualization provides the means to satisfy the scalability, performability, and quality-of-service as well as quality-of-experience requirements of modern applications, capturing fundamental redundancy, availability, reliability, and security issues.

© Springer International Publishing AG 2017
G. Eichler et al. (Eds.): I4CS 2017, CCIS 717, pp. 71–86, 2017.
DOI: 10.1007/978-3-319-60447-3_6

Following traditional approaches, modern cloud services are hosted in large data centers that fulfill all customer needs. They allow, for instance, small enterprises to establish their own distributed service delivery by the powerful cloud infrastructure and adaptive service models.

However, the new requirements of a rapidly evolving Internet-of-Things (IoT) including smart cities, smart homes, new transport and e-health services is challenging this traditional approach of service deployment (cf. [3, 4, 10]). Integrating millions of small sensors, actuators, and analysis devices provides great challenges to classical cloud computing. Today the Internet-of-Things requires a fundamental transition of many commonly used paradigms towards new lightweight protocols and processing concepts. At the edge of a high-speed network, swarms of sensors require first of all a scalable system design. At this low level of the processing hierarchy it can be based on tiny devices with small computational power and limited memory. Here heavy virtual machines and energy hungry data center technology are not suitable for sensor networks running on top of small, energy efficient processing elements. In addition, sensor networks and related data analytics that will be employed in smart private and public environments like smart homes, e-health settings, or smart cities will benefit from high-availability concepts of cloud computing and fault tolerance which is essential for critical infrastructures and their related services.

Considering traditional cloud computing for IoT purposes, an approach based on distributed data centers in the cloud would endorse much unnecessary data communication and heavily load the core network. Following Azam and Huh [1], fog computing is one possible solution to relocate virtualized services from the cloud to the network edge. In this regard the new concept of fog computing currently constitutes a challenging effort to establish the well determined concepts and services of cloud computing such as IaaS and PaaS at the edge of wireless networks based on 5G technology with their next generation optical backbones towards the cloud (see Fig. 1).

In this paper we present the design of our fog computing platform HCL-BaFog built on top of Hypriot Cluster Lab (HCL[1]) which has been developed in recent years. It is realized by suitable concepts to satisfy the computational challenges of IoT and to support services and applications, which are needed to successfully manage large data streams and communication of a large number of connected devices. In this respect HCL is able to provide a virtualized computing basis at the edge since it is running on ARM architectures, ships energy efficient features by design and can behave similar to a small data center. HCL utilizes interconnected single board computers (SBC's) with ARM architecture and HypriotOS as operating system. The HCL software platform already offers basic cloud functionality based on LINUX virtualization while running efficiently on 32-bit or 64-bit multi-core ARM processors like Raspberry Pi or Pine A64. Thus, it provides a key factor to minimize cost. Due to the fact that those processors offer less computational power, services must be packed into lightweight containers.

---

[1] See URL: https://blog.hypriot.com/downloads/.

In the HCL approach they are built by means of the framework Docker to avoid the overhead of virtual machines.

In essence, HCL provides an energy efficient micro-cloud computing platform. To support the fast development of fog computing, the developed code basis of HCL is publicly available on Github[2].

In the following we first present the design principles of our HCL-based platform HCL-BaFog and discuss its utilization for the purposes of fog computing. We illustrate how it handles redundancy and replication of service tasks between several hosts at different locations via secured wide-area networking. To enable encrypted communication between distributed hosts at layer 2 and 3, we use an interconnection approach based on overlay meshes like virtual private LANs. Our platform can establish fault tolerant, reliable and secure connections among several independent Docker Engines and provide means to achieve the QoS and performability objectives of mirco-cloud services.

To guarantee high availability and to provide failsafe data processing, we further discuss how software-defined networking and the integration of orchestration tools like Docker Swarm Mode and Kubernetes can be realized. Then we illustrate some first performance results on their application and draw a few conclusions about their suitability regarding fog computing.

The paper is organized as follows. In Sect. 2 we describe the technical basis of Hypriot Cluster Lab and discuss the establishment of secure overlay meshes among Docker hosts. In Sect. 3 we elaborate on the resource management and orchestration processes that are used in a fog cell cluster of our test bed HCL-BaFog. Then we illustrate some performance results on the container orchestration by means of Docker Swarm Mode and discuss resilience issues in related fog cell clusters. Finally, we draw some conclusions on the suitability of containerization by Docker on ARM-based architectures in fog computing scenarios.

2 Architecture of a Fog Computing Platform

The development of our fog computing platform HCL-BaFog is based on the existing Hypriot Cluster Lab (HCL). Its basic implementation of a resource management framework and runtime libraries for 64-bit ARM platforms is a Debian-based operating system called HypriotOS, that has been first deployed in February 2014. The related installations of the container virtualization framework Docker including Docker Engine, Compose and Machine as well as Docker Swarm Mode by the Hypriot team in late 2015 have been the starting point of the development described here.

2.1 The Basic Technology of Hypriot Cluster Lab

The technical basis of Hypriot Cluster Lab is provided by single board computer (SBC) systems based on a 32-bit or 64-bit multi-core ARM processor architecture. The software design is built by means of a lightweight LINUX container

---

[2] See URL: https://github.com/hypriot.

virtualization technology. Both components can provide the required hardware and software functionality of a powerful, low cost fog computing framework that includes the services, middleware and protocol stacks to interconnect sensor or actuator devices and appliances of a modern Internet-of-Things (IoT) settings at the first aggregation level of the underlying distributed infrastructure (see Fig. 1, cf. [3]).

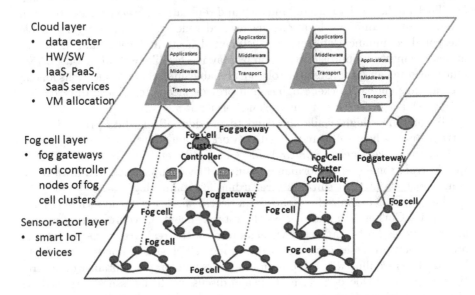

Fig. 1. Hierarchical layering of a fog computing system.

The sensor, actuator, and data sampling elements constitute the technical basis of data collection at layer 1 and distribute the information along redundant paths to the associated fog gateways. They are arranged in fog cells and controlled by more powerful cluster controller nodes that integrate software-defined networking, automatic deployment, as well as monitoring, orchestration, resource assignment, and data management functionality at a second level of the hierarchy. Putting the scalable SBC elements as first aggregation point or fog gateway at the edges of a fog cell cluster with its sensor and actuator hardware components, the virtualization offered by the container technology enables the deployment of a flexibly configurable software platform. It allows the designer to instantiate powerful processing derived from micro-cloud services in a IaaS or PaaS environment at the expense of very small latency and low cost. The architecture integrates the cell clusters by means of the secured internetworking functionality of the cluster controllers of fog cells and their interconnected gateways into the distant cloud infrastructure that offers IaaS, PaaS, SaaS and storage services at powerful data centers with their virtualized processing and storage components (cf. Fig. 1, see also [3,18]).

Hypriot Cluster Lab has adopted container virtualization since it allows the flexible realization of infrastructure and platform as a service architectures. HCL has realized the virtualization approach by means of the containerization framework Docker and its open standards running on top of all major infrastructure elements. Compared to the classical hypervisor approach or heavy LINUX container technology, a lightweight container virtualization is the appropriate design alternative for a resource constrained SBC platform like Raspberry Pi, Arduino or SolidRun'S more powerful ClearFog boards (see Fig. 2, cf. [5]). It allows to run processes efficiently at highest speed on those ARM boards without the overhead of a hypervisor using lightweight kernel namespaces derived from LINUX. The restriction caused by the binding of the container technology to the func-

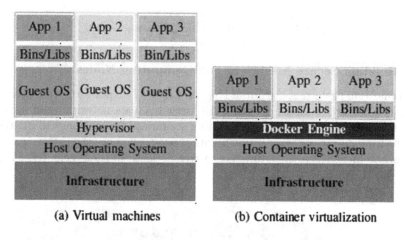

(a) Virtual machines   (b) Container virtualization

Fig. 2. Container virtualization (b) vs. a virtual machine environment (a).

tionality of the underlying host operating system HypriotOS is outperformed by the advantage of encapsulating all dependencies of an application into a single Docker image. Docker's capability regarding hierarchical layering and sharing of common images and the assignment to nodes, and the interconnection of containers using the clustering of Docker hosts by Docker Swarm Mode provides an effective way to enhance the required functionality of the edge computing nodes and to establish their interworking.

In our realized test bed we use Docker 1.12 released in June 2016. It has implemented all cluster management and orchestration features within the Docker Engine as main Docker binary. The Docker Engine consisting of a server daemon on a Docker host and a Docker client is the core of the ecosystem to create and manage containers as well as to build and manage local images. Then the Docker binary can be used in the 'Swarm Mode' which activates the cluster capabilities and allows to create the primary swarm master or leader node and all worker nodes on distributed hosts (see Fig. 3, cf. [13]).

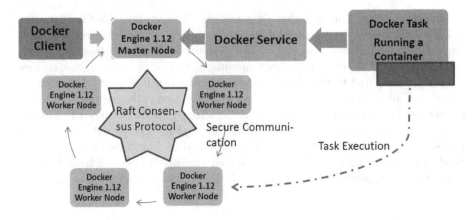

Fig. 3. Architecture of Docker Swarm Mode.

2.2 Building Secure Meshes of Fog Computing Nodes

The connection pattern of the initial Hypriot Cluster Lab platform was restricted to a local cluster paradigm derived from virtual private networking in a single domain. However, regarding fog computing scenarios it is necessary to interconnect the fog gateways as aggregation points of a fog cell above the sensor-actuator layer into a hierarchical structure, e.g. a tree or mesh of those cells (cf. Figs. 1, 4, see also [18]).

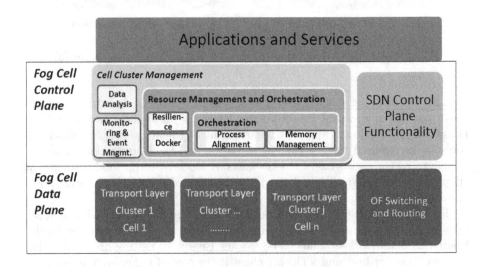

Fig. 4. Architecture of the fog computing platform.

In line with the structure of 4G and 5G networks we define the gateway as aggregation point represented by an ARM-based virtualized system as analogy to an eNodeB that is governing the control, data, and management planes of a fog cell with its attached interconnected sensor and actuator elements. Analogous to routing areas and SAE gateways these cells are interconnected among each other by gateway nodes of fog cell clusters, e.g. more powerful SBC's including software-defined network elements like programmable switches and SDN controllers. As topologies we may consider trees or mesh networks interconnected by a stationary or mobile SDN based on WiFi, NarrowBand-IoT LTE, or 5G technology (cf. Fig. 1).

To realize the interconnection topologies among fog cells in a secure way, it is necessary to establish a virtual private network as overlays among ARM based virtualized master nodes in a fog cell. Therefore, we have provided an adaptive auto-configuration process to establish a secure mesh among these fog cell control nodes and their attached Docker hosts. It extends the basic VLAN communication paradigm of HCL to a fully operational VPN system.

For this purpose the HCL configuration concept has been enhanced and new functionality including secure tunneling has been adopted. It is based on the open source LINUX framework *Tinc* (see Fig. 5) and may be substituted by evolving improved Docker functionality in the near future.

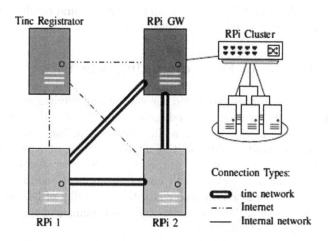

Fig. 5. Interconnection of fog cells.

The realized initialization and configuration management processes of the clustering service are adaptive and enable self-configuration. An IEEE 802.1Q VLAN mesh with a predefined ID for every node has been integrated in such a way that the existing network is not polluted by broadcast messages of the cluster. A DHCP server is configured, such that the IP addresses of nodes may be allocated dynamically. To initialize a cluster service running on top of the VLAN mesh a temporary fixed IP address of a host is used. If the service already exists, it can be recognized by a specific zeroconf notification service and the temporary IP address is replaced by a new one provided by DHCP.

If the address configuration is omitted, HCL will boot and directly use the tunnel interface. Then it reconfigures the Docker Engine to advertise the functionality of Docker Swarm Mode and initiates a Consul container on a master node. Subsequently, all other nodes join the existing Consul service by starting their own Consul containers. The master node acts as key-value store with a built-in DNS server. It is able to discover and track the liveliness of various services across a given infrastructure.

Further details on the used configuration scripts and some performance issues have been discussed in [9].

As outcome all nodes of a cluster connect with a Docker Swarm container and start another instance as a manager or replica of the cluster. The realized self-configuration management process guarantees that important components of the Docker framework such as Docker Compose, Consul, and Docker Swarm can be used to run user services and applications on a configured cluster. The feasibility of the approach has been demonstrated by a private, secured, and geographically distributed cluster running binned services across secured links (see [8,9] for more details).

Currently, the adaptation of OpenFlow switching using Open vSwitch[3] and SDN controllers to an ARM architecture and the integration of the basic *ovs-docker*[4] framework into the HCL stack is on the way and first results are available in an experimental prototype as indicated in Fig. 4.

3   Orchestration of Fog Computing Scenarios

In Subsect. 2.2 we have illustrated that fog computing requires in IoT scenarios the interworking of distinct fog cells and their management nodes, i.e. the cluster controllers. By these means layered architectures including trees and meshes of fog cells can be constructed and the interconnection of containers has to be realized. Therefore, the scalable, automatic deployment and efficient, fault tolerant operation of new services and customer applications in a lightweight virtualization environment requires tools for the clustering of Docker hosts, the deployment of containers, the monitoring and event management, as well as the powerful orchestration of processes.

In recent years several platforms offering cluster computing with LINUX containers have been developed mainly for powerful data centers, e.g. Apache Mesos[5] or Google's Kubernetes[6]. Docker has integrated Docker Swarm Mode as Engine clustering tool to enable similar orchestration features and to support container scheduling and management tasks across interconnected hosts (cf. [11, 13]). As HCL relies on those frameworks, it can enable the same functionality on cheap, energy efficient ARM-based hardware like RPi, Pine A64, or ClearFog SBC's.

---

[3] See URL: http://openvswitch.org/.

[4] See URL: https://github.com/openvswitch/ovs/blob/master/utilities/ovs-docker.

[5] See URL: http://mesos.apache.org/.

[6] See URL: http://kubernetes.io/.

3.1   Orchestration Tools for ARM Clusters

Clustering of hosts with 64-bit ARM architecture is a prerequisite for fog computing scenarios and has been studied in recent years (cf. [7,12,21]). To the best of our knowledge, in spring 2012 researchers at the University of Glasgow have started the first public project on cloud computing with Raspberry Pi 1, bundling 56 Raspberry Pi's and utilizing LXC[7] container virtualization (cf. [19,21]). After that many related projects followed (see e.g. [6,14,20]), while the largest cluster with 300 RPi's has been built at Bolzano University [2]. In mid-2015 researcher at the University of Glasgow started with in-depth experiments using Kubernetes and Docker on a cluster using the second version of Raspberry Pi's. Official support for Kubernetes on ARM has been performed by L. Kaldström's project 'Kubernetes on ARM'[8] among others (see [7,12,15,17]).

However, the performance of Kubernetes and Docker Swarm Mode has not been evaluated thoroughly by detailed measurements on those hardware platforms in any of the aforementioned experiments. The latter ended when all nodes were up and running. For instance, no experiment measured the performance characteristics of load balancing by a simple load test.

In addition, the first evidence of testing fault-tolerance capabilities of Kubernetes is provided by a talk of Tsang and Wassink at Devoxx, Belgium, in 2015[9]. Studies by Nissen and Jensen [16,17] provide the most versatile investigation about Kubernetes on Raspberry Pi's. Although they are the first to actually perform a load test on a RPi cluster, their presented measurements still don't cover other important resource consumption aspects.

In this regard our investigations on the suitability of Docker Swarm Mode and its versatile alternative Kubernetes on an ARM infrastructure clustered by HCL have been stimulated by the gaps of those studies and the evaluation is based on a hardware environment similar to that one used by Nissen and Jensen [17].

3.2   Performance Comparison of Container Orchestration

It is our objective to illustrate the comparison of major performance characteristics w.r.t. Docker Swarm Mode v1.12.2 and 1.12.3, respectively, with HypriotOS-v1.0.1[10] and the Kubernetes protocol stack on top of clustered Docker hosts with HypriotOS-v0.8 and interconnected Docker 1.11.1 containers. The latter suites have been used as basic orchestration tools for a scalable deployment and operations on ARM architectures based on the PicoCluster kit[11] due to code stability issues.

---

[7] See URL: https://linuxcontainers.org/.

[8] See URL: https://github.com/luxas/kubernetes-on-arm/releases, https://luxaslabs.com/.

[9] See URL: https://www.youtube.com/watch?v=kT1vmK0r184.

[10] See URL: https://blog.hypriot.com/downloads/.

[11] See URL: https://www.picocluster.com/collections/starter-picocluster-kits/products/pico-5-raspberry-pi-starter-kit?variant=29344698892.

Our test bed is provided by a cluster with 5 Raspberry Pi 3 Model B boards and SD cards Samsung EVO Plus, 32 GByte, with high performance of 20 MBps writing and 80 MBps reading speed. Hosts have been interconnected by a router with 100 Mbps port speed that can be utilized up to 94.4 % by RPi's and provides a DHCP service. Hosts synchronized by NTP were also interconnected to a desktop as external management and master control node with M/Monit as process monitoring server to store and visualize the performance data collected by Monit 5.11.0 clients at the RPi's (see Fig. 6).

The experiments were performed to validate whether the claims regarding the efficiency of container processing and memory access as well as the high-availability guarantees of the cluster orchestration tools Docker Swarm Mode and Kubernetes still hold in the resource constrained environment of a SBC cluster.

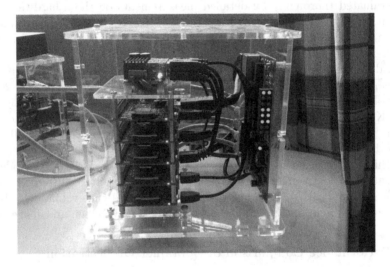

Fig. 6. A fog gateway based on a PicoCluster of RPi's controlling a cluster of fog cells.

The evaluation has considered the resource usage of the instances regarding both the manager and worker nodes of the interconnected containers hosted in a cluster as well as load balancing and resilience characteristics. Details of the used configuration scripts are publically available[12] to enable further validation tests.

In the first step, we have illustrated the exemplary resource consumption of native service clustering based on three different scenarios:

– Scenario 1 considers a fresh installation where only the service monitor *Monit* and the Docker daemon are running to get some ground-truth on the basic process load of Docker containers on the RPi's.

---

[12] See URL: https://blog.hypriot.com/post/high-availability-with-docker/.

- Scenario 2 represents a container cluster after starting the Docker Swarm Mode.
- Scenario 3 considers a cluster after starting Kubernetes as orchestration suite of the interconnected Docker containers.

In all scenarios the achieved performance results stemming from a sampling frequency of 1 Hz of the manager node (first entry) and worker nodes (second entry) have been recorded. Table 1 illustrates a typical outcome of a resource consumption test.

Table 1. Measurements of exemplary resource consumption by Docker and Kubernetes instances in our HCL-BaFog test bed.

Sce.	CPU usage [%] Manager/- Worker	Memory usage [%] Manager/- Worker	Process CPU Docker [%] Manager/Worker	Process memory Docker [%] Manager/Worker
1	0.44	4.21	0.05	2.47
2	1.43/0.83	7.87/7.4	1.1/0.44	57.45/2.42
3	14.74/2.01	34.21/12.68	5.76/1.31	479.51/160.77

As seen in Fig. 7 Docker Swarm Mode v1.12.2. is already able to balance the incoming traffic load very well among all worker nodes (node-black, node-green, node-blue, node-orange) while the master (node-red) is able to manage all aggregated traffic load.

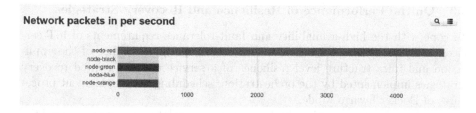

Fig. 7. Balancing incoming network traffic of the RPi cluster with Docker v1.12.2. (Color figure online)

Considering both type of nodes, one can recognize that, as expected, Kubernetes requires much more resources than Docker in Swarm Mode. Subtracting the realized consumption of scenario 1 from those of scenario 2 and 3, the resource consumption of Docker and Kubernetes can be isolated in terms of a resulting difference-in-difference model (see Table 2). Considering the CPU usage on the Raspberry Pi hosts in this exemplary cluster scenario, Kubernetes requires 14.4 and 4 times, respectively, more resources w.r.t. manager and worker nodes than

Table 2. Difference-in-difference model of an exemplary resource consumption.

Sce.	CPU usage [%] Manager/Worker	Memory usage [%] Manager/-Worker	Process CPU Docker [%] Manager/Worker	Process memory Docker [%] Manager/Worker
2	0.99/0.39	3.75/3.28	1.05/0.39	54.98/0
3	14.3/1.57	30.09/8.561	5.71/1.26	477.04/158.3

Docker in Swarm Mode. Regarding the memory usage, Kubernetes allocates 8 times respectively 2.61 times more memory than Docker Swarm Mode. In terms of process CPU seizure by Docker, Kubernetes requires 5.4 times respectively 3.23 times more CPU time than Docker Swarm Mode. Regarding process memory allocation, the resource consumption of Kubernetes is even worse. In summary, the prototypical experimental setup has revealed that Kubernetes requires on average 9.1 times more resources for the master node and 41.9 times more for worker nodes.

The reason is that the orchestration capabilities of Kubernetes are much more sophisticated and customizable compared with the current Docker Swarm Mode. Additionally, Kubernetes has a much richer feature set because it offers by default advanced operation services, such as service monitoring, centralized logging and a dashboard. The latter allows to control the cluster almost purely by the associated graphical user interface.

Thus, it is a challenging future development task to enhance the orchestration capabilities of Docker Swarm Mode while maintaining its efficient resource consumption on SBC clusters.

3.3   On the Performance of Resilience and Recovery Strategies

To cope with the high-availability and fault-tolerance requirements of IoT services in fog computing scenarios, we investigate the performance of the application and infrastructure level resilience of a service and the related recovery strategies implemented by the orchestration, scheduling and deployment procedures of Docker Swarm Mode.

The study has been inspired by Nissen and Jensen [16] who have evaluated the resilience at application and infrastructure levels of cloud computing on an ARM platform using Kubernetes. Here their infrastructure resilience experiment based on a simple Docker service has been repeated in the cluster environment of our test bed HCL-BaFog. As exemplary service of the resilience test a HTTP server is used by the swarm manager node acting as leader. When the Docker Engine is operated in Swarm Mode, a corresponding Docker service can be created to deploy the related image of the replicated HTTP application among the clustered Docker Engines of the swarm. The swarm manager schedules the service tasks onto the interconnected hosts in the swarm as one or more replica tasks which are the atomic scheduling entities. The latter instantiates a container for each task which is created and allocated by the orchestration function to an available worker node of the swarm. All tasks are then running independently of each other on the available nodes. The orchestration function performs permanent health checking of the running containers in the cluster to guarantee the level of replicas and creates a new replica task that spawns a new container at some node in case of a node crash.

The number of replicas of the container is a major tunable parameter for the level of fault tolerance provided to the service by the fog computing platform. This number of replicas in the cluster affects under varying processing loads the recovery time of a fault-tolerant distributed application running under Docker Swarm Mode and determines its response time to a requestor outside the cluster.

Therefore, a cluster recovery after a crash of a single node has been emulated with a MTBF of 5 min by the following small-scale availability test procedure of a replicated web service:

1. Docker runs a web service that is reachable from an external device, i.e. the desktop computer.
2. Variable background load is generated in terms of HTTP GET requests to the cluster using the HTTP benchmark and stress testing tool *Vegeta*[13].
3. To test the fault tolerance and recovery capabilities after a single point failure, a stopping of all processes related to the Docker service with a prescribed level of task replication and a hard rebooting of the whole cluster is performed. The following replication scenarios of the Docker service have been covered:
   (a) The Docker service runs with 1 replica.
   (b) The Docker service runs with 2 replicas.
   (c) The Docker service runs with 5 replicas.
   (d) The Docker service runs with 10 replicas.
4. During step 3, we have permanently measured the request rate processed by the cluster per seconds, the number of activated replicas, and the latency of the service response.

For comparison the results of similar experiments on a Kubernetes cluster have been adopted from Nissen and Jensen [16, Sec. 8.2, Fig. 8.5, p. 81]. The exemplary outcome of the recovery test by the Docker framework on our test bed is illustrated in Fig. 8. It is recognized that there is a sharp breaking point in the latency following a $M/G/N$ response time pattern, e.g. beyond a request rate of 900 for $N = 10$ replicas. Then the load balancing after recovery reaches a high utilization level during the redistribution and restart of replicated containers. The improvement of the service robustness due to an increasing number of replicas constitutes a positive outcome of the applied resilience strategy. Regarding the given latency threshold of 50 ms, we realize, however, that Docker Swarm Mode has still a lot of potential for an improvement beyond its current low recovery rates.

---

[13] URL: https://github.com/tsenart/vegeta, https://hub.docker.com/r/mistobaan/vegeta/.

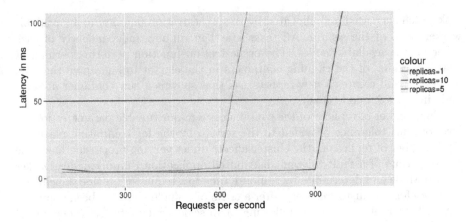

Fig. 8. Latency of the service response for Docker Swarm Mode in a recovery test.

Considering the performance of Kubernetes and Docker in Swarm Mode on more powerful systems with Intel or AMD designs or other low-cost multi-kernel ARM platforms, e.g. ONDROID-XU4 with its Octa core processor and 2 GByte RAM, of course more extensive studies are required to identify an optimal solution w.r.t the large variety of different scenarios arising from exciting IoT applications. They can provide the basis for a broader comparison on the scalability and suitability of the processing and memory units of the used hardware platforms. Regarding a monitoring and alerting application of fog computing by means of a HCL-like Raspberry Pi platform in the library depots of University of Bamberg, our current investigation already indicates that the microSD storage units may become a dependability bottleneck. In conclusion, extensive investigations of those performability issues will represent an important topic of our future research.

4   Conclusions

At present mobile edge and fog computing constitute a challenging effort to establish the distributed processing concepts and services of cloud computing at the edge of converging wireless networks and wired high-speed backbones. The need to integrate advanced transport and computing technology will increase with the rapid deployment of technology from 5G mobile networks and the fast evolution of Internet-of-Things including diverse applications from different domains such as smart energy, smart transport, smart city, smart home, and e-health.

In our paper we have discussed the concepts of our fog computing platform HCL-BaFog derived from Hypriot Cluster Lab (HCL). The latter has been developed for a resource constrained 64-bit ARM architecture, like Raspberry Pi's or ClearFog single board computers, and includes software-defined networking and lightweight LINUX container virtualization based on the open source framework

Docker. We have presented the design principles of the fog computing platform and discussed its usage to create secure overlays among Docker containers.

To guarantee high-availability features and to provide failsafe data processing, we have also elaborated on the integration of Docker Swarm Mode and Kubernetes as basic orchestration tools and drawn some conclusions on their suitability regarding fog computing on resource constrained hardware platforms.

Our results have revealed the feasibility of our approach to deploy and orchestrate automatically a small, energy efficient virtualized edge cloud on cheap commodity hardware. Regarding the cluster architecture, up to now HCL-BaFog's single point of failure is given by the master (or leader) node managing a Docker Swarm Mode. Thus, our future work will focus on fast, secure failover mechanisms based on the recently published resilience mechanisms of Docker Swarm Mode and its enhancement to scalable master-slave scenarios. Regarding the automation of a SDN deployment and traffic routing across Docker containers, further extensions of the ovs-docker framework are required on the ARM architecture such that an application can connect to the Docker REST API and start a new container with a specialized service, e.g. a caching proxy, while the container is attached to an ovs instance.

Acknowledgment. The authors are very much indebted to those members of the Hypriot Pirate team outside the University of Bamberg, including Govinda Fichtner, Dieter Reuter, and Stefan Scherer, that has developed the HCL platform during spare time and that guarantees its overwhelming success by enormous personal efforts.

References

1. Aazam, M., Huh, E.-N.: Fog computing and smart gateway based communication for cloud of things. In: International Conference on Future Internet of Things and Cloud (FiCloud) 2014, pp. 464–470, August 2014
2. Abrahamsson, P., et al.: Affordable and energy-efficient cloud computing clusters: the Bolzano Raspberry Pi cloud cluster experiment. In: IEEE 5th International Conference on Cloud Computing Technology and Science (CloudCom) 2013, vol. 2, pp. 170–175. IEEE (2013)
3. Al-Fuqaha, A., et al.: Internet of things: a survey on enabling technologies, protocols, and applications. IEEE Commun. Surv. Tutor. **17**(4), 2347–2376 (2015). (Fourth Quarter)
4. Atzori, L., et al.: Internet of things: a survey. Comput. Netw. **54**, 2787–2805 (2010)
5. Docker: What Is Docker? Comparing Containers and Virtual Machines. https://www.docker.com/what-docker#/VM. Accessed 04 Oct 2016
6. GCHQ: GCHQ's Raspberry Pi 'Bramble' - exploring the future of computing, 11. https://www.gchq.gov.uk/news-article/gchqs-raspberry-pi-bramble-exploring-future-computing. Accessed 14 Oct 2016
7. Goasguen, S.: Running Kubernetes on a Raspberry Pi, 16. http://sebgoa.blogspot.de/2015/09/running-kubernetes-on-raspberry-pi.html. Accessed 14 Oct 2016
8. Großmann, M., Eiermann, A., Renner, M.: Hypriot cluster lab: an ARM-powered cloud solution utilizing docker. In: 23rd International Conference on Telecommunications (ICT 2016), pp. 16–18, Thessaloniki, Greece, May 2016

9. Großmann, M., Eiermann, A.: Automated establishment of a secured network for providing a distributed container cluster. In: 28th International Teletraffic Congress (ITC28), 13–15 September 2016, Würzburg, Germany (2016)
10. Gubbi, J., et al.: Internet of Things (IoT): a vision, architectural elements, and future directions. Future Gener. Comput. Syst. **29**, 1645–1660 (2013)
11. Holla, S.: Orchestrating Docker. Packt Publishing Ltd., Birmingham (2015)
12. Huß, R.: A Raspberry Pi 3 Kubernetes Cluster, 27. https://ro14nd.de/kubernetes-on-raspberry-pi3. Accessed 14 Oct 2016
13. Kaewkasi, C.: Docker Swarm Mode, 2016. https://medium.com/@chanwit/docker-swarm-mode-fde1e3e392ae#p7w8sxhac. Accessed 14 Oct 2016
14. Kiepert, J.: Creating a Raspberry Pi-based Beowulf Cluster, Boise State University, 22 May 2013. Accessed 14 Oct 2016
15. Mogren, L.: Kubernetes on ARM (2016). Accessed 14 Oct 2016
16. Nissen, K., Jensen, M.: Kubecloud - a small-scale tangible cloud computing environment. Master's thesis, Aarhus University - Department of Engineering, 6 June (2016). http://kubecloud.io/files/kubecloud.pdf
17. Nissen, K., Jensen, M.: Setting up a Kubernetes on ARM cluster, 13. http://kubecloud.io/kubernetes-on-arm-cluster/. Accessed 14 Oct 2016
18. Skarlat, O., et al.: Resource provisioning for IoT services in the fog. In: 2016 IEEE 9th International Conference on Service-Oriented Computing and Applications (SOCA 2016), 4–6 November 2016. Macau, China (2016)
19. Tso, F.P., et al.: The Glasgow Raspberry Pi Cloud: a scale model for cloud computing infrastructures. In: 2013 IEEE 33rd International Conference on Distributed Computing Systems (ICDCS) Workshops, IEEE, pp. 108–112 (2013)
20. University of Southampton. Southampton engineers a Raspberry Pi Supercomputer, 11 September 2012. https://www.southampton.ac.uk/sjc/raspberrypi/Raspberry_Pi_supercomputer_11Sept2012.pdf. Accessed 14 Oct 2016
21. White, D.: Building a Raspberry Pi cloud (2014). Accessed 14 Oct 2016

Markov Random Walk vs. Higher-Order Factorization Machines: A Comparison of State-of-the-Art Recommender Algorithms

Julian Knoll$^{(\boxtimes)}$, David Köckritz, and Rainer Groß

Technische Hochschule Nürnberg Georg Simon Ohm, Keßlerplatz 12,
90489 Nuremberg, Germany
{Julian.Knoll,Rainer.Gross}@th-nuernberg.de,
Koeckritz.David@gmail.com

Abstract. World-wide research on recommender systems has resulted in great, highly effective algorithms based on a large variety of different concepts. Two of these promising recommender approaches are the Markov Random Walk and (higher-order) Factorization Machines. Unfortunately, due to the substantial effort for optimizing hyperparameters, most articles that describe new recommender approaches do not compare the obtained results with other state-of-the-art approaches in the recommender domain.

This paper demonstrates how different state-of-the-art recommender algorithms can be compared in a consistent manner. Furthermore, we investigate under which circumstances Factorization Machines should be preferred and in which situations Markov Random Walk is the most striking algorithm. In addition, we include the restart concept into a Markov Random Walk with an optimized walk length and show how the number of factors of each order in a higher-order Factorization Machine can be optimized.

Keywords: Markov Random Walk · Restart · Higher order · Factorization Machines · Collaborative filtering

1 Introduction

With the rapid growth of internet-based applications around the turn of the millennium and the associated strong increase in data volumes, software for filtering and identifying relevant information has become indispensable. Thus, it became essential to offer suitable products to prospective customers automatically, especially for companies with a business model based on digitized business processes. Recommender algorithms deal precisely with this problem and try to personalize product recommendations for customers as much as possible.

In this paper, we optimize and compare the two state-of-the-art recommender approaches Markov Random Walk (MRW) and Factorization Machines (FMs) regarding their recommendation quality. We compare these results with collaborative filtering (CF) approaches and the two simple heuristics global popularity

© Springer International Publishing AG 2017
G. Eichler et al. (Eds.): I4CS 2017, CCIS 717, pp. 87–103, 2017.
DOI: 10.1007/978-3-319-60447-3_7

and random recommendation to discover whether the additional complexity connected with the state-of-the-art algorithms results in clearly better outcomes.

We make the following main contributions. First, we present an approach concerning how to compare recommender algorithms in a consistent manner. Second, we demonstrate a new approach which incorporates the restart concept with a MRW with optimized walk length. Third, we show a way to optimize Higher-order Factorization Machines (HoFMs) regarding the number of factors. And fourth, we carry out a simulation study in order to provide a detailed analysis explaining under what circumstances the MRW approach or the HoFM approach should be preferred in a recommender system.

The remainder of this work is structured as follows. In Sect. 2, we give an overview of the related work. The theoretical background concerning the MRW and the HoFM approaches is presented in Sect. 3. After describing the simulation study conducted in Sect. 4, we discuss its results in Sect. 5. Concluding remarks and an outlook on our future work are contained in Sect. 6.

2   Related Work

In their recent survey study about recommender algorithms, Shi et al. identified three state-of-the-art algorithms that cope with various sources of contextual information (additional data which are associated with a user, an item, or the interaction between both of them) [16]: Tensor Factorization (TF), FMs, and graph-based algorithms which can be represented by the MRW approach. Due to the fact that TF is nested in the FM approach [14], it is surprising that, to date, only one publication refers to both terms "Markov Random Walk" and "Factorization Machine" [2]. Nevertheless, even in that publication neither the concepts nor the results of the algorithms were compared. Consequently, the analysis of the recommendation quality of the aforementioned approaches produces a worthwhile aim for this paper. In the following, we give a brief insight into the development of both the MRW and the FM approach in the recommender context.

2.1   Development of Markov Random Walk

The MRW recommender algorithm is based on the concept of "PageRank", which was introduced by Page et al. and served as the basis for the Google-ranking algorithm [12]. Its aim is to rank websites according to their importance by performing a random walk on a graph, which consists of websites and links. Aggarwal explained the personalized PageRank in detail, which ranks websites not entirely depending on their global popularity but, for instance, according to specific topics [1, pp. 314]. Furthermore, he provided an overview of application possibilities to generate user-specific recommendations, for example, with the algorithm "FolkRank" which was introduced by Hotho et al. and can be applied in social systems [8]. To build their model, they used a folksonomy that contained information about users which assigned items with different tags.

Konstas et al. performed a random walk based algorithm on data from the music social network "last.fm" and included a folksonomy, track playcount, and bonds of friendship in their model [11]. Like the personalized PageRank adapted by Hotho et al., this approach generated user-specific result values with the restart concept based on the stationary probability distribution. They compared this algorithm with an extended collaborative filtering method and showed that their approach generated recommendations of higher quality.

Clements et al. introduced twelve retrieval tasks in social systems, including the generation of recommendations on the basis of a tag and a specific user [4,5]. They carried out a simulation study on data from MovieLens and LibraryThing with a random walk based algorithm and measured the recommendation quality with the metric Normalized Discounted Cumulative Gain (NDCG). Furthermore, they included a folksonomy and ratings in their model. As opposed to the aforementioned methods, they optimized the walk length, configured the initial distribution specific to a tag and a user, and included the concept of self-transition. In Sect. 3.2, we show how to integrate the restart concept into the approach of Clements et al. [5].

2.2 Development of Factorization Machines

Based on prior research in the field of tensor factorization (TF) [15], Rendle introduced second-order FMs in 2010 as a concept which combined support vector machines and factorization models into one approach [13]. Though FMs serve as a general predictor in the sense of machine learning, they were always strongly connected to the domain of recommender systems.

In 2012, an open-source software library called libfm was published to support research in that area [14]. It includes several learning methods for FMs, namely: stochastic gradient descent, stochastic gradient descent with adaptive regularization, coordinate descent (alias alternating least squares), and Markov Chain Monte Carlo. In the meantime, more software tools utilizing the FM approach were developed, such as the R-package "FactoRizationMachines" used in this study.

In the 2010 article on second-order FMs, the description of a "d-way Factorization Machine model" already existed, generalizing the second-order approach to an arbitrary order without going into detail about an efficient training algorithm [13]. It took until 2016, that FMs were implemented to cope with interactions of the third or higher orders [3,10]. We will illustrate the approaches of second-order and HoFMs in more detail in Sect. 3.3.

3 Theoretical Background

3.1 Data Preparation

In order to generate recommendations, each of the considered approaches requires the input data in different representation forms. While CF and global popularity compound users, items, and ratings in one so-called user-item matrix (UI matrix), the MRW requires data in the form of an adjacency matrix, whereas FMs use these information captured in a feature matrix and a target vector. Figure 1 exemplifies the different representation forms of input data for the following situation: User u_1 rates item i_2 with four stars and tags it with tag t_1, and rates item i_3 with two stars and tags it with the tags t_1 and t_3; User u_2 rates item i_1 with three stars and tags it with the tags t_1, t_3 and t_4, and rates item i_3 with one star and tags it with tag t_3; User u_3 rates item i_2 with five stars and tags it with tag t_4, and rates item i_4 with five stars and tags it with tag t_2.

	i_1	i_2	i_3	i_4
u_1	NA	4	2	NA
u_2	3	NA	1	NA
u_3	NA	5	NA	5

(a) Exemplary UI matrix (CF and global popularity)

	u_1	u_2	u_3	i_1	i_2	i_3	i_4	t_1	t_2	t_3	t_4
u_1	1	0	0	0	4	2	0	2	0	1	0
u_2	0	1	0	3	0	1	0	1	0	2	1
u_3	0	0	1	0	5	0	5	0	1	0	1
i_1	0	3	0	1	0	0	0	1	0	1	1
i_2	4	0	5	0	1	0	0	1	0	0	1
i_3	2	1	0	0	0	1	0	1	0	2	0
i_4	0	0	5	0	0	0	1	0	1	0	0
t_1	2	1	0	1	1	1	0	1	0	0	0
t_2	0	0	1	0	0	0	1	0	1	0	0
t_3	1	2	0	1	0	2	0	0	0	1	0
t_4	0	1	1	1	1	0	0	0	0	0	1

(b) Exemplary adjacency matrix (MRW)

x_1	x_2	x_3	x_4	x_5	x_6	x_7	x_8	x_9	x_{10}	x_{11}	y
u_1	u_2	u_3	i_1	i_2	i_3	i_4	t_1	t_2	t_3	t_4	
1	0	0	0	1	0	0	1	0	0	0	4
1	0	0	0	0	1	0	1	0	1	0	2
0	1	0	1	0	0	0	1	0	1	1	3
0	1	0	0	0	1	0	0	0	1	0	1
0	0	1	0	1	0	0	0	0	0	1	5
0	0	1	0	0	0	1	0	1	0	0	5

(c) Exemplary feature matrix **X** and target vector **y** (FMs)

Fig. 1. Different forms of data representation

At first glance, it is obvious that the UI matrix contains less information than the other forms of representation. It lacks all data about users assigning tags to items. In order to compare results in a consistent manner, we analyze different cases in which either all available information is given to the algorithms, or the algorithms only receive data about the ratings.

3.2 Markov Random Walk

Theoretical Background of a Random Walk. The MRW approach was introduced by Clements et al. [4,5] and is based on a random walk on graphs.

This is a stochastic process, more precisely a Markov chain, with discrete time and states. A walk through the graph can be depicted by defining a family of random variables X_n, each associated to a specific state (node) at the time n [6, p. 29]. The graph with the set of nodes F can be described by adjacency matrix A which contains a column and a row for every node. Let g and h be any nodes of the graph ($g, h \in F$) with a_{gh} corresponding to the weight of the edge which directs from g to h in matrix A. For example, the adjacency matrix in Fig. 1b refers to a graph with 11 nodes where $a_{u_1 i_2} = 4$. In a Markov chain a future state is only dependent on the current state and not previous ones [9, p. 49]. Furthermore, we regard homogeneous Markov chains for which the transition probability is independent of the time [9, p. 59]. Therefore, a transition probability p_{gh} can be calculated by normalizing the value a_{gh} by applying $p_{gh} = \frac{a_{gh}}{\sum_{h \in F} a_{gh}}$ [6, p. 29].

The random walk begins with multiplying the row vector containing the initial probability distribution v_0 by the transition matrix P which consists of the values p_{gh} [5]. This first step of the walk results in the distribution v_1. The process continues by recursively multiplying v_n by P as shown in the following formula:

$$v_{n+1} = v_n P. \tag{1}$$

Consequently, the probability distribution of the states after n steps of the random walk is represented by the row vector v_n which consists of the probabilities $v_n(g)$ of any node g. If the regarded Markov chain is aperiodic and irreducible, a stationary probability distribution v_∞ can be calculated by iterating until $v_\infty = v_\infty P$ [6, p. 30].

Building the Model. The MRW algorithm uses the information included in a folksonomy of users who tagged items. This results in a triple relation $Y \subseteq U \times T \times I$, whereas U, T, I, respectively, are the set of users, tags, and items [8]. The MRW model is represented by the transition matrix P. The first step in generating this matrix is to build the adjacency matrix A which consists of nine submatrices (see Fig. 1b) [5]. Assuming $u_k \in U$ (with $k = 1, \ldots, K$), $t_m \in T$ (with $m = 1, \ldots, M$) and $i_b \in I$ (with $b = 1, \ldots, B$), the UT matrix and the IT matrix can be calculated according to the following formulas [8]:

$$UT(u_k, t_m) = |i_b \in I : (u_k, t_m, i_b) \in Y|, \tag{2}$$

$$IT(i_b, t_m) = |u_k \in U : (u_k, t_m, i_b) \in Y|. \tag{3}$$

This means that a cell (u_k, t_m) of UT contains the number of items which user u_k assigned to tag t_m. The value of each cell (i_b, t_m) in IT corresponds to the number of users which relate tag t_m to item i_b. Following this, the matrices TU and TI are generated by applying $TU = UT^T$ and $TI = IT^T$.

It is also possible to generate the UI matrix based on the folksonomy as shown by Hotho et al. [8]. In this case each cell (u_k, i_b) of UI is filled with the number of tags which user u_k assigned to item i_b. However, as part of a simulation study in which user-specific recommendations were generated by using a tag as a search term, Clements et al. [5] showed that using a UI matrix with explicit ratings led to better recommendations. Thus, we incorporated the ratings of the UI matrix (Fig. 1a) in the adjacency matrix A (Fig. 1b) and generated the submatrix IU by applying $IU = UI^T$.

In preparation for applying the concept of self-transition, the submatrices UU, II, and TT are generated as identity matrices. The next step in building the model is to weight the submatrices UT and IT with the "term frequency - inverse document frequency (TF-IDF)" [5]:

$$UT_{TF-IDF}(u_k, t_m) = UT(u_k, t_m) \cdot log(\frac{K}{\sum_{k=1}^{k=K} sgn(UT(u_k, t_m))}), \qquad (4)$$

$$IT_{TF-IDF}(i_b, t_m) = IT(i_b, t_m) \cdot log(\frac{B}{\sum_{b=1}^{b=B} sgn(IT(i_b, t_m))}). \qquad (5)$$

The sgn function returns the value 1 if the user u_k used tag t_m or if tag t_m is assigned to the item i_b and 0 otherwise. In this way, the cell values of UT and IT and the weights of the corresponding edges in the graph are especially diminished if a tag is used by many users or assigned too many items. Consequently, the influence of such tags on the recommendations is reduced. Furthermore, $TU_{TF-IDF} = UT_{TF-IDF}^T$ and $TI_{TF-IDF} = IT_{TF-IDF}^T$ still remains applicable.

To consider the different scaling of the data, all nine submatrices are normalized independently so that the sum of each row of every submatrix is equal to 1. The parameters α, β, γ, and δ ($\alpha, \beta, \gamma, \delta \in [0,1]$) are applied on the resulting matrix A_{norm} to generate the transition matrix P (Fig. 2). The probability of a user-tag, item-tag and tag-item step in the random walk can be controlled with β, γ, and δ. The parameter α is applied to the identity matrices UU_{norm}, II_{norm}, and TT_{norm} and thus defines the probability of a self-transition step [5].

The first step in generating recommendations for a specific user u_k starts with initializing the row vector v_0 consisting of $K + B + M$ elements by setting the element corresponding to user u_k to $v_0(u_k) = 1$ while all other elements are set to 0 [4]. Afterwards, v_0 is multiplied by the transition matrix P to obtain the probability distribution v_1 after the first step. By continuing this process (as mentioned in Eq. 1), the probability spreads from the starting node (corresponding to user u_k) to directly and indirectly connected nodes of the graph. Finally, a ranked list of items is calculated by retrieving the part of the probability distribution referring to the items ($v_n(K + 1, \ldots, K + B)$) [4]. Assuming that items which are assigned a rating or a tag by the user u_k had been already consumed by her/him, these items are removed from the list. As a last step, we obtain the recommendation list by ordering the remaining items according to their probability.

Combining Restart and Walk-Length. In deviation from the algorithm of Clements et al., we included the parameter ρ ($\rho \in [0,1]$) which dynamically adds edges to the graph during the generation of recommendations, connecting each node with the starting node. To adjust the probability of a step to other nodes,

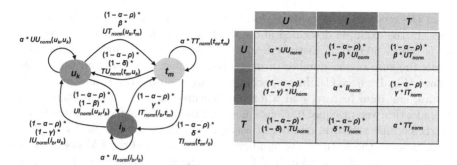

Fig. 2. Generation of the transition matrix P based on A_{norm}

a restart step, or a self-transition step, the following inequality has to apply: $\alpha + \rho \leq 1$. The final calculation of the transition matrix P is illustrated in Fig. 2. Since we add the restart with each step, the probability distribution after $n + 1$ steps is calculated with the following formula:

$$v_{n+1} = v_n P + \rho v_0. \tag{6}$$

Considering a MRW without restart ($\rho = 0$), recommendations generated based on the stationary probability distribution v_∞ are independent of the user u_k and reflect the global popularity of the items. Clements et al. [5] showed that the walk length n can be interpreted as a parameter influencing the quality of recommendations. For instance, a low n results in a probability distribution considering only nodes near the starting node u_k and thus could lead to a higher degree of personalization of the recommendations.

As an alternative approach to personalize the probability distribution with respect to u_k, the restart concept can be applied to influence v_∞ [8,11]. The parameter ρ defines the proportion of the weight flowing back into the starting node u_k with each step of the algorithm. This implies that nodes in the environment of the starting node receive a higher weight within the next steps of the walk. Although it is usually applied based on a stationary distribution, we assume that a combination of the restart concept and a non-stationary distribution with an optimized walk length n increases the personalization and thus improves the recommendation quality.

3.3 Factorization Machines

Data Representation. As a supervised machine learning approach, FMs attempt to extract structure from training examples in the form of a statistical model. Afterwards, this model can be used to predict or classify new cases. Each training example consists of a feature vector that contains information about this case and a target value which should be predicted with the specified model. The feature vectors of all training examples are collected in a feature matrix **X** and the target values in a corresponding target vector **y** (Fig. 1c).

In the recommender context, most of the features are usually binary variables. In the example described above, each user, each item, and each assigned tag is represented by a distinct feature. Thus, the total number of features q equals the sum of the number of users, the number of items, and the number of tags (Fig. 1c: $q = 11$). In a specific training example the values of one user feature, one item feature, and a few tag features equal 1 and all other values of the feature vector equal 0. Consequently, this results in a very sparse feature matrix because the total number of users, items, and tags is typically large.

In general, the features are numbered from 1 to q and the FM does not distinguish between different kinds of features. The great advantage of this representation of data is that every captured information about the training examples can be added easily to the feature matrix. For instance, if we obtain information about the weekday at which the items were rated by the users, we could simply add seven new features, each representing the corresponding day of the week.

Second-Order Factorization Machines. Based on data with q features, the following second-order FM model maps a feature vector $\mathbf{x} \in \mathbb{R}^q$ (one row of feature matrix $\mathbf{X}$ in Fig. 1c) to a corresponding target value $y \in \mathbb{R}$ (one value of target vector $\mathbf{y}$ in Fig. 1c):

$$\hat{y}(x) := w_0 + \sum_{j=1}^{q} w_j x_j + \sum_{j_1=1}^{q} \sum_{j_2=j_1+1}^{q} x_{j_1} x_{j_2} \sum_{f=1}^{k_2} v_{j_1,f}^{(2)} v_{j_2,f}^{(2)}, \tag{7}$$

with $w_0 \in \mathbb{R}$, $w \in \mathbb{R}^q$, and $V^{(2)} \in \mathbb{R}^{q \times k_2}$ as the model parameters [15]. Consequently, the second-order FM factorizes all pairwise interactions based on the dot product of two respective vectors of the matrix $V^{(2)}$. Thus, all single and pairwise interactions between the features are gathered in this model: One model parameter capturing the global intercept (w_0), q model parameters capturing a weight for each feature (w_j), and $q \cdot k_2$ model parameters capturing the second-order interactions between the features ($v_{j_1,f}^{(2)} v_{j_2,f}^{(2)}$).

By choosing the hyperparameter $k_2 \in \mathbb{N}^+$, we define the number of values factorizing the weight of the second-order interactions. Typically, k_2 is $\ll q$, and thus, in comparison to the number of second-order parameters of a naive polynomial regression (q^2), the FM model contains less parameters ($q k_2$).

Higher-Order Factorization Machines. The following HoFM model generalizes the second-order model equation with respect to higher orders:

$$\hat{y}(x) := w_0 + \sum_{j=1}^{q} w_j x_j + \sum_{l=2}^{d} \sum_{j_1=1}^{q} \cdots \sum_{j_l=j_{l-1}+1}^{q} \left(\prod_{m=1}^{l} x_{j_m} \right) \left(\sum_{f=1}^{k_l} \prod_{m=1}^{l} v_{j_m,f}^{(l)} \right), \tag{8}$$

with $w_0 \in \mathbb{R}$, $w \in \mathbb{R}^q$, and $V^{(l)} \in \mathbb{R}^{q \times k_l}$ as the model parameters [15].

In addition to the second-order FM model, this model captures interactions beyond the second-order. The term $\sum_{f=1}^{k_l} \prod_{m=1}^{l} v_{j_m,f}^{(l)}$ gathers the interactions of the arbitrary order l. Therefore, by setting k_l typically $\ll q$, the number of model parameters decreases in comparison to a naive polynomial regression from q^l to qk_l approximating the interactions of order l based the matrix $V^{(l)}$.

To identify FMs in this article, we use this representation: after the term FM, the first hyperparameter specifies whether linear weights are used in the model (1) or not (0), the following hyperparameters specify the number of factors for each order beginning with the second. The hyperparameters are set in brackets and separated by a "|". The advantage of this representation is that the number of factors of the order l is always specified by the lth hyperparameter. For example, $FM(1|2|1|0)$ represents a FM with linear weights, 2 second-order factors, 1 third-order factor, and no factors of beyond orders.

Learning Method. As shown by Rendle [15] and Knoll [10], FMs can be calculated with linear instead of polynomial complexity. This should be kept in consideration by efficient learning methods in order to retain this advantage. There are some learning methods implemented for training second-order FMs, for instance, stochastic gradient descent, stochastic gradient descent with adaptive regularization, coordinate descent, or Markov Chain Monte Carlo (MCMC) [14].

For this article, we chose the MCMC approach due to its low number of (insensitive) hyperparameters and adapted it with respect to higher orders. The intention of this learning method is to use a Gibbs-sampler based on a normal gamma hyperprior assumed for each model parameter (with unknown mean and unknown precision). Afterwards, each model parameter is estimated as the arithmetic mean over all corresponding conditional outcomes in each iteration. Regarding the (insensitive) hyperparameters of the MCMC learning method, we chose the same (trivial) values as implemented in libFM [14]. Consequently, the only hyperparameters we had to determine for our simulation study were the number of factors for each considered order.

4 Simulation Study

4.1 General Setup

We used the MovieLens 20 m data set for our simulation study and reduced it in line with the approach which Clements et al. [5] had applied to the MovieLens 10 m data set. To ensure the correct implementation of the reduction process, we could successfully reproduce the data set Clements et al. generated in their examination. Following that, all records from the original data set which did not fulfill the following requirements were removed from the data set: Each user who rated an item had to assign at least one tag to this item, each user had to rate at least five items, each item had to be rated by at least two users, and each tag had to be assigned by at least two users. This reduction process is necessary to be able to generate training and test subsets and to increase the density of the data set. It refers to the practice in which many recommender systems do not begin to suggest items unless several items were rated by the active user [5].

The reduced data set was split up randomly into a training and a test subset, each containing 1.218 users and their assigned ratings and tags. We selected a

training-validation subset containing 202 users from the training subset. Based
on these data, we optimized the hyperparameter of the MRW and the FM algorithm applying a leave-one-out approach: in each iteration we removed 20% of
the assigned ratings – including one (relevant) five star item – and the corresponding tags of the active user.

Afterwards, we applied the algorithms with the optimized hyperparameter
setting on the test subset using the leave-one-out approach once more. In total,
1,030 met the requirements to serve as an active user (at least one five-star rating
and at least one rating for a item which was rated by another user). The rest
of that simulation was the same as the aforementioned process of the training
subset. The results shown in Sect. 5 are based on the test subset.

To measure the recommendation quality of the algorithms, we chose two
different kinds of metrics: On the one hand we implemented the ROC/recall
metrics where one item is considered as relevant and should be listed by the
recommender algorithm at the first places [7]. On the other hand as opposed
to the binary approach of the ROC/recall metric, the NDCG differs between
multiple levels of relevance. It takes into account that a lower ranked item is less
useful to a user because the probability that he/she observes it decreases [5].
Consequently, we generated two ranking lists, one containing the relevant item
and 499 non-rated items (for the ROC and recall metrics), the other including
the items of the 20% removed ratings filled up with non-rated items until a total
of 500 items was reached (for the NDCG metrics).

4.2 Analyzed Data Sets

Based on the aforementioned constrains, we generated three data sets for our
simulation study, each containing more information than the one before:

- *data set "ratings"*: The reduced data set contained information about
  2,436 users giving 107,525 ratings to 7,897 items (1,580 0.5-star, 1,911 1-
  star, 1,968 1.5-star, 4,557 2-star, 6,019 2.5-star, 13,128 3-star, 17,461 3.5-
  star, 27,457 4-star, 16,726 4.5-star, and 16,718 5-star ratings). The training
  subset included 1,218 users who rated 6,954 items 51,982 times and the test
  subset 1,218 users rated 7,481 items 55,543 times.
- *data set "ratings/tags"*: This data set contained all data from data set "ratings" and additional information about 12,700 different tags which in total
  were assigned 340,192 times. The tag most frequently used was "SCI-FI"
  (3,277 times), the average number of tags per user was 139.7 and per item
  was 43.1. The data set was divided into training and test subsets in line with
  the subdivision of the data set "ratings".
- *data set "ratings/tags/genre/time"*: This data set again included all data from
  data set "ratings/tags" and additional information about the genres experts
  assigned the items to, as well as information about the time the item was
  rated. In total, the data set contained 19 different genres the movies were
  assigned to. Since a movie could have more than one genre, each of the 19
  genres was treated as either an additional tag (MRW approach) or binary

feature (FM approach). The time information was separated into the hour of day, the weekday, the month, and the year. Each of this extracted information once again served as a tag or binary feature. This data set was also divided into a training and test subset, as done with the data set "ratings".

By analyzing the recommendation quality of the algorithms between these three data sets, we can draw meaningful conclusions regarding which algorithm performs better with less information and which is able to use the additional information to improve results.

4.3   Analyzed Approaches

We considered six different recommender algorithms (MRW, FMs, item-based CF, user-based CF, the global popularity approach, and a random recommender) in our simulation study. Due to the high dependency of MRW and FMs on the hyperparameter setting, we optimized them running a grid-search over different hyperparameter constellations based on the training subset. Optimizing the hyperparameters of both approaches facilitates a consistent comparison with respect to the recommendation quality and serves as an adequate hyperparameter setting for our simulation study based on the test subset. In the following, we describe the configuration of the examined algorithms in detail:

- *MRW with restart (MRW w/ restart)*: We optimized the hyperparameters of the MRW approach, running a grid-search for the walk length n (between 1 and 150), and over the values 0, 0.33, 0.66, and 1 for the further hyperparameters α, β, γ, δ, and ρ.
- *MRW without restart (MRW w/o restart)*: To obtain the hyperparameters for a MRW without our extension (regarding the restart concept), we conducted the grid-search described above under the restriction of $\rho = 0$ which represents the approach of Clements et al. [5]. Though our approach to measuring differs from that of Clements et al. and thus the NDCG results are not comparable, we could reproduce their results in a pre-study which should ensure the correct implementation of the MRW approach.
- *restricted MRW (rest. MRW)*: To find the hyperparameters for the restricted MRW approach [4], we ran a grid-search (as explained above) restricting the values of β, γ, and δ to 0.5. The advantage of this practice is that it could save time during hyperparameter optimization by using these default values.
- *support vector machine (SVM), default FMs (def. 2oFM, def. 3oFM, def. 4oFM)*: The SVM did not include any factors and default FMs contained one factor each up to a distinct order. To be more specific, the default second-order FM included linear weights and one second-order factor ($FM(1|1|0|0)$); the default third-order FM contained linear weights, one second-order factor, and one additional third-order factor ($FM(1|1|1|0)$); and following this pattern the default fourth-order FM contained one additional fourth-order factor ($FM(1|1|1|1)$).

- *optimized second-order FM (opt. 2oFM)*: To obtain an optimal setting for the number of factors of second-order FMs, we searched for the best results varying the number of second-order factors based on the training subset over the values 0, 1, 2, 5, and 10. The outcome was that the best results are generated with 10 second-order factors ($FM(1|10|0|0)$).
- *optimized HoFM (opt. HoFM)*: We determined the hyperparameters of the optimized HoFM by running a grid-search for the number of second-, third-, and fourth-order factors based on the training subset over the values 0, 1, 2, 5, and 10. The HoFM with 10 second-order and 2 third-order factors ($FM(1|10|2|0)$) performed best.
- *item-based CF*: In the first step of item-based CF, the similarities between all pairs of items needed to be calculated. Due to the calculation performance, we decided on Pearson's correlation coefficient. The next step in the ranking process was to define items which are interesting for the active user (ratings ≥ 4 stars). In the following step, we reduced the similarity matrix to rows only containing these items. After aggregating the reduced similarity matrix by item (column), we removed the items which had already been rated by the active user from the resulting score vector. This ensured that the reduced score vector only contains not consumed items. Finally, the remaining items were ranked by the highest aggregated correlation [7].
- *user-based CF*: In contrast to item-based CF, user-based CF calculates the similarities between the active user and all other users. Again, we used Pearson's correlation coefficient for that step. In the next step, we weighted the UI matrix with the correlations between the active user and all other users. Therefore, we multiplied each rating of the UI matrix by the corresponding correlation coefficient. After aggregating the weighted UI matrix by item (column), we removed the items which had already been rated by the active user from the resulting score vector. Again, this ensured that the reduced score vector only contained items which were not consumed. Finally, the remaining items were ranked by the highest aggregated correlation [17].
- *global popularity (glob. pop.)*: This static (non-personalized) recommender is based on the average rating of the respective item over all users, so that each user gets the same recommendations structured in line with the global popularity of the items.
- *random recommender (random)*: This non-personalized recommender selects the items for each user in a completely random order.

We programmed the MRW approach, CF algorithms, the global popularity approach, and the random recommender in the programming language R (partly using the R-package "Matrix"). The HoFM approach was implemented based on the R-package "FactoRizationMachines" and extended regarding the MCMC learning method and the fourth-order interaction term.

5   Results

5.1   Results Based on Ratings

The results we obtained for the simulation based on the data set "ratings" are presented in Table 1. The MRW without restart algorithm generated by far the recommendations with the highest quality. The hyperparameter optimization for MRW with restart resulted in $\rho = 0$ which means that the algorithm cannot profit from the restart concept based on this data set. Furthermore, the restricted MRW approach cannot be applied on this data set because the restriction β, γ, and δ equal to 0.5 only affects relations to tags.

Astonishingly, the second best results are shown for the global popularity approach. This means that the higher complexity of the other approaches did not result in a better recommendation quality and thus can hardly be justified. The recommendation quality of all other considered approaches is clearly lower. The results of the analyzed FM approaches differ only slightly among each other. This is not surprising because the FM approach can only benefit from the additional higher-order terms, if interactions of higher order are existing in the data – but in the data set "ratings" only second-order interactions could possibly exist. User-based and item-based CF generated recommendations of even lower quality. For the former algorithm we measured almost similar values as for the random recommender. Only the ROC-AUC metric showed better results whereas the recall@1 and recall@10 were even worse than the ones of the random recommender.

5.2   Results Based on Ratings and Tags

The results based on the data set "ratings/tags" in Table 2 brought different insights – all results are better than the ones of the global popularity approach in Table 1, except the ROC-AUC value of the SVM with a small difference of

Table 1. Results data set "ratings"

Algorithm	NDCG					ROC	Recall		
	AUC	@10	@50	@250	@500	AUC	@1	@10	@100
MRW w/o restart	**46.26**	**34.76**	**42.28**	**47.49**	**48.58**	**90.50**	**16.12**	**47.77**	**84.37**
glob. pop	40.45	27.94	35.96	41.81	43.22	88.22	11.26	39.32	81.65
def. 2oFM	28.65	16.11	22.81	29.88	33.12	79.90	5.63	22.62	68.16
SVM	28.64	15.97	22.62	29.88	33.05	80.46	6.02	22.82	68.74
def. 4oFM	28.48	16.21	22.61	29.73	32.98	79.22	5.53	23.69	67.48
def. 3oFM	28.37	15.85	22.50	29.60	32.85	80.00	4.95	23.69	68.06
opt. HoFM	28.34	16.06	22.44	29.44	32.89	79.01	5.44	24.17	67.28
opt. 2oFM	28.26	15.90	22.49	29.47	32.78	79.59	5.44	23.69	67.48
item-based CF	<u>20.31</u>	5.67	12.25	22.42	25.09	<u>74.50</u>	0.68	7.77	58.64
user-based CF	<u>11.93</u>	0.92	2.83	13.53	19.22	<u>58.11</u>	0.00	1.46	20.87
random	11.26	1.81	4.05	11.50	19.50	50.51	0.10	1.84	20.78

Table 2. Results data set "ratings/tags"

Algorithm	NDCG					ROC	Recall		
	AUC	@10	@50	@250	@500	AUC	@1	@10	@100
opt. 2oFM	**59.79**	**53.01**	**56.79**	**60.39**	**62.42**	89.14	**46.31**	**63.20**	83.79
opt. HoFM	59.55	52.86	56.57	60.08	62.23	88.78	45.53	61.75	83.30
def. 4oFM	59.00	51.94	55.94	59.57	61.69	88.76	44.66	60.49	82.72
def. 3oFM	58.96	52.18	55.94	59.52	61.64	89.00	44.56	61.84	83.20
SVM	57.41	50.35	54.22	57.93	60.19	88.15	42.91	59.81	82.43
def. 2oFM	57.32	50.16	54.16	57.90	60.06	88.52	41.46	59.81	83.01
MRW w/restart	50.48	39.79	47.02	51.64	52.52	**92.14**	21.55	54.76	87.57
MRW w/o restart	49.93	38.96	46.35	51.06	51.99	92.02	20.78	52.91	87.38
rest. MRW	49.69	38.70	46.14	50.85	51.76	92.03	20.87	53.50	**87.67**

0.07 points. Furthermore, the FM approaches led to better results regarding the NDCG metrics, the recall@1, and the recall@10 whereas the MRW approaches were most successful considering the ROC-AUC value and the recall@100. Looking at the recall@1 values, there is an eye-catching increase of more than 20 points between the MRW and the FM approaches. In addition, we could identify a noticeable impact regarding the hyperparameter optimization of FMs. The MRW approach with restart led to slightly better results in all metrics. This indicates that the approach could take advantage of the higher weight on the starting node and thus should be further investigated.

5.3   Results Based on Ratings, Tags, Genre, and Time

The most striking point of the results regarding data set "ratings/tags/genres/ time" in Table 3 is the benefit with regard to recall@1 caused by extracting the additional information. The optimized HoFM puts 76.31 % of the relevant items at the first place of a 500 items ranking list (recall@1). The optimized

Table 3. Results data set "ratings/tags/genres/time"

Algorithm	NDCG					ROC	Recall		
	AUC	@10	@50	@250	@500	AUC	@1	@10	@100
opt. HoFM	**79.82**	**77.98**	**78.97**	**79.89**	**81.98**	91.03	**76.31**	**85.05**	89.81
opt. 2oFM	77.10	73.70	75.67	77.28	78.93	**93.62**	68.45	82.04	**91.55**
def. 3oFM	66.21	62.41	64.63	66.40	69.23	87.13	54.17	72.72	83.69
def. 4oFM	65.39	61.07	63.65	65.63	68.31	87.33	54.76	70.87	83.11
def. 2oFM	58.95	53.31	56.44	59.28	62.11	86.88	42.91	64.37	81.46
SVM	55.36	48.82	52.69	55.79	58.64	85.65	39.71	59.51	79.61
MRW w/ restart	50.03	39.14	46.57	51.21	52.10	92.07	19.32	53.50	87.96
MRW w/o restart	49.23	38.21	45.55	50.39	51.34	91.84	18.25	52.82	88.06
rest. MRW	49.06	38.00	45.44	50.25	51.16	91.91	18.54	52.52	87.77

second-order FM reached the highest ROC-AUC value in our study of 93.68. Once again, we can find a considerable gap between the recall@1 of the FM and the MRW approaches. Furthermore, we obtained a striking effect of the hyperparameter optimization improving the recall@1 of FM and HoFM (opt. HoFM vs. def. 3oFM about 26 points higher and opt. 2oFM vs. def. 2oFM 22 points higher).

5.4   General Comparison

The graphical representation of selected results (connected to the underlined values of the Tables 1, 2, and 3) is illustrated in Figs. 3 and 4. All in all, the values of the tables are a good representation of the curves. In general, FMs used more data to obtain better results whereas the MRW approach did not necessarily improve the results based on additional information.

One remarkable finding we obtained by analyzing the ROC curves in Fig. 4 is that the optimized HoFM tends to put the relevant item either on the first or on the last place of the ranking list. This is surprising because the usual expectation was that a relevant item is either recognized and put on the first place or not recognized and put on a random rank. In contrast to that, the optimized HoFM put many relevant items at the last rank which is an indication that the algorithm recognized the relevant item. Therefore, there is room for further improvement in coming investigations.

The NDCG curves in Fig. 3 show similar results because the almost horizontal curves of the FM approaches indicate that a nearly constant recommendation quality is delivered independent of the normalized ranks. In contrast to that, the other approaches show increasing NDCG curves at the first 20 % of the normalized ranks and afterwards return a constant recommendation quality on a lower level than the FM approaches.

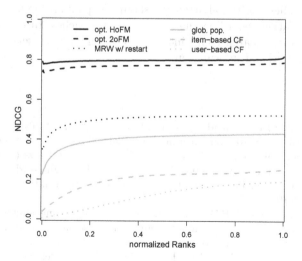

Fig. 3. Comparison of NDCG curves

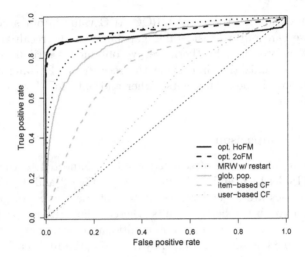

Fig. 4. Comparison of ROC curves

6   Conclusion and Future Work

In this paper, we showed how to compare two state-of-the-art recommender algorithms in a consistent manner. We came to the result, that MRW is the most striking algorithm if only data about the ratings from users assigned to items are available. If we add further information like assigned tags, genre, or time data the results can be clearly improved. In this case (higher-order) FMs outperformed the MRW approach.

Furthermore, we could present that the optimization of the hyperparameters increases the recommendation quality considerably. This means that in future comparative studies additional attention should be paid on the field of hyperparameter optimization regarding the individual approaches. In order to confirm our results, future research could incorporate different data sets which potentially contain additional information.

References

1. Aggarwal, C.C.: Recommender Systems. Springer, Cham (2016)
2. Alhamid, M.F.: Towards context-aware personalized recommendations in an ambient intelligence environment. Ph.D. thesis, University of Ottawa (2015)
3. Blondel, M., Fujino, A., Ueda, N., Ishihata, M.: Higher-order factorization machines. In: Proceedings of the Conference Neural Information Processing Systems 2016 (2016)
4. Clements, M., Vries, A.P.D., Reinders, M.J.T.: Optimizing single term queries using a personalized Markov random walk over the social graph. In: Workshop on Exploiting Semantic Annotations in Information Retrieval (2008)
5. Clements, M., Vries, A.P.D., Reinders, M.J.T.: The task-dependent effect of tags and ratings on social media access. ACM Trans. Inf. Syst. (TOIS) **28**, 1–42 (2010)

6. Fouss, F., Saerens, M., Shimbo, M.: Algorithms and models for network data and link analysis. Cambridge University Press, Cambridge (2016)
7. Grottke, M., Knoll, J., Groß, R.: How the distribution of the number of items rated per user influences the quality of recommendations. In: Proceedings of the 15th International Conference on Innovations for Community Services, pp. 1–8 (2015)
8. Hotho, A., Jäschke, R., Schmitz, C., Stumme, G.: Information retrieval in folksonomies: search and ranking. In: Sure, Y., Domingue, J. (eds.) ESWC 2006. LNCS, vol. 4011, pp. 411–426. Springer, Heidelberg (2006). doi:10.1007/11762256_31
9. Ibe, O.: Markov Processes for Stochastic Modeling, 2 edn. Newnes (2013)
10. Knoll, J.: Recommending with higher-order factorization machines. In: Bramer, M., Petridis, M. (eds.) Research and Development in Intelligent Systems XXXIII. Springer, Cham (2016)
11. Konstas, I., Stathopoulos, V., Jose, J.M.: On social networks and collaborative recommendation. In: Proceedings of the 32th International ACM SIGIR Conference on Research and Development in Information Retrieval (2009)
12. Page, L., Brin, S., Motwani, R., Winograd, T.: The PageRank citation ranking: bringing order to the web. In: Proceedings of the 7th International World Wide Web Conference, pp. 161–172 (1998)
13. Rendle, S.: Factorization machines. In: Proceedings of the 10th International Conference on Data Mining, pp. 995–1000 (2010)
14. Rendle, S.: Factorization machines with libFM. ACM Trans. Intell. Syst. Technol. 3, 1–22 (2012)
15. Rendle, S., Schmidt-Thieme, L.: Pairwise interaction tensor factorization for personalized tag recommendation. In: Proceedings of the 3rd ACM International Conference on Web Search and Data Mining, pp. 81–90 (2010)
16. Shi, Y., Larson, M., Hanjalic, A.: Collaborative filtering beyond the user-item matrix: a survey of the state of the art and future challenges. ACM Comput. Surv. 47, 1–45 (2014)
17. Su, X., Khoshgoftaar, T.: A survey of collaborative filtering. Adv. Artif. Intell. 10, 1–19 (2009)

Finding the Intersection Points of Networks

Niels Neumann[1,2] and Frank Phillipson[1(✉)]

[1] TNO, The Hague, The Netherlands
{niels.neumann,frank.phillipson}@tno.nl
[2] Radboud University, Nijmegen, The Netherlands

Abstract. Two algorithms have been constructed that find the intersections between two sets of line segments in practical networks used for planning and routing, solving the implementation issues of existing algorithms. One of the algorithms is a generalisation of the Bentley-Ottmann-algorithm, relaxing the assumptions in the original algorithm, the other is a *smart* brute force algorithm. In this article the algorithms are elaborated and will be tested, using real data sets constructed from street networks and trench networks. Both algorithms find all the intersections but with a difference in calculation time.

Keywords: Intersections · Networks · Algorithms

1 Introduction

In networks the shortest, or least cost, path between two points is often of interest. In some cases this path can use multiple networks. Consider for instance Fibre-to-the-X planning in telecommunication (e.g., [11]) where new active equipment has to be connected with an existing fibre network, where the route can use a trench network, a street network and a network of existing ducts. Another example is routing in multi-modal or synchro-modal logistic networks [8,14]. Here an end-to-end path using street, rail and water networks has to be found. In all these cases, connection points have to be found to go from one network to the other, which is only possible if it is known where the two networks intersect[1]. Once the intersections have been determined, routes through all networks can be found to connect any starting point with the required endpoints.

In this paper two algorithms are presented for this problem. The first is a smart version of a brute force algorithm. The second is inspired by an algorithm by Bentley and Ottmann [4], but relaxing the strict assumptions that do not work in real life networks. In Sect. 2 first a formal description of the problem and a literature background is given. In Sect. 3 both constructed algorithms are presented and in Sect. 4 the two algorithms are compared and conclusions are drawn.

---

[1] Intersection means intersection in the two dimensional projection.

© Springer International Publishing AG 2017
G. Eichler et al. (Eds.): I4CS 2017, CCIS 717, pp. 104–118, 2017.
DOI: 10.1007/978-3-319-60447-3_8

2   Problem Description

The problem under investigation is to find the intersections between two sets of line segments and the possible intersections between two line segments from the same set.

In literature, algorithms have been constructed which find all intersection points between two sets of line segments. Typically one thinks of the sets as being a set with red line segments and a set with blue line segments. In Fig. 1 an example is given of two such sets and the desired intersection points. Already existing algorithms will not find all intersections points, i.e., will not find intersections between two red or between two blue line segments. Intersections between two red or two blue line segments are also called self-intersections as two line segments from the same set intersect. The algorithms presented in this paper do find all shown intersections, also the self-intersections. Algorithms that solve this so called *Red-Blue Line Segment Intersection*-problem can for instance be found in [1, 2, 7]. However, using this approach will not give a complete answer. Namely, self-intersections will not be found using these algorithms, while these intersections are also of interest. Therefore, treating the problem as a *Red-Blue*-problem will not give the complete answer.

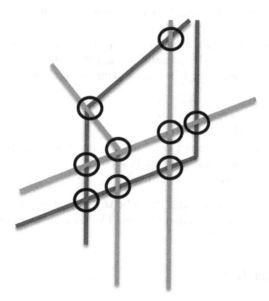

Fig. 1. Example of two sets of connections and their interconnections to be found. (Color figure online)

In 1976 Shamos and Hoey published an article [13] in which they present an algorithm that determines, when given a set of n line segments, if any two intersect. This algorithm was extended by Bentley and Ottmann [4] to an algorithm which could detect and give all the intersection points of a set of n line segments. The time complexity of this algorithm is $\mathcal{O}((n+k)\log(n))$, where k is the number of intersections[2]. The memory space required to run the algorithm, i.e., the space complexity was $\mathcal{O}(n)$. Hence, even in extreme cases where almost all line segments pairwise intersect, the required space is limited by $\mathcal{O}(n)$. This algorithm was improved even further to have a time complexity of $\mathcal{O}(n\log(n)+k)$. For instance by Chazelle and Edelsbrunner [5] and by Mulmuley [10], however both algorithms presented were randomised algorithms. Chazelle and Edelsbrunner also showed that the time complexity found in their algorithm was optimal. Apart from the fact that the algorithms were randomised, another drawback was that improved time complexity was traded for worse space complexity. Clarkson and Shor [6] were the first to present an algorithm with $\mathcal{O}(n\log(n)+k)$ time complexity and $\mathcal{O}(n)$ space complexity. This algorithm also used a randomised approach of the problem. The first deterministic algorithm for the problem with optimal time and space complexity was given by Balaban [3].

Over time multiple algorithms were presented which gave better results than the original algorithm by Bentley and Ottmann in terms of time or space complexity. However, the Bentley-Ottmann-algorithm remains the most popular choice. This is due to its simplicity and the low memory requirements. Other, faster algorithms often use more memory space to run the algorithm or use a randomised algorithm. Furthermore, these faster algorithm are more difficult to understand and implement.

Another reason this paper focuses on improving and applying the Bentley-Ottmann-algorithm, is that the assumptions made on the line segments are most easily tackled using the original Bentley-Ottmann-algorithm. The assumptions made are:

1. No line segment is vertical;
2. No two line segments overlap;
3. An endpoint of a line segment does not lie on another line segment;
4. At most two line segments intersect in a point;
5. Every event has a different x-coordinate.

Even though the assumptions simplify the algorithm, in most real world applications these assumptions do not hold. The assumptions made are resolved in Sect. 3.1.

3   The Algorithms

In this section two algorithms are constructed, the first being a modified Bentley-Ottmann-algorithm, the second being a smart brute force-algorithm. They will be referred to as *mBO* and *SBF*. Both determine all intersection points between two networks, which consist of multiple line segments in $\mathbb{R}^2$. Note that the endpoints of the line segments are points $(x,y) \in \mathbb{R}^2$. Recall that an intersection of

---

[2] Note that the Bentley-Ottmann-algorithm is output-sensitive, meaning that the complexity and therefore the running times depend on the size of the output.

two line segments from the same network, a self-intersection, is also of interest and therefore has to be found as well.

In Sect. 3.1 the modified Bentley-Ottmann-algorithm is considered. First the original Bentley-Ottmann-algorithm is explained, after which the modifications and implementation issues will be discussed. Section 3.2 explains the smart brute force-algorithm and in Sect. 3.3 an analysis of the complexity of both algorithms is made.

3.1   Modified Bentley-Ottmann

The first algorithm considered is a modified version of the Bentley-Ottmann-algorithm. The Bentley-Ottmann-algorithm gives exact results within reasonable time, however there are a few drawbacks. For instance, the assumptions presented in Sect. 2 do not need to hold in practical applications. Next to this, some dynamic structures such as binary search trees are important for the outperformance, but are not always implementable, for example when using MATLAB.

First the Bentley-Ottmann-algorithm as originally constructed will be discussed. Afterwards the relaxation of the assumptions made in the original algorithm and the implementation issues will be considered. Together this gives the modified Bentley-Ottmann-algorithm.

Bentley-Ottmann-Algorithm.   The Bentley-Ottmann-algorithm is a line sweep algorithm, meaning that a sweep line is used which sweeps through the plane looking for intersections. At some points during the sweep, non-trivial things happen. These points are for instance starting points of line segments, endpoints of line segments or the intersection between two line segments. Such points are called events. As input the algorithm takes n line segments. The $2n$ corresponding endpoints are then sorted according to the x-values of the endpoints. This data is then stored in a *priority queue* E, also referred to as event list E, used to keep track of the future events. Now all intersecting pairs of line segments have to be determined as well as the coordinates of the intersection points.

The event queue E is initialised with only starting points and endpoints. Intersections are added to E during the algorithm. In each step of the algorithm, the event with the minimum x-value in E is taken and the type of event is determined. The three, fundamentally different events are:

- *Start point.* If the event happens to be the start of a line segment, the line segment is inserted in the sweep line L. The line segments in L will be stored according to the y-coordinates.
- *Intersection.* If the event is an intersection, it will be reported and deleted from E. Also the order of the corresponding lines in L is flipped.
- *Endpoint.* If the event is an endpoint, the corresponding line segment is removed from L.

In Fig. 2 we see the three different events possible. This is a situation at the start of the algorithm with sweep line L at the first event a. The starting points are a and c, while the endpoints are b and d. The intersection point is given by point e.

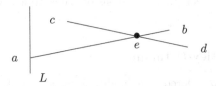

Fig. 2. A small example of the setup of the Bentley-Ottmann-algorithm.

After an event is treated, it will be removed from the priority queue. First it is checked if there are possible new intersections, then the next event is determined. This continues until the priority queue is empty, at which point all intersections have been found. After that, output is generated such that every intersection point is a node in the new network.

Line segments for which the right endpoint is to the left of L are said to be *dead* line segments. Once a line segment is removed from the sweep line it is of no interest anymore. After each event is treated, new neighbours in L are checked for a possible intersection. New intersections to the right of L are added to E. For example after removing a line segment, we have to check if the two old direct neighbours of the line segment intersect. If these new neighbours intersect and the intersection point is to the right of L, it will be inserted in the event list E. Note that in Fig. 2 the intersection point e will only be found after the line segments ab and cd are neighbours in the sweep line. Hence, only after the starting point c was processed. In Fig. 3 we see an example where an intersection is found, but it is to the left of the sweep line. Once the sweep line has processed the intersection point between line segments ab and ef, the line segments ab and cd become neighbours in the sweep line again. These two line segments intersect, however the intersection was already processed. Hence, only intersections which are to the right of the sweep line must be considered.

To give an idea of the structure of the sweep line: Right before the intersection point between line segments ab and ef is treated, the structure of the sweep line is $L = (ab; ef; cd)$. After the intersection point is processed, the sweep line is $L = (ef; ab; cd)$.

The assumptions made for the Bentley-Ottmann-algorithm (see Sect. 2) are made to prove that the algorithm finds all intersections. This way it is certain that every event has different coordinates and that every intersection is a proper intersection (not in an endpoint). The Bentley-Ottmann-algorithm relies on the fact that two line segments can only intersect if they are adjacent in the sweep line. If that is not the case, there must be an event prior to the event where they intersect such that the two segments become direct neighbours.

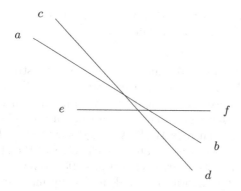

Fig. 3. After the intersection between ef and ab is reported, segments ab and cd become neighbours in the sweep line again.

Relaxation of the Assumptions. The best way to take care of the assumptions is to generalise the definitions of the events and the way the events are processed in the algorithm. If events are allowed to have the same x-coordinate, but events with the same x-coordinate are sorted according to the y-coordinate, assumptions 1 and 5 are solved. The approach for solving assumption 2 is to consider lists of line segments corresponding to a certain event instead of considering individual line segments. This way, overlapping line segments are treated at the same time, which solves the problem. Assumption 3 can be taken care of by generalising the definition of an intersection. Instead of considering only proper intersections, also intersections where three of the endpoints are collinear are allowed. Assumption 4 can be solved by generalising the definition of an intersection point. Instead of two line segments which intersect, more line segments may intersect in a single point. When treating intersections, we must be careful. Instead of swapping the position of two line segments, the order of the multiple line segments has to be reversed. Note that for two line segments this is the same as swapping the position. So we have the following solutions for the five assumptions given above.

1. For vertical line segments, define the endpoint with the higher y-coordinate to be the starting point and the event with the lower y-coordinate to be the endpoint;
2. Consider overlapping line segments at the same time instead of one after the other;
3. The definition of an intersection is generalised;
4. Multiple line segments may intersect in a single point. At the intersection point, we reverse the order of the corresponding segments in the sweep line;
5. Events with the same x-coordinate are sorted according to the y-coordinate. Events with the same x- and y-coordinate are treated in groups at the same time.

For the original Bentley-Ottmann-algorithm it is proved that all intersections are found. Due to the generalisations of the definitions of events and intersections this proof no longer holds for *mBO*. The proof relies strongly on the fact that no two events had the same x-coordinate.

Implementation Issues. To take care of the data structures used in the Bentley-Ottmann-algorithm, binary search trees (see [12]) can be used. These are used for both the event list E and the sweep line L and very important for the outperformance. However, binary search trees are not always supported by programming languages such as MATLAB, as Binary Search Trees are dynamic structures. Packages have been created which recreate the structure of binary search trees using other structures, for instance [9]. However, it turned out that the running time of the algorithm would drastically increase and *mBO* would in this case take longer than *SBF*, which will be explained in the next section. Therefore, such packages will not be used. In order to deal with the data structures problem, the structures are recreated using arrays. Both structures are described here.

Event List. An event list contains all events that did not happen yet. This includes both the starting points and endpoints of the line segments and the, once known, intersection points between line segments. This event list is recreated using two arrays. The start and endpoints are listed in the first array. The intersection points in the second. Also some characteristics of the line segment are added to each entry in both arrays to make future calculations easier.

The intersection events are listed in another array, as inserting the intersection events in the array with line segments is very time-consuming. Once an intersection has been found, both the intersection point and the coordinates of the corresponding line segments are added to the array. The next event is determined using the x-values of the events. For the array containing the intersections this means finding the minimum x-value among the intersection points. Note that sorting this array every time a new intersection is added takes at least as long as determining the minimum x-value.

Once an intersection is treated, it is deleted from the array. Now the next event has to be determined, which means that the event with the minimum x-coordinate has to be found. This means taking the minimum over the x-coordinates of the events in the array of intersections. For the array containing the start and endpoints an index is used to process through the events, hence it is easy to determine the next event in this case. This follows as the array is sorted. This was most efficient time-wise. This gives two possible next events, one for the array with intersections and one from the list with starting points and endpoints. The event with the minimum x-coordinate is taken as the event which is processed next.

Sweep Line. Also for the sweep line an array is used. Again the start- and endpoints of the line segments are denoted in the array, together with the corresponding indices of the line segment in the original network. At an intersection, the events have to be swapped. Given the implementation this means swapping the rows of the array. Furthermore, new line segments can be added to the sweep line. However, to be able to do that, the y-value of the line segments needs to be compared. A function is constructed which only checks for the middle value of the sweep line and then continues the calculation with half of the previous array. Which half is used depends on the y-value calculated and the y-value of the line segment considered. This way, in every iteration the size of the sweep line halves, hence we do not have to do the calculations for every entry. Note that this technique is also used in the Binary Search Trees resulting in their complexity $\mathcal{O}(\log n)$ to insert or delete an event or to locate it.

3.2   The *Smart Brute Force*-Algorithm

The second algorithm is a smart version of a *brute force*-algorithm. In a brute force-algorithm one would check for every possible pair of two line segments if they intersect. This method certainly finds all intersection points, however, the running time of this approach also blows up as its complexity is $\mathcal{O}(n^2)$, where n is the number of line segments. Algorithm 1 shows the pseudo code of *SBF*.

Algorithm 1. Smart brute force-algorithm

Input: A network consisting of line segments
Output: A network of non-intersecting line segments

Initialisation: Determine the minimum and maximum x- and y-value of every line segment

1: **for** every pair of line segments **do**
2:       **if** bounding rectangles overlap **then**
3:             **if** there is an intersection **then**
4:                   Report the intersection
5:             **end**
6:       **end**
7: **end**
8: Given the intersections found, create the network with no intersecting line segments

---

The output produced by the algorithm is an array consisting of line segments which were given as input, where every intersection point is now treated as an endpoint of a line segment. Hence, two intersecting line segments as input give four non-intersecting line segments as output.

Note that two line segments can only intersect if they have overlapping x-values and also overlapping y-values. In Fig. 4 we see two line segments which have overlapping x- and overlapping y-values. Such pairs of line segments are said to have overlapping bounding rectangles. We chose the orientation of these rectangles such that one side is parallel to the x-axis, while the other is parallel to the y-axis, however other orientations will work similarly.

Note that the same figure also tells us that overlapping bounding rectangles does not imply intersecting line segments. In the algorithm we make use of the

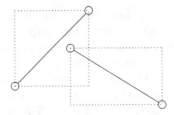

Fig. 4. Two line segments with overlapping x- and y-values.

bounding rectangles in the sense that if the bounding rectangles do not overlap, we do not check if the line segments intersect.

If the bounding rectangles overlap however, we do check for an intersection. This will be done using the following theorem. For the proof we make the embedding $(x, y) \in \mathbb{R}^2 \mapsto (x, y, 0) \in \mathbb{R}^3$. A sketch of the proof is given.

Theorem 1. *Given two line segments, the first with endpoints A and B and the second line segment with endpoints C and D. The line segments intersect if and only if both*

$$((A - B) \times (B - C))_3 \cdot ((A - B) \times (B - D))_3 < 0$$

$$((C - D) \times (D - A))_3 \cdot ((C - D) \times (D - B))_3 < 0.$$

Here $((A - B) \times (B - C))_3$ is the third component of the cross product of the vectors $A - B$ and $B - C$.

Proof. Two line segments intersect if we can extend one line segment to a line, thus creating two half-spaces, and the two endpoints of the other line segment lie in different half-spaces. Say line segment CD is extended to a line. In order to determine if A and B lie in different half-spaces, we determine whether the points (C, D, A) and (C, D, B) are traversed clockwise or counter-clockwise. We now have an intersection if one of the two is traversed clockwise and the other counter-clockwise.

Due to our embedding of the points in $\mathbb{R}^3$, we can take the outer-product. The result now follows as the signs of the outer-products are different if the points are traversed differently.   □

If two line segments intersect, the intersection point is determined. When all line segments have been found, the output is generated. This is done such that each line segment is subdivided in multiple smaller line segments according to the intersection points. Two intersecting line segments now result in four non-intersecting line segments.

Note that some extra calculations are done such as determining the bounding rectangles. In cases where most of the line segments pairwise intersect, this will lead to more computations and therefore longer running times. However, in most cases data sets are considered where most line segments do not pairwise intersect.

Using techniques as mentioned above, it is guaranteed that line segments which certainly do not intersect, are not considered in further calculations. As line segments which might intersect are still considered, we can conclude that all intersections are found.

3.3   Complexity of Algorithms

Let us now determine the complexity of the two algorithms. Let n be the number of line segments of the two networks together and let k be the number of intersections.

Let us first consider *SBF*. Given the n line segments, there are at most $\frac{1}{2}n(n-1)$ intersecting pairs of line segments. For every pair, it is determined if the two line segments have overlapping rectangles and if they do, it is determined if they intersect. Determining if the bounding rectangles overlap and if the line segments intersect, takes $\mathcal{O}(1)$ time. After the intersection points have been found, the output needs to be generated. This takes $\mathcal{O}(1)$ time and has to be done $\mathcal{O}(k)$ times. This results in a complexity of

$$\mathcal{O}\left(n^2 + k\right)$$

for *SBF*. Note that k is $\mathcal{O}(n^2)$, hence leaving us with

$$\mathcal{O}\left(n^2\right).$$

Now consider *mBO* and its complexity. First the events are determined and sorted, that is, the starting points and endpoints of all line segments are taken and sorted according to the x-coordinates. Finding and sorting the endpoints takes $\mathcal{O}(n \log(n))$ time. Now the main part of the algorithm, the iteration over the event queue, starts. The running time for every event that is processed is bounded by $\mathcal{O}(\log(n))$. Recall that, as the k intersection points are events as well, this complexity also applies to these k events. Note that the term $\mathcal{O}(\log(n))$ holds given the used implementation. After all events have been processed, the output needs to be generated. The time this takes scales according to k. This leads to a complexity of

$$\mathcal{O}\left((n + k) \log(n)\right).$$

Summarising *mBO* performs the best in terms of the complexity. Note however that *mBO* is output-sensitive. Hence, if k becomes large, the complexity might increase drastically. In fact, if $k = \Theta(n^2)$ the complexity of *mBO* will be $\mathcal{O}(n^2 \log(n))$, which is even worse than the complexity of *SBF*. Hence, in those cases *SBF* is preferred in terms of complexities.

4   Results

In order to compare the running times of both algorithms we take an example from Fibre-to-the-X planning. In this example street and trench networks of different Dutch cities are used for routing. These networks have to be combined to find a path from an origin to a destination point. The algorithms will be executed for these networks. For all data sets considered, the intersections found were the same for both algorithms.

In Table 1 the data sets used for validation are shown. Note that the first column gives the name of the data set and the second and third column give the number of line segments in the street network and in the trench network, respectively. To give an idea of the size of the real data sets relative to others, in column four and five the (approximate) size of the regions the data sets are derived from are given in terms of the population and the area.

Table 1. For each used data set: the name, the number of streets and trenches, the population ($\times 1,000$) and the area (in km^2)

Data sets	Street network	Trench network	Population ($\times 1,000$)	Area (in km^2)
Venray	8,547	53,030	28	17
Tilburg	31,829	184,597	213	90
Amsterdam	211,268	1,085,434	840	219
Southwest of the Netherlands	1,102,610	3,656,964	2,600	6,500

In Sect. 4.1 it is analysed whether it is better to consider the data set as a whole, or to subdivide the data set in multiple smaller data sets (or blocks) and run the algorithm for each smaller data set. In Sect. 4.2 the scalability of the algorithms is tested with two larger data sets.

For the running times, median results are considered for a number of runs of the algorithm. In the first section, twenty runs will be considered, while in the second section the median of five runs is taken. Median running times are considered as in every run the data set does not change. Hence, it is expected that the running times will be fairly equal for each run. Taking the median, reduces the effect of bad runs.

All tests were conducted on a Latitude E6430 laptop with dual core i5-3210M 2.5 GHz processor and 4 GB RAM. During the test, no other programs were running on the laptop. Connection with Internet was maintained to prevent licensing-issues.

4.1 Subdivide the Data Set in Smaller Blocks

In this section the running times of both algorithms will be considered and it will be checked if it is beneficial to split the data set in multiple smaller data sets and run the algorithms on the smaller data sets separately. First note that making a subdivision in disjoint data sets (or blocks) requires information on which line segments intersect, hence non-disjoint blocks will be used. The number of different blocks the data set is subdivided in will be referred to as the block-number or c.

The blocks will be made using the bounding rectangles of the line segments. First the width of the entire data set is determined, that is, the minimum and maximum x-value among all line segments is determined and the difference is the width. This width is divided by c, which gives the *width of each block*. The smaller data sets now consist of those line segments which bounding rectangle overlaps with the block itself. Note that it is possible for line segments to appear in multiple blocks.

Note that taking $c = 1$ implies that the data set is not subdivided in multiple smaller data sets. In the following block-numbers of 1, 5, 20, 100 and 500 are considered.

The first data set considered is Venray. The running times for *SBF* and *mBO* are shown in Table 2.

Table 2. Venray: median running times of twenty runs in seconds.

Block-number	1	5	20	100	500
SBF	63.37	34.28	29.87	30.19	71.81
mBO	12.39	14.32	17.13	31.97	67.97

For *SBF* it is observed that the usage of blocks does decrease the running time if only a few blocks are used. However, if the data set is subdivided in a large number of blocks (e.g. 500) the running time starts to increase. In fact, the running time when using 500 blocks is longer than the running time when the data set is not subdivided in smaller blocks. This is most likely due to the fact that for this block-number, many connections appear in multiple blocks. Hence, they have to be checked multiple times. Moreover, more calculations have to be done in order to construct the blocks. For this data set it can be seen that the usage of blocks is preferred if the data set is subdivided in 5 to 100 blocks. For *mBO* it can be seen that the algorithm is most efficient if the data set is not subdivided into multiple smaller blocks.

Now let us consider a larger data set, that of the Dutch city Tilburg. The results found for this data set can be found in Table 3.

Table 3. Tilburg: median running times of twenty runs in seconds.

Block-number	1	5	20	100	500
SBF	1,232.26	303.32	248.46	157.27	242.43
mBO	46.21	58.80	88.44	158.27	292.98

Again it can be seen that the usage of blocks is preferred over using no additional blocks for *SBF*. However, note that in this situation, the block-number hundred is preferred over the other considered block-numbers. Again the running times for *mBO* are the lowest when the data set is not subdivided in smaller blocks. It can also be observed that if the data set is subdivided in many blocks, the running time of *mBO* will become larger than that of *SBF*.

Given the data sets it appears that a block-number around hundred is optimal, however, this does not need to be the case. In fact, it will be very hard to determine the optimal number of blocks in general. This number can differ from one data set to another. This again has to do with the gains of using more blocks compared to the extra calculations needed to divide the data set in these blocks. Moreover, even if two data sets have the same number of line segments, this does not imply that the optimum number of blocks is equal for both. This has to do with the way the line segments are clustered within the data set. If all line segments are spread uniformly over a region, subdividing the data set in blocks will be much more beneficial compared to the situation where almost all line segments are clustered in a small region.

4.2   The Results for Increasingly Large Data Sets

To test the scalability of the algorithm, in this section data sets are considered greater than typical data sets. One could think of data sets from multiple cities instead of one, or a data set of a larger city including smaller villages in its surroundings. The largest data set considered spans the entire southwest of the Netherlands. Block-numbers 1, 75, 125 and 175 are considered.

First let us consider the Dutch capital Amsterdam together with some surrounding villages. The running times can be found in Table 4.

Table 4. Amsterdam and its surroundings: median running times of five runs in seconds.

Block-number	1	75	125	175
SBF	17,255.60	1,756.41	1,423.15	1,473.68
mBO	720.80	902.35	1,080.55	1,108.88

As was concluded for the smaller data sets, *mBO* again has the shortest running time for block-number 1. The running times of *SBF* are shortest when block-numbers around 125 are used, however even in that case, this algorithm takes longer than *mBO*.

Lastly, a data set covering the southwest part of the Netherlands, including the provinces Zeeland and Noord-Brabant, is considered. In practice data sets of this size will not be considered as multiple cities are included in this set and the resulting clustering of line segments makes the algorithms take longer than running the algorithm for the individual cities separately. The running times found for this data set are shown in Table 5.

Table 5. The southwest of the Netherlands: median running times of five runs in seconds.

Block-number	1	75	125	175
SBF	36,682.43	9,124.52	6,464.52	6,181.74
mBO		4,624.87	7,273.83	7,925.26	10,035.91

Note that the running times for *SBF* are decreasing for block-numbers 125 and 175. If the block-number is increased even further, the running times might drop below that of *mBO*. Hence, the running times are also determined for block-number 250, as can be seen in Table 6.

Table 6. The southwest of the Netherlands: running times in seconds for block-number 250.

SBF	mBO
6,215.05	14,657.97

Note that the running times for *SBF* start increasing again, while the running times of *mBO* keep increasing. Hence, it can be concluded that the running times will not drop below the running times of *mBO*.

5 Conclusion

Two algorithms have been constructed to find all intersection points between two networks: a modified Bentley-Ottmann-algorithm (*mBO*) and a smart brute force-algorithm (*SBF*). Also possible intersections between line segments from the same set are found using these algorithms. Such intersections are called self-intersections.

The first algorithm, *mBO*, is a sweep line-algorithm. A sweep line is used to sweep through the plane and find the intersections. The second algorithm, *SBF*, is a smart version of a brute force-algorithm. In a brute force-approach, all pairs of line segments are considered. Smart techniques are used to decrease the number of possible intersections pairs of line segments that need to be considered.

The two algorithms constructed have been tested with different data sets. We saw that in all cases both algorithms find all intersections, however *mBO* performs better in terms of running times. For small data sets *mBO* gives results within seconds, for larger data sets, it takes up to a few minutes. For the largest practical data set *mBO* takes up to only three minutes, while *SBF* takes more than ten minutes.

It is also considered whether it would be beneficial to subdivide the data set in multiple smaller data sets (also called blocks) and run the algorithm on each block. It was observed that such subdivision of the data set in smaller blocks is preferred for *SBF*. However, in all cases *mBO* without subdividing the data set was faster. Determining which block-number gives the optimal results for a network is hard beforehand as this depends heavily on the topology of the network. However, we saw in our analysis that a block-number around a hundred will give acceptable results in most practical cases for *SBF*. Further research on the optimal block-number is needed and will most likely heavily depend on the topology of the network.

As mentioned before, we cannot prove that *mBO* finds all intersections, due to the relaxation of the assumptions of the Bentley-Ottmann-algorithm. However, in the analysis above we saw that for all data sets considered *mBO* does find the same intersections as *SBF* and *SBF* does find all intersections.

References

1. Agarwal, P.K., Sharir, M.: Red-blue intersection detection algorithms, with applications to motion planning and collision detection. SIAM J. Comput. **19**(2), 297–321 (1990)
2. Arge, L., Mølhave, T., Zeh, N.: Cache-oblivious red-blue line segment intersection. In: Halperin, D., Mehlhorn, K. (eds.) ESA 2008. LNCS, vol. 5193, pp. 88–99. Springer, Heidelberg (2008). doi:10.1007/978-3-540-87744-8_8
3. Balaban, I.: An optimal algorithm for finding segments intersections. In: Proceedings of the Eleventh Annual Symposium on Computational Geometry, SCG 1995, pp. 211–219. ACM, New York (1995)
4. Bentley, J., Ottmann, T.: Algorithms for reporting and counting geometric intersections. IEEE Trans. Comput. **28**(9), 643–647 (1979)
5. Chazelle, B., Edelsbrunner, H.: An optimal algorithm for intersecting line segments in the plane. J. ACM **39**(1), 1–54 (1992)
6. Clarkson, K., Shor, P.: Applications of random sampling in computational geometry, II. Discret. Comput. Geom. **4**(5), 387–421 (1989)
7. Mantler, A., Snoeyink, J.: Intersecting red and blue line segments in optimal time and precision. In: Akiyama, J., Kano, M., Urabe, M. (eds.) JCDCG 2000. LNCS, vol. 2098, pp. 244–251. Springer, Heidelberg (2001). doi:10.1007/3-540-47738-1_23
8. Mes, M.R., Iacob, M.E.: Synchromodal transport planning at a logistics service provider. In: Zijm, H., Klumpp, M., Clausen, U., ten Hompel, M. (eds.) Logistics and Supply Chain Innovation, pp. 23–36. Springer, Heidelberg (2016)
9. Moore, B.: Data structures (2014). http://www.mathworks.com/matlabcentral/fileexchange/45123-data-structures
10. Mulmuley, K.: A fast planar partition algorithm. I. In: 2013 IEEE 54th Annual Symposium on Foundations of Computer Science, pp. 580–589 (1988)
11. Phillipson, F.: Efficient algorithms for infrastructure networks: planning issues and economic impact. Ph.D. thesis, VU Amsterdam (2014)
12. Sedgewick, R., Wayne, K.: Algorithms, 4th edn. Addison-Wesley, Boston (2011)
13. Shamos, M., Hoey, D.: Geometric intersection problems. In: 2013 IEEE 54th Annual Symposium on Foundations of Computer Science, pp. 208–215 (1976)
14. SteadieSeifi, M., Dellaert, N.P., Nuijten, W., Van Woensel, T., Raoufi, R.: Multimodal freight transportation planning: a literature review. Eur. J. Oper. Res. **233**(1), 1–15 (2014)

Infrastructure Planning

Distributed Network Infrastructure for Community Services in the Framework of Next Generation Mobile Networks

Dirk von Hugo$^{(\boxtimes)}$ and Gerald Eichler

Deutsche Telekom AG, Technology and Innovation,
Deutsche-Telekom-Allee 7, 64295 Darmstadt, Germany
{dirk.von-hugo,gerald.eichler}@telekom.de

Abstract. The concept of next generation networks as is currently consolidating within research and standards defining organizations foresees beside provision of higher flexibility and adaptability to different services' requirements also increased resource efficiency to enable affordable access in a sustainable way. To this end, a truly universal access has to be provided integrating multiple wireline, wireless, and cellular technologies to support residential and mobile entities of different size/shape/capability sets as is reflected by the variety of typical 5G use cases. Multiple logically separate networks (slices) shall be operated across the same infrastructure offering a performance and user experience meeting the diverse demand as exact as possible. This could include, beside traditional commercial operator services, a type of best effort connectivity to access e.g. urban community information and support daily life within a future smart city environment. This paper addresses a framework concept to integrate such a usage scenario within a future converged 5G system. Main focus of the reported exemplary results is on the issues of flexible service support (including varying mobility requirements) and efficient use of resources which seem to be most relevant for 5G success from a commercial point of view.

Keywords: Community communication · Service requirements · 5G mobile network · Universal broadband access · Quality of experience · Internet of Things

1 Introduction

LTE advanced, the recently executed fifth generation of mobile network (5G) technology research projects [1–3] address architecture and functionality of next generation integrated communication systems to support a wide range of use case and application families which are grouped into three main categories:

- Enhanced Mobile Broadband (eMBB)
- Massive Internet of Things (mIoT)
- Critical Communications (CC)

© Springer International Publishing AG 2017
G. Eichler et al. (Eds.): I4CS 2017, CCIS 717, pp. 121–136, 2017.
DOI: 10.1007/978-3-319-60447-3_9

According to [7], Next Generation Mobile Networks (NGMN) or 5G shall address demands of 2020 and beyond and "is expected to enable a fully mobile and connected society and to empower socio-economic transformations in countless ways many of which are unimagined today, including those for productivity, sustainability and well-being." Subsequently, there is the aim of introducing 5G systems directly related to supporting community services via community networks to the benefit of people as individuals and social groups.

According to the European Information Technology Observatory (EITO), evaluation of Information and Communication technologies (ICT) market data in cooperation with the Organization for Economic Co-operation and Development (OECD) and the EU Commission (DG Enterprise and Industry, DG Information Society and Media) [6], the ICT key technology trends in 2016/17 that are currently reshaping the ICT environment and industry focus on:

- High performant and reliable **mobile communications**,
- User interaction in **social media**,
- Secure operation of **cloud solutions**, and
- New data driven business based on **big data analytics**.

A recently announced technology program on Smart Services [5] shall promote cross-cutting flagship solutions for small and medium enterprises (SME) addressing following fields of application:

- **Employment** (use of smart services e.g. to safeguard employment or to alleviate the skills shortage, etc.)
- **Mobility** (e.g. new logistics solutions, services for multimodal local transport use, etc.)
- **Housing** (e.g. digital services to help older people, increase the safety/security and comfort of buildings, etc.)
- **Basic services** (e.g. smart services for energy supply, the supply of goods and services, basic medical care, etc.)

Affordability of network usage for the end user and a positive business case for the infrastructure operator and service provider in terms of proper costs and investments seems to be essential for successful deployment. Therefore the communication concepts of tomorrow shall be capable to support such basic human needs and allow for true community services. This contribution tries to address this topic. After associating results of currently ongoing projects in Sect. 2 a summary of commonly agreed 5G architecture concepts and solution approaches is given outlining a basis for the considerations of this paper. Section 3 presents requirements and a model for envisaged community service including traffic and demand model for an exemplary smart city scenario. A high level design of an end-to-end system architecture and representative network functions to achieve the envisaged service offering are described in Sect. 4. Section 5 presents estimated results on performance and capacity figures to allow for assessment of the proposed strategy while Sect. 6 highlights open issues requiring further investigation and summarizes the key conclusions of the work.

2 5G Architecture Principles

The attempt to define novel architectures for 5G systems has been undertaken by several joint research initiatives, sometimes with overlapping scope, coherent goals, and similar achievements. A relevant example is 5G NORMA (5G NOvel Radio Multiservice adaptive network Architecture) [2], which aims at developing a software-controlled End-to-End (E2E) 5G mobile network architecture enabling multi-service, context-aware adaptation of network functions, and supporting usage of multiple infrastructures (multi-tenancy), while focusing on cellular radio systems. Similarly, Metis II [1] aims at an overall 5G radio Access Network (AN) design and at providing technical enablers to integrate new wireless technologies and components currently being developed. Beyond the scope of cellular radio systems, the joint cooperation named CONFIG (COntrol Networks in FIve G) [3] was dedicated to the design of a 5G convergent Core Network (CN) architecture with the goal to achieve architecture flexibility, support heterogeneous access, and allow for vertical business integration, leveraging on recent advances on Network Function Virtualization (NFV) and Software Defined Networking (SDN). Focusing on the CN and resource efficient Control Plane (CP) approaches an E2E 5G system which embeds the abstraction for AN is discussed and described here. One of the main goals from an operator perspective is less to increase the data rate but rather to exploit on tools to grant a stable user perception at affordable effort in terms of service performance requirements as e.g. in terms of reliable connectivity, latency, and security, described henceforth as Quality of Experience (QoE).

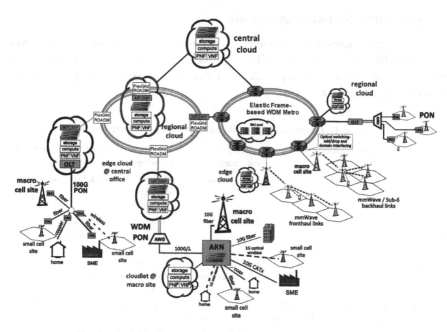

Fig. 1. Architecture overview of 5G network heterogeneity [8]

According to latest agreements in standardization (see e.g. [14] for 3GPP), the 5G system architecture shall minimize the dependency between AN and CN, being defined with a converged access-agnostic core integrating different cellular (i.e. here: 3GPP) and non-3GPP access types (such as WiFi and other fixed wireless etc.). Parallel work is also ongoing at International Telecommunication Union (ITU) with International Mobile Telecommunications for 2020 and beyond (IMT-2020) [20] and correspondingly for fixed networks at and in cooperation with Broadband Forum (BBF). The envisaged heterogeneity is depicted in Fig. 1, including also generalized resources for transport infrastructure and how and where to implement the required control and management functionality.

Exemplary requirements for supporting new wireless broadband community services based on Wi-Fi (IEEE 802.11) technology over residential architectures have been identified in [4] covering also scenarios demanding mobility tools which meanwhile have been partly standardized in IETF (Internet Engineering Task Force) (see e.g. [21]). Such an approach could prospectively be used for developing a next generation system concept enabling integration of the foreseen heterogeneous 5G access network architectures.

3   Community Services

Within this section both, a classification of different typical categories of communities are introduced and corresponding emerging requirements will be identified. A potential mapping to exemplary applications which will be used also in future smart city environments and a comparison to foreseen basic 5G use case scenarios will be given.

3.1   Community-Specific Requirements

According to their purpose, communities are created on demand as well as decompose themselves after reaching their aim. The time frame of a community establishment is an important indicator for their requirements (Table 1). Furthermore, security and data protection requirements might differ.

Table 1. Community classification regarding its living time

	Ad-hoc community	Short-term community	Mid-term community	Long-term community
Community living time	Order of hours	Order of days	Order of weeks or months	Order of years
Typical exchange objects	Resources	Contacts	Messages	Information, documents
Information exchange focus	Capability view, location information	Profile building, interest exchange	Task status, progress report	Offer generation, product distribution
Community example	Emergency task force, single social, sport or cultural event	Conference participants, trade fair actors	Project team, learning groups	Association, club, forum, standardization group

With respect to the requirements to the underlying communication network, there are different grades of requirements regarding the service quality (time and reliability) and quantity (throughput). While ad-hoc communities have stronger quality requirements, long-term communities look for stable quantitative offers (Table 2).

Different social groups have various expectations regarding their favorite tools, communication offers and usability. [15] summarizes requirements of a student interaction community.

Table 2. Service requirements depending on the community type

	Ad-hoc community	Short-term community	Mid-term community	Long-term community
Media real-time aspect	Very strong	Near real-time	Medium	Low
Media type	Status info	Attribute set	Code, document piece	Multimedia file
Average media piece size	Very small	Small	Medium	Large
Media storage place	Distributed devices incl. meshed network	Peering entity	Cloud repository	Centrally hosted server
Communication device	Smart phone, Tetra device	Tablet	Laptop	Desktop
Communication support	App	Web service	Application integration	Client-server system

With increased user mobility, today an increasing number of communication devices without built-in support of connectivity to latest cellular networks (such as 3GPPs LTE, Long Term Evolution technology) rely on a LTE attached nodes as relays, e.g., WIFIonICE [18] with the multi-provider MNO Icomera background technology, connected car with WiFi to mobile network support, or the simple local hotspot capability of today's smartphones. Such a sometimes awkward work-around solution will be needless in a future integrated 5G system.

3.2   Community Service Model and Scenario

As outlined e.g. in [11, 12], so-called smart services include city-wide traffic management and monitoring, smart parking assistance, public transportation, information services (e.g., bus, train, taxi, plane), logistics, real-time traffic, and road speed limit monitoring and management, among others. The definition of a smart city in [13] denotes 'a collection of entities (living and non-living) in an urban area that is always connected, fully aware, auto-managed, self-secure, adaptive, and well-informed.'

Other authors discuss enabling communication and networking technologies actually used and potentially to be improved for smart cities concluding that utilization of existing communication technologies cannot provide error-free connectivity in smart cities because these technologies are designed only for a limited number of devices and supported for a specific range of communication. The attention of future research has to focus on enabling unimpaired connectivity in smart cities with research challenges identified pointing to interference management, scalability of wireless solutions, interoperability support among heterogeneous wireless networks, mobility management, and measures to reduce the high energy consumption. Such issues are typically addressed also by 5G research projects as executed within the framework of 5GPPP [8].

Table 3. Use case description for community services

	Main performance specifics	Typical applications	
		Consumer oriented	Commercial
mMTC	Many devices, low data volume	Smart home	Industry 4.0
eMBB	Variable data rates and services	Triple play (data, audio, video)	Office communication
CC	Strictly low delay	Assisted living	Smart grid

The smart city community service scenario as seen from a 5G viewpoint would face the challenge to provide a bunch of diverging applications with both wide ranges of service and user device demands via a single physical network infrastructure efficiently. To illustrate the broad variety of somewhat contrasting demands out of the multitude of use cases as identified e.g. in [7] a set of three typical use case families is included in Table 3 together with typical performance requirements and exemplary applications. In Fig. 2 the view of 3GPP on 5G or Next Generation use cases including vehicular communication (V2X) is depicted together with aspects of operational ease as vertical axis.

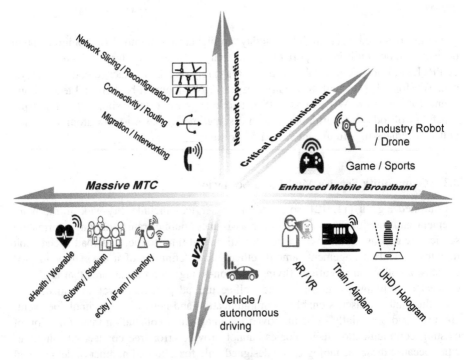

Fig. 2. 3GPP proposed classification into a plane of use case families and exemplary operational issues (vertical) (source: [19])

The subsequent sections detail three exemplary use cases, further following [1]. Generally not all such services can and have to be offered within one specifically configured logical network. Flexibility to allow adaptation of multiple logical network slices on the same physical infrastructure to fulfil each tenants' or verticals' (service providers) request is essential for an appropriate 5G system concept with respect to reliability and scalability.

3.2.1   Ubiquitous Broadband Access Use Case

The Ubiquitous Broadband Access Use Case (or enhanced Mobile BroadBand, eMBB) covers fixed, portable, and mobile applications between a multitude of user equipment and servers in the network which may be characterized by large bandwidth requirements, support of moving devices, and resemble typical multimedia services exchanging content between multiple human individuals or between humans and network nodes (e.g. servers, data bases) to only name a few. These services cover mainly exchange of text, audio, and video content between different individuals or between humans and data storage in the network.

Figure 3 shows an exemplary heterogeneous network structure where all current cellular access technologies (GSM, UMTS, LTE) as well as New Radio (5G) and popular WLAN (Wireless Local Area Network) access nodes with their different site dimensions and cell sizes are included for a dense urban coverage scenario. However also other so-called 'alternative' access opportunities as detailed e.g. in [9] can be taken into account here. A forthcoming approach for combination of multiple links is described in detail in [10].

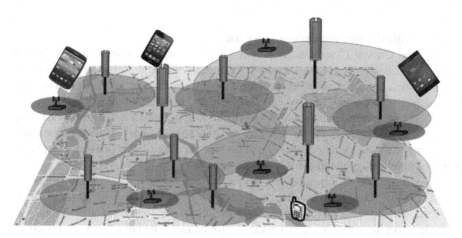

Fig. 3. Urban deployment of radio access via small (micro, pico) and large macro cells providing broadband connectivity terminals and services (eMBB use case)

3.2.2   Massive Deployment of Machines Use Case

The use case of a huge number of deployed connected machines (massive Machine-Type Communication, mMTC) describes generally a large amount and dense deployment of devices (sensors, metering) as smart grid or of Industry 4.0 type, but also may include vehicular communication. Such applications are also denoted as Internet of Things (IoT).

Figure 4 illustrates a scenario where machines of the same type contact via wireless or fixed access technology specific Gateways (GWs) (here: GW$_a$, GW$_b$, GW$_c$) for e.g. aggregation and admission control. This is applied to enhance scalability by aggregation and achieve tailored security before data is transmitted for final processing to respective servers.

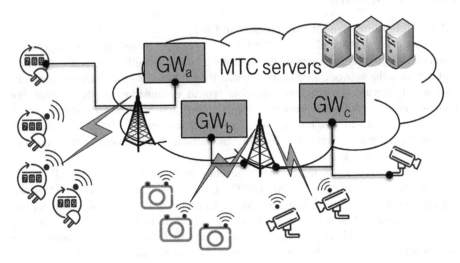

Fig. 4. Exemplary types of machines heterogeneously connected via dedicated gateways to application servers for massive IoT/MTC use case

3.2.3 Critical Communications Use Case

Finally, the Critical Communications (CC) use case demands for a strictly limited transmission delay, Ultra-Low Latency (ULL), and Ultra-High Reliability (UHR) constraint to be considered since services are time-critical ('tactile internet') and/or need high delivery probability (e.g. so-called 'five nines' referring to 99.999% uptime and availability of the electricity grid). As shown in Fig. 5 a direct device to device communication may be required for reducing the transmission delay while increased reliability may demand for interconnection of devices via network functionalities, deployed e.g. in a mobile edge cloud (MEC) environment.

To achieve such a service-aware provision of communication means within the framework of 5G a network slice is defined as an independent logical end-to-end network, defined by a set of specific network functions configured and designed to provide a specific network characteristic (performance). The basic Network Functions can be both physical and virtual in nature, and comprise Control (C)-plane and user or Data (D)-plane tasks (maybe supplemented by management), and should be independently instantiated and operated.

Network function adaption according to service demands which includes as well parameter settings as their logical and spatial location within the network topology is e.g. task of a newly specified Software Defined Mobile network Controller (SDM-C) as defined in project 5G NORMA [2]. The underlying architecture model assumed here is briefly outlined in the following section.

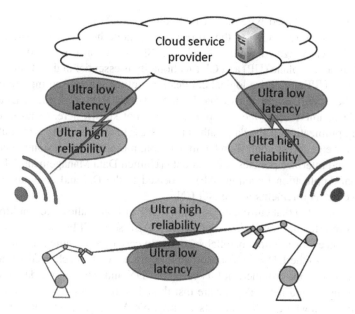

Fig. 5. Possible communication paths for UHR and ULL use cases as proposed by METIS project [1]

4 Functional Architecture

The high level design of an end-to-end system architecture as discussed within several Standard Driving Organizations (SDOs) and a description of modularization and interworking of representative network functions to implement capabilities and features for provision of the multitude of envisaged service offering are described here.

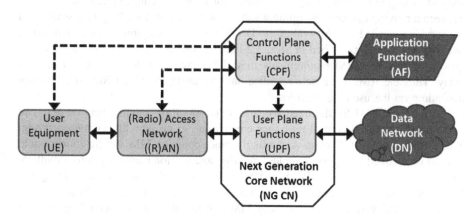

Fig. 6. Simplified 5G System architecture representation (according to [14])

As shown in Fig. 6 the (mobile or fixed) terminal device or User Equipment (UE) is connected via an Access Network (AN) - which may be either a general one (e.g. copper or fibre-based wireline) or of Radio type, (R)AN – and the Next Generation Core Network (NG CN) to the corresponding node hosting the desired application. As is basically agreed within all relevant SDOs (see also e.g. [20, 21]) a split between data or user plane (UP) and CP functionality is essential in the 5G architecture. UP Functions (UPF) comprise logical entities for routing and forwarding the user data exchanged between UE and an external Data Network (DN) (or another UE) and may also include or interface to the transport network not shown here. Control, configuration, and optimization of the data path is task of CP functions (CPF) which also have to account for e.g. access control and authorization, mobility and session management, to consider and interface policies and user data (Unified Data Management, UDM), etc. The external Application Function (AF) is located in the DN and communicates e.g. service specific requirements to the NG CN.

It should be noted that current approach in 3GPP [14] also allows for multiple UPFs and/or DNs interfacing the (R)AN concurrently. Also some CPFs may be available in multiple instances for multiple parallel sessions. In case of a roaming scenario the connection of a UE to the UDM in a subscribers' home network is achieved via a foreign visited access network provider. In this case both DN and AF may reside either in the home or in the visited network – or are distributed across both. The 5G concept also includes scenarios where a UE connects via multiple ANs (e.g. a cellular one and a so-called non-3GPP one, i.e. typically WLAN), which may require an additional Non-3GPP Inter-Working Function (N3IWF) to the NG CN. Details on modularization of CPFs and UPFs and the interfaces as well as their representation are discussed e.g. in [14].

As an exemplary modular network function the AMF (Access and Mobility Function) terminates all traffic from the AN as well as access independent messages from the UE on CP level and is responsible for management of registration, connectivity, and mobility. In case of concurrent access via 3GPP technology to home network and via a foreign WiFi access point also multiple AMFs have to interwork.

A Mobility Management (MM) sub-function within AMF is required for actual support of ongoing connectivity and uninterrupted service consumption via a session between a moving device (e.g. within a vehicle or carried by a walking pedestrian) and the service provided by host within the DN. Here any of the applications included in one of the use cases described in Sect. 3.2 may be considered. As described above the quality of service (QoS) requirements may differ greatly in terms of e.g. handover delay. Thus the AMF for a network slice has to choose a modular MM sub-function depending on the use case specifics.

As a default MM for the fixed scenario a "no-mobility" module may be designed without any overhead control massages created due to no mobility events occurring, e.g., in the static mMTC case. Accordingly more complex MM sub-functions would have to be invoked to support seamless mobility and session continuity across multiple technologies or domains – and/or to increase the service reliability by securing e.g. the handover procedure in terms of more robust message exchange mechanisms. The dedicated AMF with its corresponding MM sub-function is instantiated per service specific network slice in order to tailor the capabilities according to meet as precisely as possible the demanded performance. A detailed description on such an approach including message sequence chart definitions has been given in [16].

The expected outcome in terms of increased performance figures and efficient use of scarce radio resources thanks to service aware network configuration will be visualized in the estimated result of the evaluation of mobility concepts as derived during two research collaborations.

5 Preliminary Results

A comparison of performance figures for 4G and 5G for the mMTC use case has been achieved in the framework of CONFIG [17] based on first analytically calculated estimations. An approach to deal more efficiently with a great amount of smart devices thanks to 5G than can be reached with current LTE/4G radio variant for Narrow-Band IoT (NB-IoT) is shown in Fig. 7. Here a hexagonal cell structure and a low volume data transmission between the devices and the application server once per minute have been considered. For 40 up to 60 Bytes of data transmitted once per minute and device the cellular capacity in terms of amount of supported devices is depicted as a function of cell radius (dashed and dotted lines). Here different average transmission rates available for upcoming LTE (NB-IoT) technology have been assumed. An exemplary 5G mMTC logical network slice would employ intelligent combined handling of multiple (physical) entities (device types) with similar characteristics in terms of common Virtual Devices (represented in Fig. 4 by dedicated gateways). For more details please see project outcome reported in [17]. The improvement by 5G approach (denoted as by solid lines) results in a factor of up to eight – depending on the chosen parameters (Fig. 7).

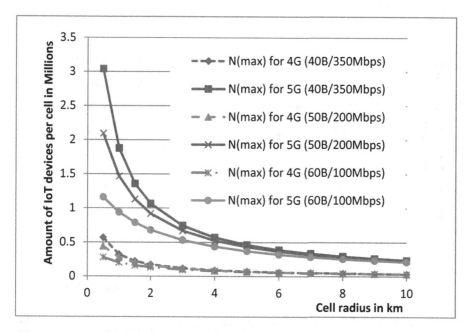

Fig. 7. Amount of IoT devices supported per dedicated cell in case of CONFIG 5G model

For the eMBB and mobile CC use case the impact of different MM approaches was estimated within project 5G NORMA to assess the applicability of a modular MM design concept. Here the seamlessness of the service during handover (HO) is proposed to be adjustable by applying different MM schemes, exemplarily differentiated for the type of HandOver (HO) enabled between adjacent cells or access nodes: as well a simple Horizontal HO (HHO), i.e., within the same access technology, as HHO together with maintaining concurrent connectivity to multiple cells to achieve Ultra-Low Delay (ULD) during HO is considered. Enhanced support of also vertical HO (across multiple technologies) could provide enriched (in terms of bandwidth or coverage) eMBB+ service while a mobility protocol allowing for cross domain (X-D) HO would facilitate to provide UHR services (e.g., continuing connectivity in case of failure or outage of the primary serving domain).

For LTE-typical data rates of 350 Mbps and an assumed data consumption of 20 MB per minute and terminal, the amount of the average signaling overhead and potential latency due to signaling was estimated. The amount of concurrently supported users per cell only slightly varies since higher spectrum efficiency for smaller cell size is counteracted by increased effort and loss due to higher HO rate. Depending on the applied MM scheme the expected additional signaling overhead ranges between 0.05% for 30 km/h maximum speed in 1000-m-cells and eMBB to more than 0.28% for ULD in 500-m-cells when terminals may move with up to 50 km/h. The network slicing concept is applied here such that the (limited) radio access resource for the mobility use cases is shared with an IoT service as provided by a logically separate 5G-slice without any MM support, as described above and resulting in case of fully dedicated radio resources in the performance shown in Fig. 7.

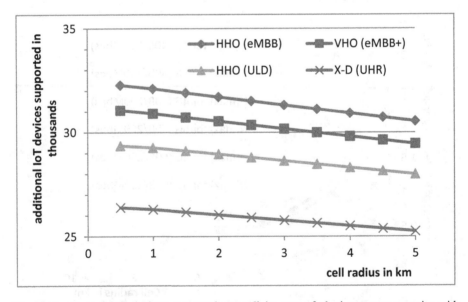

Fig. 8. Amount of IoT devices supported per cell in case of sharing access capacity with different types (e.g. quality in terms of seamlessness) of mobility services

In case of joint usage of the cellular transmission capacity for both slices the amount of additionally supported IoT devices in addition to a fixed amount of mobile users (here: at 70% load) is shown in Fig. 8. As can be seen the number of concurrently supported IoT devices per cell increases with decreasing cell size and required MM capability and complexity – however only in a nearly linear way. While in case of the "complex mobility support" (X-D), e.g., within cells with up to 2 km radius, about 26,000 IoT devices can be served in parallel the capacity increases to nearly 32,000 when the mobile service requires "simple mobility support" (eMBB) only. This 22% gain is achieved since a simplified mechanism for handover only can be chosen requiring less effort in terms of signaling and related radio resource consumption. Whereas here a vehicular speed of 30 km/h has been assumed, the corresponding figures for up to 50 km/h (not shown in Fig. 8) would be reduced by between 5% (eMBB) and 20% (UHR).

6   Analysis and Next Steps

The results presented in Sect. 5 shall illustrate mainly two features of next generation 5G communication namely the flexibility to provide service tailored sub-network configurations and the aspect of common resource sharing for multiple network slices concurrently. Design and selection of different instantiations of network (sub) functions for Mobility Management was chosen were the MM feature ranges between "no" and "full seamless highly reliable" mobility support. A static IoT slice (mMTC) built up by 5G could increase the performance (in terms of device amount) by a factor of up to eight utilizing the same frequency resources. A highly sophisticated MM scheme would require much more overhead than a simple one resulting in fewer resources available for a parallel, e.g., best effort type of service.

While the rough estimation only can give a qualitative result further investigations are needed taking into account a detailed analysis of the information exchanged between functional entities of a 5G system architecture and the protocols and interfaces required. Such aspects as well as simulations for realistic scenarios and partially also experimental verifications are planned within the project 5G NORMA. In addition other types of (e.g. specifically vehicular) types of mobility support between cars or vehicles and dedicated roadside infrastructure or between neighboring end user terminals have not yet been considered here. The overall system concept however including increasing computerization of traditional radio hardware in AN and CN as is envisaged in cloud computing, software defined (mobile) networking, and network function virtualization should be flexible enough to allow for such extensions.

The ongoing research activities continue to investigate and evaluate means to efficiently provide prospective future community communication services beside other business driven services to end customers. The perspective of both, operators and service providers as well as a wide range of community types and tenants end users is in focus of these activities. Analysis and assessment of different solution proposals, currently under discussion, is foreseen as well as contributions of prospective approaches to standards defining organizations and bodies which is a major step to make the vision of a flexible service-aware network architecture reality.

7 Conclusions

This paper has attempted to link the partly still unresolved basic and enhanced needs of people and communities with the currently ongoing research and concepts of next generation communication systems denoted as 5G. Starting from requirements and sketching the diverse range of demands – here, e.g., for both machine-type services as well as data-hungry mobile communication typical in an urban environment (smart city) – the concept of flexible provision of service specific logical subnetworks has been explained. Such network slices are configured to meet diverse needs and thereby efficiently make use of scarce resources as has been outlined in the contribution. Deutsche Telekom stated at the Mobile World Congress (MWC 2017): 5G is driven by customer use cases and thus will encompass three main classes of mobile networks [22]:

- **Extreme Mobile Broadband** for consumer digital interactive services,
- **Massive Machine-Type Communication** for Internet of Things and sensor applications, and
- **Mission-Critical Machine-Type Communication** for low-latency and reliable robotics.

Recent exemplary results achieved within of two collaborative research projects executed in the framework of 5GPPP have been reported for illustrative reason. As has been shown via simplified calculations new approaches to be introduced with 5G as efficient IoT support and service-aware network slicing can improve the overall system performance considerably. At the same time the overall required effort in terms of spent resources and costs for investment and operation can be reduced by joint and coordinated access to these common resources.

There is still a gap between not clearly defined community requirements, resulting from expected QoE which still is a kind of "moving target" and the actual mobile network performance in terms of QoS which can be offered with the new 5G concepts. Future research activities will have to address these open questions.

Acknowledgements. The authors want to thank the members and partners of the projects 5GNORMA and CONFIG as well researchers and standardization delegates in- and outside the project for the very fruitful discussions.

Research work performed in the framework of project 5G NORMA has partly been funded by EU under contract H2020-ICT-2014-2. The views expressed are those of the authors and do not necessarily represent the project or the EU. The cooperation CONFIG [17] is not funded by the international and national funding authorities and runs on a self-funding basis.

References

1. Elayoubi, S.E., et al.: 5G Service Requirements and Operational Use Cases: Analysis and METIS II Vision. In: Proceedings of the EuCNC 2016, Athens (2016)
2. Rost, P., et al.: Mobile network architecture evolution toward 5G. IEEE Commun. Mag. **54**(5), 84–91 (2016)

3. Einsiedler, H.J., Gavras, A., Sellstedt, P., Aguiar, R., Trivisonno, R., Lavaux, D.: System design for 5G converged networks. In: 2015th European Conference on Networks and Communications (EuCNC) (2015)
4. Gundavelli, S., Grayson, M., Seite, P., Lee, Y.: Service Provider Wi-Fi Services Over Residential Architectures, work in progress, April 2013. https://tools.ietf.org/html/draft-gundavelli-v6ops-community-wifi-svcs-06.txt. Accessed Feb 2017
5. Smart Services World II – new examples of applications for digital services and platforms, BMWi. http://www.digitale-technologien.de/DT/Navigation/EN/Foerderprogramme/Smart-Service-Welt-2/smart-service-welt-2.html. Accessed Feb 2017
6. EITO: Key Technology Trends in Europe 2016/17, Thematic report, September 2016. http://www.eito.com/epages/63182014.sf/en_GB/?ObjectPath=/Shops/63182014/Products/635-1609. Accessed Feb 2017
7. NGMN Alliance: 5G White Paper, February 2015. http://www.ngmn.org. Accessed Mar 2017
8. 5GPPP: 5G Architecture – White Paper, updated July 2016. https://5g-ppp.eu/white-papers/. Accessed Feb 2017
9. Lange, C., Behrens, C., Weis, E., Kraus, J. Krauß, S., Grigat, M., Droste, H., Rosowski, T., Monath, T., Bunge, C.-A., Bogenfeld., E., Amend, P., Bayer, N., Düser, M., Westphal, F.-J., Gladisch, A.: Bridging the Last Mile – Evaluating Alternative Connectivity Options, Breitbandversorgung in Deutschland, 10. ITG-Fachkonferenz, Berlin, Deutschland, April 2016. https://www.vde-verlag.de/proceedings-de/454193008.html. Accessed Feb 2017
10. Bayer, N., Girmazion, A.T., Amend, M., Hänsge, K., Szczepanski, R., Hailemichael, M.D.: Bundling of DSL resources in home environments. In: IEEE 17th International Symposium on a World of Wireless, Mobile and Multimedia Networks (WoWMoM), June 2016
11. Reis, A.B., Sargento, S.: Statistics of parked cars for urban vehicular networks. In: IEEE 17th International Symposium on a World of Wireless, Mobile and Multimedia Networks (WoWMoM), June 2016
12. Bouk, S.H., Ahmed, S.H., Kim, D., Song, H.: Named-data-networking-based ITS for smart cities. IEEE Commun. Mag. 55(1), 105–111 (2017)
13. Yaqoob, I., Hashem, I.A.T., Mehmood, Y., Gani, A., Mokhtar, S., Guizani, S.: Enabling communication technologies for smart cities. IEEE Commun. Mag. 55(1), 112–119 (2017)
14. 3GPP TS 23.501: System Architecture for the 5G System; Stage 2 (Release 15), work in progress, March 2017
15. Eichler, G., Erfurth, C., Lüke, K.-H.: Student interaction communities – social requirements reflected by a tool and system landscape. In: IEEE-Proceedings of the 14th International Conference on Innovations for Community Services (I4CS 2014), pp. 47–56, June 2014
16. Yousaf, F.Z., Gramaglia, M., Friderikos, V., Gajic, B., von Hugo, D. Sayadi, B., Sciancalepore, V., Rates Crippa, M.: Network slicing with flexible mobility and QoS/QoE support for 5G networks. In: Paper Accepted for 4th International Workshop on 5G Architecture at ICC, May 2017
17. CONFIG cooperation Deliverable 2.1: Intelligent Connectivity and Showcases (2017). Available on request at the project web site https://www.5g-control-plane.eu/. Accessed Feb 2017
18. Deutsche Bahn: WiFi on board trains and at stations. https://www.bahn.de/en/view/trains/on-board-service/wifi.shtml. Accessed Feb 2017
19. 3GPP TR 22.891: Feasibility Study on New Services and Markets Technology Enablers; Stage 1 (Release 14) (2016)
20. ITU-T: ITU towards "IMT for 2020 and beyond". http://www.itu.int/en/ITU-R/study-groups/rsg5/rwp5d/imt-2020/Pages/default.aspx. Accessed Mar 2017

21. IETF: Distributed Mobility Management (dmm), active WG, Charter. https://tools.ietf.org/wg/dmm/charters. Accessed Mar 2017
22. Ledl, P.: 5G – Redefining Connectivity for the Digital Society. Mobile World Congress (MWC), Barcelona, February 2017. http://www.mwcguide.telekom.com/. Accessed Mar 2017

Constrained Wireless Network Planning

Timotheus J.C. Vos[1,2] and Frank Phillipson[1(✉)]

[1] TNO, The Hague, The Netherlands
frank.phillipson@tno.nl
[2] Erasmus University, Rotterdam, The Netherlands

Abstract. In this paper we define the Constrained Wireless Network Planning problem. Given is an orientation of access points which, if supplied with network connectivity, is able to provide a required level of coverage to clients. The goal is to find a division of these access points in source locations and repeater locations such that each of the access points is provided with network connectivity, while not all need to be directly connected to an existing network. The origin of the constraints in this problem are threefold. First, there is a restriction on the allowed distance between a source and a repeater location. Second, there is a restriction on the number of repeaters which may be provided with network connectivity by a source. Third, a repeater location may not provide another location with network connectivity. In this paper we propose an Iterated Local Search procedure to solve this problem. We apply this procedure to a problem arising in the field of multi-service planning in Smart Cities.

Keywords: Capacitated Vertex Cover · Single-Source Capacitated Facility Location Problem · Wireless Network Planning

1 Introduction

Information density is condensing more and more in our daily life. Not only the need for receiving information is increasing, but also the need for processing information gathered by, for example, sensors. Denser networks are required to be able to satisfy these increasing needs and to process all the data in an efficient way.

This trend is already visible in the mobile telecommunication industry, where in the case of 5G and 4G-small cells the area covered by a base station is decreasing, which in effect condenses the network. A benefit of dense networks is that higher transmission rates can be reached as the distance to a connection point is smaller.

In Smart Cities also other services or monitoring systems will arise, like security cameras, air quality and pollution monitoring systems, event detection systems and communication systems for smart vehicles enabling congestion control, smart parking and (smart) road condition systems. These applications assist in the transition to 'smart cities' for which the ultimate goal is to improve

© Springer International Publishing AG 2017
G. Eichler et al. (Eds.): I4CS 2017, CCIS 717, pp. 137–152, 2017.
DOI: 10.1007/978-3-319-60447-3_10

the quality of life in a city. However, where mobile telecommunication operators are already limited in the search for locations for their equipment, in the
near future this will be worse. A potential solution will be the integration of
these locations with (already existing) street furniture like lamp posts and bus
shelters, which are a dense infrastructure and are close to the place people live
and work. Then the question arises how to choose the right locations (of the
many options) to deliver the required coverage of the services at minimal costs.
For this, in earlier work [26], the Multi-Service Location Set Covering Problem
(MSLSCP) is proposed. There a set of locations is selected and each location in
that set is equipped for a selection of services such that the coverage requirements of all services is met. However, in that work each selected location is
assumed to be connected to a core network. A possible alternative for this is
a (hypothetical) radio overlay network providing access to the core network for
a number of locations by a central location. The goal here is to find a division
of the locations in source locations, directly connected, and repeater locations,
connected by the overlay network, such that each of the access points is provided
with network connectivity. This is defined as the Constrained Wireless Network
Planning problem (CWNP).

In this paper we first give a formal formulation of the problem in Sect. 2 and
a literature review is performed on both the Single-Source Capacitated Facility
Location Problem and the Capacitated Vertex Cover in Sect. 3. The CWNP
possesses characteristics of both these types of problems. In Sect. 4 an Iterated
Local Search procedure will be proposed to solve the CWNP which is tested on
a number of instances in Sect. 5. Finally, in Sect. 6 some concluding remarks will
be given.

2   Problem Formulation

Given is a set of (geo-spatial) locations for access points $\mathcal{L} = 1, \ldots, L$, which
should be supplied with network connectivity such that coverage for a service
can be provided. To prevent connecting each of these locations to an existing
network directly, a division in source locations and repeater locations is made.
Here, only the source locations need to be connected to an existing network
directly. The repeater locations are then able to provide the service using a
(hypothetical) radio overlay network to a source location.

Some constraints should be taken into account when finding such a division.
First, a source and repeater location are unlikely to be able to communicate with
each other when the range between them is too large. The second constraint is
that a location that services as a source for repeater locations is subject to bandwidth restrictions. This is expressed by a maximum number of repeater locations
per source location. Finally, a repeater location may not provide another location with network connectivity as this is believed to degrade the quality of the
service too much. Envision for example a row of locations with an equal distance
between each other. If the signal degrades by 20% between each location than
by the fifth location we have only 40.94% of our original signal quality.

Let f_j be the cost of realizing a connection to an existing network for location $j \in \mathcal{L}$. This source location $j \in \mathcal{L}$ is then able to provide at most k_j repeater locations with a network connection. The parameter $a_{ij} = 1$ when location $i \in \mathcal{L}$ is within range of location $j \in \mathcal{L}$ and $a_{ij} = 0$ otherwise. When each location has the same range, the a_{ij} matrix is symmetric. Decision variable y_j equals 1 when location $j \in \mathcal{L}$ is connected to an existing network and to 0 otherwise. The choice to have location $j \in \mathcal{L}$ act as a source for location $i \in \mathcal{L}$ is made by setting $x_{ij} = 1$ and $x_{ij} = 0$, otherwise. Now the optimisation problem is:

$$\text{Min} \sum_{j \in \mathcal{L}} f_j y_j \tag{1}$$

$$\text{s.t.} \sum_{i \in \mathcal{L}} x_{ji} + y_j = 1 \qquad \forall j \in \mathcal{L} \tag{2}$$

$$\sum_{i \in \mathcal{L}} x_{ij} \leq k_j y_j \qquad \forall j \in \mathcal{L} \tag{3}$$

$$x_{ij} \leq a_{ij} y_j \qquad \forall i, j \in \mathcal{L} \tag{4}$$

$$x_{ij}, y_j \in \{0, 1\} \qquad \forall i, j \in \mathcal{L} \tag{5}$$

The goal is to minimize the total costs of connecting locations to an existing network (1) while taking the following into account. First, each location should be either connected to a source location, or it should be a source location itself (2). Secondly, constraint set (3) states that a source location can provide at most a prespecified number of repeater locations with network connectivity. The constraint set (4) represents the requirement that a connection between a source and repeater location can only exist when they are in range of one another. Finally, the decision variables are binary.

The CWNP has properties of both the Single-Sourced Capacitated Facility Location Problem (SSCFLP) and the Capacitated Vertex Cover (CVC) problem, however, there are some fundamental differences. In the SSCFLP one searches for a set of facilities which can supply a set of customers at the least amount of costs. There is no restriction on distance between customer and facility. Also, not all facilities have to be used to supply all customers. In the CWNP we can not make such a distinction between facilities and demand locations and thus can not fit our problem in the SSCFLP formulation. In the CVC problem the goal is to find a minimum weight vertex cover where each vertex is able to cover a capacitated number of edges. In the CWNP we can take the locations as vertices and the possible connections as edges. However, we do not want each possible connection to be covered as connections between two connected locations need no longer be covered.

Both the SSCFLP [12] and the CVC [24] are proven to be NP-hard, however we have difficulty mathematically relating the CWNP to either of these problems. Because of this we can make no hardness claims about the CWNP, though we do have a strong impression that the CWNP is, in fact, NP-hard.

3   Literature Review

As indicated in the previous section, the CWNP problem has features from both the Single-Source Capacitated Facility Location Problem and the Capacitated Vertex Cover Problem. For both problems a short literature overview is given.

As the SSCFLP is a NP-hard problem most solution methods have focused on finding good approximations of an optimal solution. Among the heuristics Lagrangian relaxation is used most often. The applications of Lagrangian relaxation to the SSCFLP differ in which constraint is relaxed. A choice can be made to either relax the assignment constraint, the capacity constraint or both. Additionally, Lagrangian relaxation methods differ in the way a feasible solution is generated from the solution to the relaxed problem.

One of the first to propose a Lagrangian relaxation were Klincewicz and Luss [22]. In their approach they relax the capacity constraint. The resulting problem now is a UFLP, which they solve using a dual ascent algorithm. The solution to the relaxed problem is then made feasible by using a so-called add heuristic. A final adjustment heuristic is used to improve the best solution generated.

Lagrangian relaxation approaches are used by [2], resulting in several knapsack subproblems which are solved to obtain feasible solutions, [17], combining a greedy heuristic and restricted neighborhood search to obtain feasibility and [3], presenting extensive computational results for the Lagrangian relaxations.

Chen and Ting [6] implement a Multiple Ant Colony System as well as a hybrid algorithm of both Lagrangian relaxation and an Ant Colony System to solve the SSCFLP.

Recently several heuristic methods have been proposed which use methods other than Lagrangian relaxation to obtain solutions to the SSCFLP. In [1] a Very Largescale Neighborhood Search is applied, [8] use scatter search to solve the SSCFLP and [18] presents a simple iterated tabu search algorithm. In [15] the Kernel Search heuristic is extended to general Binary Integer Linear Programming problems.

Several exact solution approaches have been proposed as well. [20] proposes a branch and bound method where in each iteration they calculate a lower bound using a Lagrangian heuristic and an upper bound using a strong primal heuristic. [9] implements a column generation procedure in a branch and price framework. A cut-and-solve based algorithm is presented in [27].

The Capacitated Vertex Cover (CVC) has first been proposed by Guha et al. [16]. They applied the CVC with soft constraints and arbitrary weights to a problem arising in the field of glycobiology. For the resulting problem a 2-approximation algorithm using a primal-dual approach and a 4-approximation algorithm based on LP-rounding are given. Gandhi et al. [14] give a 2-approximation algorithm for the same problem based on LP-rounding.

For the CVC with hard constraints the problem becomes significantly harder. In [7] is shown that the CVC with hard constraints is at least as hard to approximate as the Set Covering Problem when arbitrary weights are used. They give a

3-approximation algorithm for the unweighted case based on randomized rounding of an LP-relaxation followed by an alteration step. In [13] this is improved in two crucial ways to obtain a 2-approximation for the unweighted case of the CVC with hard constraints. They add a pre-processing step and they modify the alteration step from [7].

4   Solution Approach

We propose an Iterated Local Search (ILS) procedure to solve the CWNP. ILS is for a large part based on the well-known Local Search (LS) method. LS is an intensification-oriented, single-solution based metaheuristic. In a LS method it is repeatedly attempted to improve the current best solution by applying slight changes and accepting these changes when they lead to improvements. This is done till either a local optimum is found or a stopping criterion is reached. Whereas the LS method is strong in its intensification of a solution, it lacks in the diversification of the found solutions.

The ILS method, proposed by Lourenço et al. [23], tries to improve on the LS method by introducing diversification through perturbation of a solution stuck in a local optimum. When for a solution a local optimum is found or a stopping criterion is reached, the search is restarted using a perturbed version of the current best solution. A good perturbation of a solution is achieved when the perturbed solution has the right balance between being a randomly chosen solution and the original solution. Usually, the restart is performed a fixed number of times, always starting from the current best solution.

A framework for the ILS method is given in Algorithm 1. In this framework there are several steps, such as creating an initial solution, local search and perturbing an existing solution, which will be discussed in the following subsections.

Algorithm 1. Iterated Local Search [23].

1: Initialize $f(s^*) = \infty$
2: Create an initial solution s using a Greedy Heuristic
3: Apply the local search method to s to obtain s'
4: **if** $f(s') < f(s^*)$ **then**
5:     $s^* = s'$
6: **end if**
7: **for** A fixed number of iterations **do**
8:     Perturb solution s^* to obtain p
9:     Apply the local search method to p to obtain p'
10:     **if** $f(p') < f(s^*)$ **then**
11:         $s^* = p'$
12:     **end if**
13: **end for**
14: Return the overall best solution

4.1   Initial Solution

An initial solution to the CWNP is generated using a greedy heuristic, as shown in Algorithm 2. In the first step locations are identified which are always connected to an existing network. These are the locations which are not in range of any other location, i.e. for which $\sum_i a_{ij} = 0$. All locations for which this holds are added to the set $\mathcal{F}$, containing all locations which are either connected to an existing network or to another location.

Then, using the remaining locations $j \notin \mathcal{F}$, a value is calculated which represents the likeliness of a location to occur in good solutions. This is calculated as follows.

$$V_j = \min\{1 + \sum_{i \notin \mathcal{F}} a_{ij}, k_j\}/f_j \qquad \forall j \notin \mathcal{F} \qquad (6)$$

The presented ratio can be seen as the number of locations one can add over the costs of connecting a location to an existing network. The location for which the highest value of V_j is reached is most likely to occur in a good solution and is chosen to be connected to an existing network. This results in a greedy heuristic.

This procedure can also be randomized. Based on the values V_j a probability can be assigned to each of the locations which can be used to choose which location to add to the solution. This probability is calculated as in (7). This is a common way of assigning probabilities, see Murata et al. [25].

$$P_j = \frac{(V_j - \min_j V_j)^2}{\sum_j (V_j - \min_j V_j)^2} \qquad \forall j \notin \mathcal{F} \qquad (7)$$

When a location is selected to be connected it is checked which other locations are within range of the newly connected location. When there are less locations within range than the specified capacity, then all locations within range are connected to the newly connected location. When there are more locations within range than the specified capacity than randomly locations are selected to be connected to the newly connected location with equal probability till the capacity is reached.

All newly connected locations are added to the set $\mathcal{F}$ and the previous steps are repeated till all locations are either connected to an existing network or to a source location.

4.2   Local Search

The neighborhood of a feasible solution to the CWNP is defined as follows. For any feasible solution it is given that there are small clusters of locations of which one is connected to an existing network. In the greedy heuristic which is used to create an initial solution, there are always as much as possible locations connected to an opened location. Intuitively this might seem the best thing to do. However, this need not lead to the best possible solution.

To try and improve on a solution, the following method is proposed. Of all locations which are connected to an opened location, choose one at random to

Algorithm 2. (Randomized) Greedy Heuristic.

1: Initialize $\mathcal{F}$ with all locations which are always opened
2: Set $y_j = 1 \; \forall j \in \mathcal{F}$
3: **while** Not all locations connected **do**
4:      Calculate $V_j \; \forall j \notin \mathcal{F}$
5:      **if** Greedy **then**
6:          Identify location to open $j = \operatorname{argmax} V_j$
7:      **else if** Randomized Greedy **then**
8:          Calculate $P_j \; \forall j \notin \mathcal{F}$
9:          Randomly choose location j to open using P_j
10:      **end if**
11:      Set $y_j = 1$
12:      Identify all locations within range $I = \{i | A_{ij} = 1, i \notin \mathcal{F}\}$
13:      **if** $|I| > k_j$ **then**
14:          Randomly remove $|I| - k_j$ locations from I
15:      **end if**
16:      Set $x_{ij} = 1 \; \forall i \in I$
17:      $\mathcal{F} = \mathcal{F} \cap \{I \cap j\}$
18: **end while**

---

investigate whether disconnecting from the opened location is profitable. Disconnecting can only be profitable when the disconnected location is within range of one or more opened locations other than the location it was connected to, before disconnecting.

When a location has been identified for which disconnecting might be profitable then this location will be disconnected and consequently opened. All opened locations, other than the location the disconnected location was connected to, will be connected to the newly opened location if possible. Now these opened locations which have been connected to the newly opened location could have locations connected to them. These will then be disconnected and using the greedy heuristic will be opened again.

The total creation of a neighboring solution is as in Algorithm 3. This algorithm is implemented in a LS procedure as follows. Repeatedly, neighbouring solutions which might be improvements are proposed. When the neighbouring solution is of a better quality then it is accepted as the new solution. When for a certain number of iterations the LS procedure is unable to find an improved neighbouring solution than the search is stopped and the current solution is returned.

4.3 Perturbation of a Solution

In the perturbation of a solution the goal is to introduce a large amount of diversification in the solution. In this perturbation step large changes are made to a given solution by purposefully breaking and consequently repairing the solution in a randomized greedy way.

Algorithm 3. Neighborhood Heuristic.

1: Identify all locations connected to an opened location $C = \{i|\exists x_{ij} = 1\}$
2: Randomly choose $i \in C$, was connected to $J = \{j|x_{ij} = 1\}$
3: Open the location i, $x_{ij} = 0 \ \forall j \in \mathcal{L}$, $y_i = 1$
4: Identify all opened locations in range of i, $O = \{k|a_{ik} = 1, y_k = 1, k \neq J\}$
5: Disconnect all $k \in O$, $y_k = 0$ and $x_{jk} = 0 \ \forall j \in \mathcal{L}$
6: Let $N = \{i|y_i = 0, \nexists x_{ij} = 0\}$
7: Identify all locations within range of i, $I = \{j|a_{ij} = 1, j \in N\}$
8: **if** $|I| > k_j$ **then**
9:     Randomly remove $|I| - k_j$ locations from I
10: **end if**
11: Set $x_{ji} = 1 \ \forall j \in I$
12: $N = N \backslash I$
13: Greedily connect all remaining locations in N

For any feasible solution the locations can be divided in a set of opened locations and a set of locations connected to an opened location. In the set of opened locations there might be a subset of locations which are opened in all feasible solution and locations which are opened in the specific solution. The opened locations which are not fixed in any feasible solution is the part of a solution which will be perturbed.

Of these non-fixed, opened locations 20% is closed. Additionally, all locations connected to these closed locations are disconnected. This results in a large part of the locations being disconnected and an infeasible solution. All locations which are closed and not connected to an opened location are added to the set N, thus indicating the locations requiring a repair.

The purposefully broken down solution is then rebuilt using a randomized greedy heuristic for all locations still requiring a connection. The complete algorithm is given in Algorithm 4.

5   Application and Performance

This section is divided into two parts. In the first subsection benchmark approaches are presented. In the second subsection the results of the ILS procedure are presented and compared with the results of the benchmark approaches. All of the approaches have been implemented in Matlab.

5.1   Benchmark Approaches

GRASP. Greedy Randomized Adaptive Search Procedure (GRASP) is a single-solution based metaheuristic which has been introduced by [10,11]. A GRASP procedure repeatedly initializes a solution s using a randomized greedy heuristic which is consequently improved using a simple local search method to obtain s'. Each time the local search method terminates the resulting solution is compared against the current best solution s^*. If it is found that the newly created solution

---

Algorithm 4. Perturbation Heuristic.

1: Initialize $\mathcal{F}$ with all locations which are always opened
2: Initialize $C = \{j|y_j = 1, j \notin \mathcal{F}\}$
3: Randomly pick 20% of locations in C to obtain T
4: Set $y_j = 0 \; \forall j \in T$, $x_{ij} = 0 \; \forall i \in \mathcal{L}, \forall j \in T$
5: Let $N = \{j|y_j = 0, \nexists x_{ji} = 0\}$
6: **while** $N \neq \emptyset$ **do**
7:     Calculate $V_j \; \forall j \in N$
8:     Calculate $P_j \; \forall j \in N$
9:     Identify location to open $j \in N$
10:    Set $y_j = 1$
11:    Identify all locations within range $I = \{i|A_{ij} = 1, i \notin \mathcal{F}\}$
12:    **if** $|I| > k_j$ **then**
13:         Randomly remove $|I| - k_j$ locations from I
14:    **end if**
15:    Set $x_{ij} = 1 \; \forall i \in I$
16:    $N = N \backslash \{I \cap j\}$
17: **end while**

---

is an improvement compared to the current best solution then the current best solution is replaced with the new solution.

This is done for a specified number of iterations, after which the algorithm terminates and the overall best found solution is returned. A general framework is given in Algorithm 5.

Algorithm 5. Greedy Randomized Adaptive Search Procedure [10,11].

1: Initialize $f(s^*) = \infty$
2: **for** A fixed number of iterations **do**
3:     Create an initial solution s using a Randomized Greedy Heuristic
4:     Apply the local search method to s to obtain s'
5:     **if** $f(s') < f(s^*)$ **then**
6:         $s^* = s'$
7:     **end if**
8: **end for**
9: Return the best solution

Simulated Annealing. Another often used metaheuristic is Simulated Annealing (SA). This metaheuristic has been independently proposed by [5,21]. SA is a nature-inspired, single-solution metaheuristic, based on annealing metals. SA uses this analogy by introducing controlling parameter T, called the temperature. After the initialization of a solution and a high temperature a neighboring solution is searched. When the objective value of the neighboring solution is better than the objective value of the original solution, then the original solution is replaced by the neighboring solution. When the neighboring solution is worse than the original solution, then the neighboring solution is accepted as the new solution with a probability based on the temperature and the objective values of both solutions. A general form of a probability function is $P(T, f(s'), f(s)) = \exp(-(f(s') - f(s))/T)$ where T is the temperature, s' is the neighboring solution and s is the original solution. When the temperature is high the probability of accepting a worse solution is large and as the temperature decreases the probability of accepting a worse solution decreases.

Accepting worse solutions can be seen as a diversification step to escape from local optima. For a temperature $T = 0$ a worse solution is never accepted and the SA method is equal to a LS method. Generally the SA method is terminated when either the temperature is below a certain threshold value or when the objective value no longer improves.

A general framework for SA can be found in Algorithm 6. In this algorithm the value η represents the threshold temperature. When the temperature drops below this temperature it is expected that a good solution has been found by this time.

Algorithm 6. Simulated Annealing [5,21].

1: Create an initial solution s using a Greedy Heuristic
2: Initialize temperature T
3: **while** $T > \eta$ **do**
4:     Search neighboring solution s' of s
5:     **if** $f(s') < f(s)$ **then**
6:         $s = s'$
7:     **else**
8:         $s = s'$ with probability $P(T, f(s'), f(s))$
9:     **end if**
10:     Decrease T
11: **end while**
12: Return the best solution

Genetic Algorithm. Genetic Algorithms (GA), first designed by [19], are commonly used to generate high-quality solutions for optimization and search problems by relying on bio-inspired operators such as mutation, crossover and selection.

For the CWNP the GA has been implemented as follows. First the exogenous parameters are initialized, the population size S, the maximum number of generations G, the crossover probability p_c and the mutation probability p_m. The population is then initialized by calling a randomized greedy heuristic S times. For all the individuals in the population a fitness is calculated by evaluating the objective function of the CWNP. Based on the fitness of each of the individuals a selection of the individuals are used in the next generation. This is done (see [25]) by assigning to each of the individuals a probability ($p \in S$ as in Eq. (8)) of being selected as a parent. The second parent is chosen by assigning equal probabilities to the remaining parents.

$$P_p = \frac{(f(p) - \min_{s \in S} f(s))^2}{\sum_s (f(p) - \min_{s \in S} f(s))^2} \qquad \forall p \in S \qquad (8)$$

The two parents recombine in the next generation with probability p_c. Here the recombination is chosen as follows. Let parent 1 be represented by x_{ij}^1 and y_j^1 and parent 2 is x_{ij}^2 and y_j^2. For each location in these solutions it follows that they are either connected to an opened location, or they are opened themselves.

A breakpoint is randomly chosen for the two solutions. Then locations are crossed by taking all choices made for the locations from the first parent till the breakpoint and all choices made for the locations from the second parent from the breakpoint till the end. For the second new solution this is done by taking the choices made for the locations till the breakpoint from the second parent and additionally all choices made for the locations from the breakpoint till the end from the first parent. Each solution should be checked for feasibility and, if necessary, undergo repair.

Repair is done by searching for all locations which are connected to a location which is not opened in the new solution. These are the invalid locations. For each of these locations it is checked whether there is another opened location within range which has not yet reached its capacity. If so, the location is connected to this opened location. Otherwise, the location is disconnected from all opened locations and opened itself. This is repeated till there are no more invalid locations.

When the recombination phase has ended a new population is obtained. However, before moving to the next generation, each of the individuals in the new population might undergo mutation. To each of the solutions in the population a random variable is assigned drawn from a uniform distribution between [0,1]. When for any solution the random variable is smaller than p_m the individual undergoes mutation. This is done by moving the individual to a neighboring solution as has been described in the implementation.

These steps are then repeated for the prespecified number of generations G. At the end the best found solution is returned.

5.2   Results

The proposed Iterated Local Search procedure is applied to a problem arising in the field of multi-service planning. Given is a set of geospatial locations for access points, here lampposts, in which a division in source locations and repeater locations is searched such that the total costs of connecting the locations to an existing network are minimized. There are several other test instances which the ILS procedure has been applied to. These are displayed in Table 1. Here the starting position of the CWNP is shown. This starting position is defined by the results of the MSLSCP obtained through the SSC method on the test instances, as shown in [26]. In these solutions a certain amount of lampposts is connected to an existing network and there is a corresponding connection costs associated with this.

Algorithm 7. Genetic Algorithm [4].
───
1: Initialize exogenous parameters S, G, p_c and p_m
2: Initialize population by calling the Randomized Greedy Heuristic S times
3: **for** G generations **do**
4:     Select parents
5:     **if** $x \in U(0,1) < p_c$ **then**
6:         Recombine parents
7:     **else**
8:         Pass parents to next generation as they are
9:     **end if**
10:     Select individuals to mutate from new population
11: **end for**
12: Return the best solution
───

Table 1. Comparison of connection results after the MSLSCP and after CWNP. For solution times marked with †, the Gurobi solver reached the time limit before finding an optimal solution.

Service Area	MSLSCP		Exact CWNP		
	Connected	Costs (€)	Connected	Costs (€)	Time (s)
Schiermonnikoog	163	441,049	55	120,478	0.15
Rozendaal	196	506,227	48	73,958	0.29
Noordwijk	544	1,434,866	142	233,330	2.00
Lisse	1,075	2,511,543	261	393,003	89.09
Amsterdam Center	1,401	2,729,674	307	357,287	1536.70
Delft	2,792	5,851,939	648	855,452	†25,200.00

In the table also the results of the exact algorithm for the CWNP can be found. The results indicate an increasing computational effort required to solve the CWNP.

The results for the ILS method can be found in Table 2. As the ILS method is randomized to a certain extend it is chosen to apply the method three times to each of the test instances. In the table the best objective value from the three solutions is presented, as well as the average objective value and the average time required to come to a solution. The goal of the research was to find a method that can be used in an interactive planning tool, meaning that calculation times up to a few minutes are acceptable.

The comparison with the benchmark approaches can also be found in Table 2. Here also the methods were applied three times to each of the test instances. In the table the best objective value from the three solutions is presented, as well as the average objective value and the average time required to come to a solution. First, the ILS and GRASP methods are shown. Both methods restarted the search 10 times from a perturbed version of the best solution. At the end the overall best solution is returned for which the results are shown in the table.

Table 2. Results on CWNP for ILS, GRASP, SA and GA.

Service area	ILS			GRASP		
	Costs (€)	Avg	Time (s)	Costs (€)	Avg	Time (s)
Schiermonnikoog	134,851	135,450	0.21	132,874	134,140	0.76
Rozendaal	76,791	81,091	0.37	85,829	87,312	1.17
Noordwijk	255,015	256,550	2.15	267,084	279,010	10.94
Lisse	501,235	511,790	15.93	545,337	555,790	64.53
Amsterdam Center	516,017	538,388	32.25	550,556	561,990	136.65
Delft	1,186,504	1,196,515	147.39	1,276,910	1,287,202	318.24
Service Area	SA			GA		
	Costs (€)	Avg	Time (s)	Costs (€)	Avg	Time (s)
Schiermonnikoog	143,149	146,025	0.14	145,901	147,714	3.38
Rozendaal	93,514	96,734	0.23	95,074	99,251	5.17
Noordwijk	308,813	320,027	1.72	342,396	346,415	19.43
Lisse	550,193	551,091	12.37	612,893	620,898	75.62
Amsterdam Center	565,008	583,935	53.23	617,867	629,034	119.78
Delft	1,225,352	1,241,628	201.21	1,395,782	1,413,018	333.49

Secondly, the SA and GA methods are shown. These methods allow some control over the behavior of the methods through the tuning of several parameters. For the SA method the same initial temperature has been used for all test instances which is chosen to be a temperature of 10,000. This initial temperature yields suitable acceptance probabilities of worse solutions. Differing cooling schemes have been used. For the Schiermonnikoog, Rozendaal and Noordwijk test cases the temperature is decreased by 50 after each iteration. For Lisse the temperature is decreased by 25 in each iteration and for Amsterdam Center and Delft by 10 in each iteration. When the temperature is decreased with a smaller number then this ultimately results in a larger number of total iterations, which for the larger test instances is useful as the search space is larger for these test instances. For all test instances the search is terminated once the temperature falls below 500.

The GA has the same parameters for all test instances. The population size is initialized to be 20. In accordance with existing literature the mutation rate has been selected to be 5% and the crossover rate is set to 80%, see [4]. The GA terminates after 50 generations. In this way there is a sufficient number of iterations to allow the algorithm to investigate a large part of the search space. A high crossover rate is chosen to give good solutions the opportunity to obtain good characteristics of other solutions. Mutation of a solution is not necessarily preferred as this might result in a decreasing quality of a solution which is why this rate is set relatively low.

From the results it can be seen that the ILS method returns the most promising results. Generally, this method is able to find the best solutions while requiring the least amount of computation time. This indicates that this method is able to find a good balance between intensification and diversification. The other methods are unable to find a similar balance between intensification and diversification, however this can be explained.

For the GRASP method it is found that it is able to obtain solutions which are not far off from the solutions found by the ILS method. This can be attributed to the fact that these methods use the same local search method. However, the solution times for GRASP are noticeably worse than the solution times which are required for the ILS method. This can be attributed to the initialization of these solutions.

The GRASP method always restarts from a randomized greedy solution, whereas the ILS method starts from a greedy solution and restarts from a perturbed version of the current best solution which is likely to still be of a better quality than the randomized greedy solutions. This leads to a smaller number of overall iterations for the ILS method and thus better computation times.

The SA method also starts from a greedy solution. However, this method sometimes moves to worse solutions for the purpose of diversification. As the algorithm progresses the amount of diversification is lowered and the amount of intensification is increased. Apparently the method is unable to obtain a suitable starting point for the intensification of a solution after the diversification of the solutions.

The GA method is overall the method which results in the least favorable solutions and computation times. The GA method is also the method which is the most distinct from the other methods. The reason why the GA method is unable to find good solutions can be attributed to the fact that it is rather difficult to suitably recombine two solutions. Generally after each recombination the solutions have to be repaired in order to adhere to the restrictions imposed by the CWNP. This repairing of a solution prevents the GA method from converting to better and better solutions.

This shows that ILS is the preferred method for solving the CWNP. For this method the solutions are of a sufficient quality while requiring the least amount of computation time. A possible solution is displayed in Fig. 1.

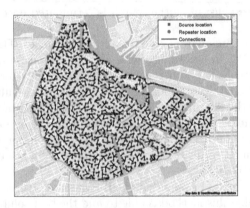

Fig. 1. Possible division in source and repeater locations.

6   Conclusion

This research addresses a problem which is likely to require an answer in the near future, namely, the existing networks becoming increasingly dense. To be prepared, we propose to divide a set of access points in source locations and repeater locations, such that the directly connected source locations can provide the repeater locations with a network connection through a (hypothetical) radio overlay network.

In this paper the CWNP is presented which has characteristics of both the Single-Source Capacitated Facility Location Problem and the Capacitated Vertex Cover. We proposed an Iterated Local Search procedure to solve the CWNP. To test the ILS procedure we created test instances of differing sizes in which we searched for a division in source and repeater locations.

Based on the results it was found that solving the test instances to optimality quickly turns computationally intractable. However, the proposed Iterated Local Search procedure achieved seemingly good and efficient solutions. This method was able to quickly find good solutions to the CWNP, even for the larger test instances.

References

1. Ahuja, R.K., Orlin, J.B., Pallottino, S., Scaparra, M.P., Scutellà, M.G.: A multi-exchange heuristic for the single-source capacitated facility location problem. Manag. Sci. **50**(6), 749–760 (2004)
2. Barceló, J., Casanovas, J.: A heuristic lagrangean algorithm for the capacitated plant location problem. Eur. J. Oper. Res. **15**(2), 212–226 (1984)
3. Beasley, J.E.: Lagrangean heuristics for location problems. Eur. J. Oper. Res. **65**(3), 383–399 (1993)
4. Boussaïd, I., Lepagnot, J., Siarry, P.: A survey on optimization metaheuristics. Inf. Sci. **237**, 82–117 (2013)
5. Černỳ, V.: Thermodynamical approach to the traveling salesman problem: an efficient simulation algorithm. J. Optim. Theory Appl. **45**(1), 41–51 (1985)
6. Chen, C.H., Ting, C.J.: Combining lagrangian heuristic and ant colony system to solve the single source capacitated facility location problem. Transp. Res. Part E: Logist. Transp. Rev. **44**(6), 1099–1122 (2008)
7. Chuzhoy, J., Naor, J.: Covering problems with hard capacities. SIAM J. Comput. **36**(2), 498–515 (2006)
8. Contreras, I.A., Díaz, J.A.: Scatter search for the single source capacitated facility location problem. Ann. Oper. Res. **157**(1), 73–89 (2008)
9. Diaz, J., Fernández, E.: A branch-and-price algorithm for the single source capacitated plant location problem. J. Oper. Res. Soc. **53**(7), 728–740 (2002)
10. Feo, T.A., Resende, M.G.: A probabilistic heuristic for a computationally difficult set covering problem. Oper. Res. Lett. **8**(2), 67–71 (1989)
11. Feo, T.A., Resende, M.G.: Greedy randomized adaptive search procedures. J. Global Optim. **6**(2), 109–133 (1995)
12. Fisher, M.L., Jaikumar, R., Van Wassenhove, L.N.: A multiplier adjustment method for the generalized assignment problem. Manag. Sci. **32**(9), 1095–1103 (1986)

13. Gandhi, R., Halperin, E., Khuller, S., Kortsarz, G., Srinivasan, A.: An improved approximation algorithm for vertex cover with hard capacities. J. Comput. Syst. Sci. **72**(1), 16–33 (2006)
14. Gandhi, R., Khuller, S., Parthasarathy, S., Srinivasan, A.: Dependent rounding in bipartite graphs. In: Proceedings of the 43rd Annual IEEE Symposium on Foundations of Computer Science, pp. 323–332. IEEE (2002)
15. Guastaroba, G., Speranza, M.G.: A heuristic for bilp problems: the single source capacitated facility location problem. Eur. J. Oper. Res. **238**(2), 438–450 (2014)
16. Guha, S., Hassin, R., Khuller, S., Or, E.: Capacitated vertex covering. J. Algorithms **48**(1), 257–270 (2003)
17. Hindi, K., Pieńkosz, K.: Efficient solution of large scale, single-source, capacitated plant location problems. J. Oper. Res. Soc. **50**(3), 268–274 (1999)
18. Ho, S.C.: An iterated tabu search heuristic for the single source capacitated facility location problem. Appl. Soft Comput. **27**, 169–178 (2015)
19. Holland, J.H.: Adaptation in Natural and Artificial Systems: An Introductory Analysis with Applications to Biology, Control, and Artificial Intelligence. U Michigan Press, Ann Arbor (1975)
20. Holmberg, K., Rönnqvist, M., Yuan, D.: An exact algorithm for the capacitated facility location problems with single sourcing. Eur. J. Oper. Res. **113**(3), 544–559 (1999)
21. Kirkpatrick, S.: Optimization by simulated annealing: quantitative studies. J. Stat. Phys. **34**(5–6), 975–986 (1984)
22. Klincewicz, J.G., Luss, H.: A lagrangian relaxation heuristic for capacitated facility location with single-source constraints. J. Oper. Res. Soc. **37**(5), 495–500 (1986)
23. Lourenço, H.R., Martin, O.C., Stützle, T.: Iterated local search. In: Glover, F., Kochenberger, G.A. (eds.) Handbook of Metaheuristics, pp. 320–353. Springer, Heidelberg (2003)
24. Michael, R.G., David, S.J.: Computers and Intractability: A Guide to the Theory of NP-Completeness. WH Free. Co., San Francisco (1979)
25. Murata, T., Ishibuchi, H., Tanaka, H.: Genetic algorithms for flowshop scheduling problems. Comput. Ind. Eng. **30**(4), 1061–1071 (1996)
26. Vos, T.J., Phillipson, F.: Dense multi-service planning in smart cities (2017, under review)
27. Yang, Z., Chu, F., Chen, H.: A cut-and-solve based algorithm for the single-source capacitated facility location problem. Eur. J. Oper. Res. **221**(3), 521–532 (2012)

Energy Management

Multi Objective Approach for Tactical Capacity Management of Distributed Generation

Frank Phillipson[✉]

TNO, The Hague, The Netherlands
frank.phillipson@tno.nl

Abstract. Stakeholders in an electricity system can have different objectives. For this reason, in this paper a model is presented that can handle uncertainty in demand and supply and can do multi-objective analysis to show the sensitivity of the capacity management to the different objectives. Four possible objectives are presented to be considered by the model: Self-sufficiency rate, Maximum Import, Overcapacity and Return on investment. A case study is presented to show the capabilities of the model and give some results and insight into a particular case study.

Keywords: Distributed generation · Tactical capacity management · Multi criteria optimization

1 Introduction

Although the introduction of distributed generators (DGs) looks promising, one important challenge will be to optimally integrate the increasing number of small generation units in an electricity system that up to now has been very centralised, integrated and planned. Since most DGs rely on exploitation of natural sources of energy they exhibit high fluctuations in production over time. This means that electricity generated by DGs will probably not match load demand and can cause over- or underproduction of electricity. The current technological solution to solve resulting transport problems is to reinforce the existing grid. This is very expensive and has to be avoided as much as possible. Another solution, still in development, is to make the grid smarter by controlling fluctuations in production and consumption, using smart grids and production planning. Next to this, many trials have been done to manage the behaviour of customers. Before grid reinforcements is done and smart grids are created, there is a need for sophisticated tactical load balancing. We should have some idea about the global demand and supply characteristics and perform tactical planning: try to find an optimal mix of DGs while keeping network capacities in mind. In earlier work [7] the optimal mix was found, minimising transportation losses. However, losses are not the key objective in practice; losses of renewable energy are considered less important. From the investor (owner) side more important are the

© Springer International Publishing AG 2017
G. Eichler et al. (Eds.): I4CS 2017, CCIS 717, pp. 155–166, 2017.
DOI: 10.1007/978-3-319-60447-3_11

financial drivers and the decrease in used fossil fuels. From the network operator side the network balance is important. This leads, for example, to situations
driven by investors where many, cheap, solar cells are placed with a total (yearly)
capacity that covers the total (yearly) demand, leading to a huge mismatch of
demand-supply over time. It is obvious that different stakeholders have different objectives. This urges the need of an optimisation model that can answer
the question: How much of what kind of decentralised generator do I need in a
neighbourhood such that:

- The district is self-sufficient with probability $x\%$ over time;
- The return on investment (RoI) is as large as possible;
- The use of fossil fuels is minimised;
- The central added capacity is maximised on x kW;
- etcetera.

Or even combined questions, like for example: How to get a system with a self-
sufficient rate of $x\%$, where the RoI is at least $r\%$.

There is a wide range of different types of energy models with different
approaches and objectives known in literature. The review papers [11,12] give a
good overview of energy models presented in the literature. In [12] an overview
is given of energy models that have been emerging over the last few years. The
following types of energy models are discussed: energy planning models, energy
supply-demand models, forecasting models, optimisation models, energy models
based on neural networks and emission reduction models.

From the energy planning models two articles stand out: [14] on special programming models and [5] on the pay-off matrix technique. In [14] elementary spatial programming are discussed such as Quadratic Programming, Mixed Integer
Linear Programming and Linear Complementarity Programming models. These
models are used to optimise energy production, transportation, distribution and
utilisation with respect to cost.

In the articles on optimization models the objective is to minimise (only)
costs. See for example [6,8,11,15,17,18]. Those papers minimise cost or maximise
GNP/energy ratio and try to find an optimal mix of energy sources.

In [16] the authors present a multi period optimisation model for a micro
grid, aimed at maximising its benefit, i.e. revenues-costs. The optimisation model
includes the use of DGs relying on wind and solar, an electrochemical storage
and interruptible load. DGs are incorporated into the low voltage grid where
both technical and economic aspects are considered. They allow the DGs and
storage system to be controllable. This creates a system resembling the smart
grid.

In [10] a method is presented for locating and sizing of DGs, with respect
to mainly voltage stability and a reduction of network losses. They use a static
approach and optimise using dynamic programming.

In [4] a management strategy is presented for a renewable energy system with
storage capacity that integrates tactical and operational decisions in a single
mathematical model that makes use of an updated probabilistic wind speed

forecast. They use a stochastic model but consider only wind energy and optimise the profit obtained from the energy sold during the next hour.

To handle the stochastic nature, in [2] a robust approach is proposed for the design of distributed energy systems in a neighbourhood, minimizing the present value of all costs for a regional energy system. In this paper a model is presented that can handle both uncertainty in demand and supply and multi-objective analysis to show the sensitivity of the capacity management to the different objectives as input for the discussion between investors and network owners. With this model, that is presented in Sect. 2, some analysis is presented in a case study to show the capabilities of the model and give some results and insight into a particular case study, which are shown in Sect. 3. Conclusions are drawn in Sect. 4.

2   Model

In the model a neighbourhood of n houses is assumed. The demand for electricity and the supply from solar panels and wind turbines are stochastic. Given is a base pattern for demand per house, the average production pattern per solar panel (with characteristics: 1.65 m2, 250 Wp, €500)) and the average production pattern per (micro) wind turbine (hypothetical, €10.000 [3]). From here, realisations are drawn per hour using a uniform distribution, where the mean is time dependent (the base pattern) and a half width of σ_d, σ_s, σ_w respectively for demand, solar and wind. An example of such a realisation can be found in Fig. 1. One simulation covers T hours and is repeated N times to get the results.

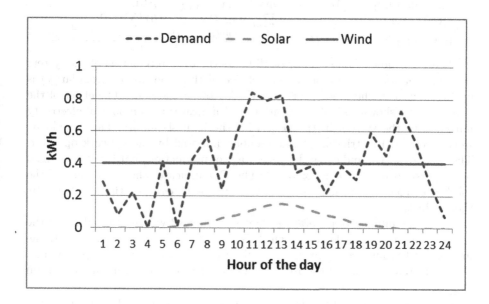

Fig. 1. Example of realisation.

The following notation is used:

- $D_{i,t}$ = total (n houses) demand for hour t on day i.
- $P_{i,t}$ = total production by the solar panels and the wind turbines for hour t on day i.
- P_u = Price paid for regular kWh.
- P_d = Price earned for each kWh that is not used and delivered to the network.
- P_s = Price of a solar panel.
- P_w = Price of a wind turbine.
- N_s = Number of solar panels.
- N_w = Number of wind turbines.

Note that in many countries there is a yearly 'netting' method. There P_u is paid for all generated electricity during a year as long as it meets the total yearly own consumption, and a lower price (not defined here) is paid for the generated electricity that is (yearly) above the own consumption. In such a system it is interesting to choose the number of solar panels such that you generate your own yearly consumption. However, if everybody would do this, the overcapacity on some time moments will be huge[1]. Here it is assumed that there is no 'netting' method. A produced kWh that is used directly has the same price as a purchased kWh from the network, P_u. A produced kWh that is delivered to the network is sold for a price P_d.

As said before, different stakeholders have different objectives. Now some measures are defined that can be used as objective in the model:

Self-sufficiency rate (SSR) $= \sum_{i,t} 1_{\{P_{i,t} >= D_{i,t}\}}/T.$
Maximum Import (M) $= \max_{i,t} \max(D_{i,t} - P_{i,t}; 0).$
Overcapacity (C) $= \sum_{i,t} \max(P_{i,t} - D_{i,t}; 0)/\sum_{i,t} P_{i,t}.$
Return on investment (RoI) $= \dfrac{P_u \sum_{i,t} \min(P_{i,t}, D_{i,t}) + P_d \sum_{i,t} \max(P_{i,t} - D_{i,t}, 0)}{N_s P_s + N_w P_w}.$

The SSR indicates how many of all hours the total production of the system is higher than the consumption. The choice of the time frame (granularity) is up to the user in the model, but here chosen to be one hour. The effect of the granularity is shown in [13]. The variable M indicates the amount of electricity imported to the system in the hour with the highest import. There could be some (technical) restriction to this number, imposed by the network operator. The overcapacity C indicates the percentage of production that is not consumed by the system itself, but is exported. The RoI indicates the percentage of the total investment in production capacity, here the generators, that is earned by the production.

When the number of generators increases, the SSR will increase also and the amount imported will decrease, which is in most cases positive. However, the increase of the number of generators will also lead to higher overcapacity and, probably, in a decrease of the RoI, which are both negative. Finding a solution

---

[1] For this reason we expect 'netting' to disappear in the near future. In the Netherlands this is expected shortly after the year 2020.

that provides an acceptable value of all these four, partly conflicting, objectives can be seen as Multi Objective Optimisation, see for example [9]. Bringing them together into one combined (normalised) objective function gives a number of optimal solutions, depending on the weights of the normalisation. All these optimal solutions are called Pareto Solutions, combined (as a set) to a Pareto frontier [1]. Sometimes an objective can be removed if the optimisation is not needed, but some maximal or minimal value is desired. Then that objective has become a restriction to the optimisation problem. An example of the remaining problem is, with normalisation weights w_1 and w_2:

$$\max(w_1 SSR - w_2 C),$$

under the constraints:

$$RoI \geq r,$$

$$M \leq m.$$

Here the SSR and the overcapacity are in some combination of weights optimised[2], under constraints for the RoI and the maximum import.

3   Case Study

To show the capabilities of the model a case study is presented, assuming a certain scenario. The chosen values for the variables in the scenario are shown in Table 1. First some experience on the effect of input parameters is shown. Then some different combinations of objectives and constraints are used. Finally some idea is given of controllable measures to reach a stable desirable solution.

Table 1. Details for the case study.

Parameter	Value
n	100
σ_d	0.6
σ_s	0.3
σ_w	1.3
P_u	€0.20
P_d	€0.20

3.1   Introduction

First, to get some experience on the effect of input parameters on the objectives, some results, as a function of the number of solar panels, are shown. In Fig. 2 both the RoI and the SSR are depicted under these parameters, where the

---

[2] SSR is maximised, the overcapacity, by the minus sign, minimised.

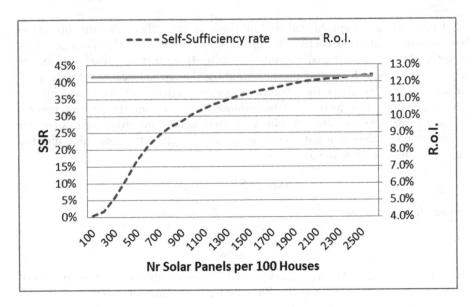

Fig. 2. SSR and RoI in first example.

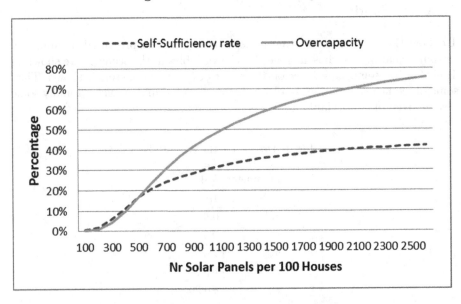

Fig. 3. SSR and overcapacity in first example.

number of solar panels varies and the number of wind turbines is set to zero. The (yearly) *RoI* is constant here, 12.3%. This constant value is caused by the fact that $P_u = P_d$. The *SSR* grows from 0% to 47% (asymptotically). In Fig. 3 for the same example the *SSR* and the overcapacity C are shown. The figure shows that the overcapacity grows quickly. To reach a high SSR with solar panels only, a high overcapacity is unavoidable.

Now P_d is set to zero. Then there is no benefit for the owner of the solar panels when the production is higher than the demand in the system in a certain period, the periods of overcapacity. The RoI decreases quickly when the capacity of installed solar panels grows, as shown in Fig. 4.

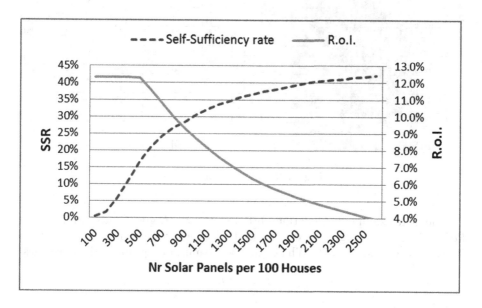

Fig. 4. Effect of $P_d = 0$ in example.

3.2 Playing with Constraints and Objectives

Still under the assumption that $P_d = 0$ some restrictions are introduced, possibly by government or network owner, to the value of SSR and M. For example, say that $SSR \geq 40\%$ and $M \leq 70kWh$. The optimisation problem then becomes:

$$\max RoI$$

under the constraints:

$$SSR \geq 40\%$$

$$M \leq 70$$

Optimising the RoI under these constraints gives as solution (500/45): the installation of 500 solar panels (5 per house) and 45 micro turbines, see Fig. 5. The RoI here is 6.7%. If the SSR constraint is set to 30%, then the optimal solution is (400/35) leading to a RoI of 7.4%.

							Nr Wind Turbines						
	0	**5**	**10**	**15**	**20**	**25**	**30**	**35**	**40**	**45**	**50**	**55**	**60**
100													
200													
300													6.2%
400											6.6%	6.3%	6.1%
500										6.7%	6.4%	6.2%	5.9%
600									6.6%	6.4%	6.2%	5.9%	5.7%
700								6.5%	6.3%	6.1%	5.9%	5.7%	5.5%
800							6.4%	6.2%	6.0%	5.8%	5.7%	5.5%	5.3%
900						6.2%	6.1%	5.9%	5.7%	5.6%	5.4%	5.3%	5.1%
1000					6.0%	5.9%	5.8%	5.6%	5.5%	5.3%	5.2%	5.1%	4.9%
1100					5.7%	5.6%	5.5%	5.4%	5.2%	5.1%	5.0%	4.9%	4.7%
1200					5.4%	5.3%	5.2%	5.1%	5.0%	4.9%	4.8%	4.7%	4.6%
1300					5.2%	5.1%	5.0%	4.9%	4.8%	4.7%	4.6%	4.5%	4.4%
1400					4.9%	4.8%	4.8%	4.7%	4.6%	4.5%	4.4%	4.3%	4.2%
1500					4.7%	4.6%	4.6%	4.5%	4.4%	4.4%	4.3%	4.2%	4.1%
1600					4.5%	4.4%	4.4%	4.3%	4.3%	4.2%	4.1%	4.0%	4.0%
1700					4.3%	4.2%	4.2%	4.2%	4.1%	4.0%	4.0%	3.9%	3.8%
1800					4.1%	4.1%	4.0%	4.0%	4.0%	3.9%	3.8%	3.8%	3.7%
1900					3.9%	3.9%	3.9%	3.9%	3.8%	3.8%	3.7%	3.7%	3.6%
2000					3.8%	3.8%	3.8%	3.7%	3.7%	3.7%	3.6%	3.6%	3.5%
2100					3.7%	3.6%	3.6%	3.6%	3.6%	3.5%	3.5%	3.4%	3.4%
2200					3.5%	3.5%	3.5%	3.5%	3.5%	3.4%	3.4%	3.3%	3.3%
2300					3.4%	3.4%	3.4%	3.4%	3.4%	3.3%	3.3%	3.3%	3.2%
2400					3.3%	3.3%	3.3%	3.3%	3.3%	3.2%	3.2%	3.2%	3.1%
2500					3.2%	3.2%	3.2%	3.2%	3.2%	3.1%	3.1%	3.1%	3.0%

(Left axis label: Nr Solar Panels)

Fig. 5. Result of optimisation.

The next example formulation optimises the SSR, given constraints on the RoI and M. Say a regulator decides that 6% is a nice return for the owners of the equipment and $M \leq 70$kWh again. The optimisation problem then becomes:

$$\max SSR$$

under the constraints:

$$RoI \geq 6\%$$

$$M \leq 70$$

Now an SSR of 48.2% can be reached by choosing the solution (600/50), 600 solar panels and 50 wind turbines.

As a last example the combination of SSR and RoI is optimised. The optimisation problem then becomes:

$$\max w_1 SSR + w_2 RoI$$

under the constraints:

$$C \leq 50\%$$

$$M \leq 70$$

If $w_1 = 1$ and $w_2 = 0$, the optimum is reached taking the solution (600/100), resulting in a SSR of 65% and a RoI of 4.4%. However if $w_1 = 0$ and $w_2 = 1$ the optimum is reached at the solution (300/40), resulting in a SSR of 30% and a RoI of 7.2%. Taking the intermediate values results in the Pareto frontier of the optimisation problem, as depicted in Fig. 6. Also the Pareto frontiers for several values of P_d can be generated. For three values this is depicted in Fig. 7.

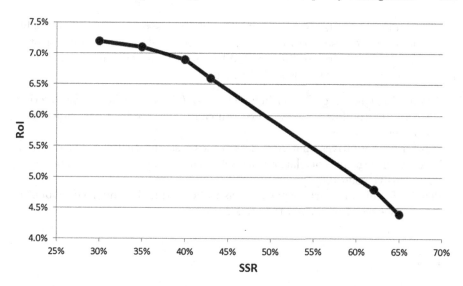

Fig. 6. Pareto Frontier.

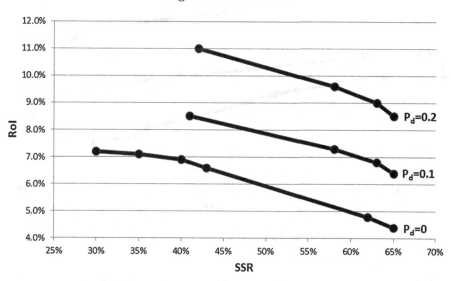

Fig. 7. Pareto Frontiers for values of P_d.

3.3 Policy Making

Then the problem of policy makers and network owners is touched. They have goals, constraints and a number of buttons they can use to influence. For example, a high value for SSR is desirable. However, too much certainty may induce overproduction too many of a certain generator, probability the most profitable for the investor, will cause overproduction on certain moments. Reducing the price the consumer gets for electricity that is not used directly will probably cause a lower SSR (resulting from Fig. 7). Which incentive can be given to steer the system in the desirable direction? What are the actual buttons the policy makers can use? Some options and thoughts:

- Setting P_d. Choosing P_d too high (close to P_u) will cause overproduction. Choosing P_d too low (close to zero) will cause a choice for the cheapest generator and a low SSR.
- Subsidise alternatives that have less peak or stochasticity in generation or have low or negative correlation with solar panel generation. This is, probably, an expensive solution.
- Penalty for high import. A penalty has to be paid if the imported amount of electricity exceeds a certain threshold.

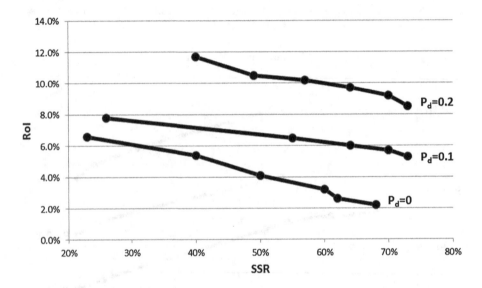

Fig. 8. Frontiers with penalty.

For the latter some exercises are presented. If the threshold is set on 40 kWh and both the penalty and P_d are varied, three frontiers are available that can be realised, as depicted in Fig. 8. Per value of P_d a frontier is given, where the left values are reached by using a low penalty (e.g., €10), the right values by using high penalty (e.g., €100). The RoI is calculated including the penalty. The advantage is that these frontiers can be exploited by the policy makers, while these are results of parameters they can influence. Note however that the difference in RoI between the three lines have to be paid by someone. When the overproduction is used (for example by industrial parties) or stored for later use, this is real economic gain. Otherwise this has to be paid by electricity companies or government. The cost of 1% per house equals (around) in this example €180 euro per year. This means that going from the line $P_d = 0$ to $P_d = 0.2$ costs 6%, which is around 1500 euro per house per year. To go to the line $P_d = 0.1$ this costs around 500 euro per house per year. On total level for 100 houses, this is shown in Table 2, solution 1,2 and 3.

Table 2. Details for the test instances.

Nr	P_d	SSR	RoI	Costs (€/year)	Investment	Penalty	Solution
1	€0.00	50%	4.1%	€−40k		€40	500/60
2	€0.10	51%	6.8%	€−5k		€20	1200/40
3	€0.20	49%	10.5%	€78k		€30	2000/20
4	€0.10	51%	37.4%	€−10k	€880k	€0	100/100

To compare this approach another option is considered. To reach the same SSR in an equilibrium without penalty at $P_d = 0.1$, the price of the wind turbine should drop almost 90%. This costs around €8,800 per house, however, around €50 per house per year is saved on the solution with penalty (at $P_d = 0.1$) that has more solar panels and thus more overcapacity to be sold. This is the fourth solution in Table 2.

4   Conclusions

In this paper a model was presented that can handle uncertainty in demand and supply and do multi-objective analysis to show the sensitivity of the capacity management for the different objectives as input for the discussion between investors and network owners. Four possible objective were introduced to be considered by the model: Self-sufficiency rate, Maximum Import, Overcapacity and Return on investment. With this model some analysis was done in a case study to show the possibilities of the model and give some results and insight in the particular case study. Following the model, the most effective way to control the user behaviour is the introduction of a penalty on high electricity import to the system. Other options turn out to be expensive in the model, not effective or difficult to realise in practice.

References

1. Abbass, H.A., Sarker, R., Newton, C.: PDE: a pareto-frontier differential evolution approach for multi-objective optimization problems. In: Proceedings of the 2001 Congress on Evolutionary Computation. vol. 2, pp. 971–978. IEEE (2001)
2. Akbari, K., Jolai, F., Ghaderi, S.F.: Optimal design of distributed energy system in a neighborhood under uncertainty. Energy **116**, 567–582 (2016)
3. Association, C.W.E.: Small wind turbine purchasing guide: offgrid, residential, farm & small business applications. Developed by the Pembina Institute and eFormative Options, LLC (2008)

4. Azcárate, C., Mallor, F., Mateo, P.: Tactical and operational management of wind energy systems with storage using a probabilistic forecast of the energy resource. Renew. Energy **102**, 445–456 (2017)
5. Belyaev, L.S.: Pay-off matrix technique. Energy **15**(7/8), 631–643 (1990)
6. Chedid, R., Mezher, T., Jarrouche, C.: A fuzzy programming approach to energy resource allocation. Int. J. Energy Res. **23**, 303–317 (1999)
7. Croes, N., Phillipson, F., Schreuder, M.: Tactical congestion management: the optimal mix of decentralised generators in a district. In: Integration of Renewables into the Distribution Grid, CIRED 2012 Workshop, pp. 1–4, IET (2012)
8. De Musgrove, A.: A linear programming analysis of liquid-furl production and use options for Australia. Energy **9**, 281–302 (1984)
9. Deb, K.: Multi-objective optimization. In: Burke, E.K., Kendall, G. (eds.) Search methodologies, pp. 403–449. Springer, Heidelberg (2014)
10. Esmaili, M., Firozjaee, E.C., Shayanfar, H.A.: Optimal placement of distributed generations considering voltage stability and power losses with observing voltage-related constraints. Appl. Energy **113**, 1252–1260 (2014)
11. Hiremath, R., Shikha, S., Ravindranath, N.: Decentralized energy planning; modeling and application - a review. Renew. Sustain. Energy Rev. **11**, 729–752 (2007)
12. Jebaraj, S., Iniyan, S.: A review of energy models. Renew. Sustain. Energy Rev. **10**(4), 281–311 (2006)
13. Kools, L., Phillipson, F.: Data granularity and the optimal planning of distributed generation. Energy **112**, 342–352 (2016)
14. Labys, W.C., Kuczmowski, T., Infanger, G.: Special programming models. Energy **15**(7/8), 607–617 (1990)
15. Luhanga, M., Mwandosya, M., Luteganya, P.: Optimisation in computerized energy modeling for Tanzania. Energy **18**, 1171–1179 (1993)
16. Mashhour, E., Moghaddas-Tafreshi, S.: Integration of distributed energy resources into low voltage grid: a market-based multiperiod optimization model. Electr. Power Syst. Res. **80**(4), 473–480 (2009)
17. Satsangi, P., Sarma, E.: Integrated energy planning model for India with particular reference to renewable energy prospects. In: Energy Options for the 1990's: Proceedings of the National Solar Energy Convention held at Indian Institute of Technology, pp. 596–620. Tata McGraw Hill, New Delhi (1988)
18. Suganthi, L., Jagadeesan, T.: A modified model for prediction of Indias future energy requirement. Int. J. Energy Environ. **3**, 371–386 (1992)

DP and RL Approach Optimization for Embedded System Communications with Energy Harvesting

Mohammed Assaouy[1(✉)], Ouadoudi Zytoune[1,2], and Driss Aboutajdine[1]

[1] Mohammed V University, Rabat, Morocco
assaouy.med@gmail.com, aboutaj@fsr.ac.ma
[2] Ibn Tofail University, Kénitra, Morocco
zytoune.ouadoudi@uit.ac.ma

Abstract. In this paper, we consider a point-to-point wireless communication in embedded system. This system is supposed to be battery powered and equipped with an energy harvester. According to the battery level and the harvested energy, the transmitter has to make decision following an optimal policy in order to maximize its reward over the operating period. We first consider a prior stochastic knowledge of the transition matrix probabilities to find out the optimal policy using algorithm originated from DP methods. With no such stochastic knowledge, we will adopt algorithms from RL methods to find out the optimal policies. The resulting performances are then compared.

Keywords: Wireless communications · Energy harvesting · MDP · Dynamic programming · Reinforcement learning

1 Introduction

Internet of things has emerged as a promising technology and a new way of connectivity [1]. The wireless senor networks play a crucial role in the field of IoT as they are part of several applications such as environmental monitoring, security of traffic reporting and controlling, military target tracking [2,3].

In wireless sensor networks field of research the consumption still the most important difficulties that we need to deal with [4,5]. The energy harvesting technology appears like to give a solution that guarantees a theoretical unlimited working time for sensors that are deployed densely in harsh environments.

The recent development in the harvesting field of technology makes the harvesters able to capture even the very small amount of energy from the environment surrounding the sensors. They transform it into electrical energy.

In addition, the performance efficiency achieved thanks to the recent development in the microprocessor technology contributes significantly to reduce the energy consumption of sensors [6].

An unlimited time horizon of work for the sensors is just a theoretic assumption because the operation times of the wireless sensor networks are limited by

© Springer International Publishing AG 2017
G. Eichler et al. (Eds.): I4CS 2017, CCIS 717, pp. 167–182, 2017.
DOI: 10.1007/978-3-319-60447-3_12

other factors such as discounted rewards, depending on the nature of the information being collected, and the quite small amounts of energy harvested from the ambient environment [7].

The transmitter needs to take advantage of the harvested amount of energy arriving at the sensor by making the right transmission decisions [8]. For this purpose, we need to compute optimal policies based on strategies that takes into account the information available concerning the stochastic behavior of the system [9].

In our paper, we consider a point to point wireless sensor communication system that could be a part of a traffic management system for smart highways [10]. Actually, in-road battery powered sensors are charged to gather real traffic information that are sent directly to a traffic control base station where many treatments are performed in order to improve the safety and the flows of vehicles [11].

The proposed model is energy-independent thanks to its harvesting skills and energy managing capabilities. In fact, Many application-oriented research institutions conduct projects on that field and could be interested in new generation of independent and self energy managing sensors, e.g. the Daedalus Project conducted in the Fraunhofer IIS that care about efficient self-powered tracking systems [12].

Two scenarios are considered depending on the available information for the optimal policies calculation. In the first scenario, a stochastic knowledge of the environment behavior is already available and the optimal policy can then be computed into each sensor or broadcasted by the gateway to all the concerned sensors in order to address the making decision ability of the transmitter according to the system states. In the second scenario, no information is available about the stochastic behavior of the operating environment, the policies are then learned directly from the decisions made and improved from one episode to another.

We assume that the transmitter is battery-powered. The battery in use is connected to an energy harvesting system and can be replenished infinitely. The whole system model is described in Fig. 1.

We assume that data arrives at the transmitter in a time slotted way. At the beginning of each time slot (TS), a data packet is received and is supposed lost if not transmitted within the following time slot. The harvested energy that arrives within a time slot is stocked if and only if the battery is not full, otherwise this energy is lost. We also consider that the transmission of data is the main dominant source of energy consumption. We assume that the state of the wireless channel doesn't change during the laps time of a slot but may vary from one time slot to another. We consider that the data arrivals, the energy harvesting and the attenuation levels of the wireless channel are all modeled as Markov processes [13].

The only objective of the transmitter is the maximization of the expected cumulative transmitted data to the destination during its operating time under the energy availability constraints. For this purpose, we provide a complete

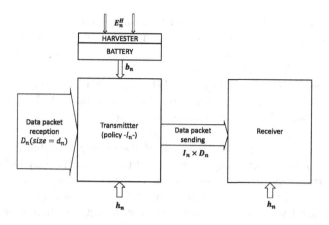

Fig. 1. Battery-powered system with energy harvesting

analysis of the optimal communication system based on a stochastic modelization of the system. We present a computing methods to obtain an optimal policy according to the availability of information. The information considered are the transition matrix probabilities of data sizes, energy harvesting amounts and the channel states. Both of the model-based and the model-free approaches are treated. The main contribution of this paper can be summarized as follows:

- Based on the models of different components of the system studied, we provide a complete analysis to obtain the optimal policy for a maximum expected cumulative transmitted data.
- We compare through the numerical results obtained the performance achieved by our optimal policies in terms expected cumulative transmitted data.

the rest of this paper will be divided in Sect. 2 that is dedicated to the system modeling and the presentation of the computing methods to obtain the optimal policies as a resolution of the subsequent MDP models, Sect. 3 where the results are presented and compared by numerical analysis and simulation using matlab, and finally Sect. 4 that concludes this paper.

2 System Modeling and Optimization Strategies

2.1 System Modeling

In this work we consider a wireless system with a transceiver powered by battery equipped by an energy harvesting process [14]. We assume that the battery has limitation storage capacity and will often be subject of replenishment by the energy harvester.

We assume also that our system operates according to a time-slotted fashion with fixed duration periods of equal values TS. The data arrives in packets at each time slot TS with different packet sizes. The environmental energy is harvested with different amounts within each time slot and may be lost whenever the battery is full. We consider that the communication channel takes a constant state over each TS and we assume that channel state changes would only be possible from one TS to the next one.

We consider that a received data packet will be transmitted over the next TS duration otherwise it will be destroyed. The energy harvested during a giving time slot TS_n serve for the replenishment of the battery in the following time slot TS_{n+1}.

Our main objective is to do good use of the energy available in the battery with the purpose of maximizing the expected total data transmitted during the whole operating time of the system in association with a discounted rewards process in terms of transmitted data according to a factor rate γ.

We modelize the data packet sizes arriving during the current time slot TS as a stochastic process characterized by a first order Markov model. We made the choice to consider that the data packet sizes arriving during TS_n is d_n that belongs to the set of all possible data packet sizes such as $\{d_1, d_2, \ldots, d_{N_D}\}$, where N_D is the total number of all possible packet sizes considered. We note that the transition probability that the considered data packet size shifts from one packet size d_j to d_k within one time slot TS as $p_D(d_j, d_k)$.

In addition, we assume that the amount of harvested energy during TS_n follows also a stochastic process characterized by a first order Markov model. We consider that the harvested energy during TS_n is E_n^h that belongs to the set of all possible harvested energy amounts such as $\{e_1, e_2, \ldots, d_{N_E}\}$, where N_E is the total number of all possible harvested energy amounts considered. We note that the transition probability that the considered harvested energy amounts shifts from one amount e_j to e_k within one time slot TS as $p_e(e_j, e_k)$.

Also, we consider the channel attenuation level evolution from one time slot TS to the next as a stochastic process characterized by a first order Markov model. We make the choice to consider that the channel attenuation level during TSn is h_n that belongs to the set of all possible channel states such as $\{d_1, d_2, \ldots, d_{N_H}\}$, where N_H is the total number of all possible channel states considered.

We note that the transition probability that the channel state switches from one channel state h_j to h_k within one time slot TS as $p_D(h_j, h_k)$.

We note, E_n^{TS} the amount of energy being spent when the transmitter is performing a data packet transmission of size d_n over the channel being in state h_n towards a receiver, no matter whether the transmission is being performed successfully or not. And we note, e the elementary amount of energy which is equivalent to the minimum of energy needed to transmit a data packet of minimal size across the channel that presents the minimal attenuation.

We consider that a transmission is performed successfully if the E_n^{TS} amount of energy consumed is equal to the right quantity of energy needed in terms of charge units according to both d_n and h_n values. It appears trivial that for long data packet sizes and/or bad channel conditions we would need more than one charge unit to perform a successful transmission.

We assume that all the information related to the battery charge level, the energy being harvested, the size of the arrived data packet, the current channel state are known at the transmitter side, and so are the information related to the channel state during the considered time slot is known at the receiver side.

At the beginning of each TS the transmitter makes the decision, according to the information available concerning the remained battery charge, the data packet size and the channel attenuation level, of either to transmit the incoming packet or to drop it when following a designed policy or according to a learning process. We consider I_n as an indicator function of the decision being made by the transmitter whether to transmit ($I_n = 1$) or to drop it ($I_n = 0$). I_n is then belonging to the set of values $\{0, 1\}$. The transmitter fixes the transmission rate and power at the beginning of each time slot and cannot be changed therefore.

Some constraints must be taken into account to insure a good achievement of the optimization objectives, such that:

$$I_n E_n^{TS} \leq B_n, \tag{1}$$

$$B_{n+1} = \min\left\{B_n - I_n E_n^{TS} + E_n^h, B_{max}\right\} \tag{2}$$

where B_n is the current battery charge, B_{max} the maximal charge capacity of the battery. After each iteration, the battery state is then updated to the next state according to energy spent for the transmission and the harvested energy received and stocked.

The main goal of the optimization problem is to maximize the expected total transmitted data over the whole operating time which will be equivalent to the total activation time duration of the transmitter. The objective of this optimization will be described as follows:

$$\max_{\{I_i\}_{i=1}^{\infty}} \sum_{n=1}^{\infty} \gamma^{n-1} I_n D_n \tag{3}$$

$$\text{subject to} \quad (1) \; and \; (2) \tag{4}$$

Our system will be then approximated by a finite-state discrete-time MDP model [15]. The MDP model will constitute the basic platform for the decision making giving the randomness nature of the states taken by the system and its environment that will be considered fully observable so that the current state completely characterizes the process. Our considered system state is composed of four element that are E_n^h representing the quantity of energy that would be harvested during the current time slot, D_n the data size packet received in the previous time slot TS_{n-1} and being ready to be transmitted during the current time slot, H_n the actual attenuation of the channel and B_n the available capacity charge in the battery at the beginning of the time slot, so S_n is $\langle E_n^h, D_n, H_n, B_n \rangle$.

At each period T_{S_n}, the system state is S_n. The components of the system state are then discrete, and the set of all the possible system state S is of a finite number of elements. S is denoted by $S = \{S_1, S_2, \ldots, S_{N_S}\}$ where N_S is the total number of all the possible system states obtained by combining all the component values of the three dimensional S_i element.

The set of the possible actions that the transmitter can take is either to transmit the data packet or to drop it, so this set is denoted as $I = [0, 1]$.

A policy will defines the behavior of the transmitter at each time according to the evolution of the system state S_n, i.e. it is the linking map between the set of the observed system state and the set of the actions to be taken by the transmitter as a decision maker agent. This policy will be denoted by π.

The reward function considered represents the goal of the transmitter as an agent, i.e. it translates the pair vector composed of the action applied to the system and the current state being taken to a single reward number. In our case, the reward represents the quantity of bits being transmitted when evolving from one system state to the next according to the decision made by the transmitter and is denoted by $R_n = I_n D_n$.

The main transmitter objective is to maximize the sum of the resulting rewards in the long run of the system considering the discounted aspect of the data being transmitted. This objective is addressed by the state-value function $v_\pi(S_i)$ of the MDP system which represents the expected total discounted amount of rewards when starting from state S_i, and then following the policy π. The state value function will be our main tool for solving the resulting MDP system is defined as follows:

$$V^\pi(S_i) \triangleq \sum_{\forall S_k \in S} p_{\pi(S_i)}(S_i, S_k)[R_{\pi(S_i)}(S_i, S_k) + \gamma V^\pi(S_k)] \tag{5}$$

The state-value function $V^\pi(S_n)$ is then expressed as a combination of the expected immediate reward and the next state-value function denoted by $V^\pi(S_{n+1})$.

In the case of a learning policy, the transmitter objective becomes to maximize the reward in long run interaction with the environment on the basis of his own experience. To act like this, the transmitter has to consider the value of the action-state value function in each step when starting from state S_i, taking action X_l and then following policy π. The action-state value function is defined as follows:

$$Q^\pi(S_i, I_l) \triangleq \sum_{\forall S_k \in S} p_{I_l}(S_i, S_k)[R_{I_l}(S_i, S_k) + \gamma V^\pi(S_k)] \tag{6}$$

The state-action value function $Q^\pi(S_n, I_n)$, when starting from state S_n, taking action I_n and then following policy π, is by the same way expressed as a combination of the expected immediate reward and the next state-value function denoted by $V^\pi(S_{n+1})$.

We can say that a policy π' is better than or equal to policy π, denoted by $\pi' \geq \pi$, if and only if the expected total discount amount of rewards obtained following policy π' is greater than or equal to that when following policy π which means that $V^{\pi'}(S_i) \geq V^\pi(S_i)$. The optimal policy π^* is defined as the policy which is better or equal to any other possible policy conducting to the optimal state value functions $V^{\pi^*}(S_i)$ with $i = 1, 2, \ldots, N_S$. So is the case of the action state value $Q^{\pi^*}(S_i, I_i)$ being greater or equal to any action state value following other policies strategies. The optimal state value is linked to the optimal action state value by the following relationship:

$$V^{\pi^*}(S_i) = max_{I_i \in A} Q^{\pi^*}(S_i, I_i) \tag{7}$$

According to the system state S_i, the optimal policy is then greedy over the set the action state values of all possible pairs (S_i, I_i). That is, the problem to solve become which action should the transmitter take to maximize his rewards and then starts following the policy π. To reach to optimal expected total reward one should consider that the action state value is the combination of the maximum immediate reward obtained by choosing the action to take according to the greedy policy and the maximum action state value for the next state so that:

$$Q^{\pi^*}(S_i, I_l) = \sum_{\forall S_k \in S} p_{I_l}(S_i, S_k)[R_{I_l}(S_i, S_k) + \gamma max_{I_i \in A} Q^{\pi^*}(S_i, I_i)] \tag{8}$$

Two approaches will be taken into account in our study in order to solve the resulting MDP problem depending on whether we manage to know the system model so that we are dealing with a model based Markovian decision problem or we will then in the situation of a model free control problem.

In a model based configuration, we assume that we have good knowledge of the stochastic behavior of the model with prior information on the different components of the MDP model, as it can be described by a 5 tuple $\langle S, A, P, R, \gamma \rangle$, where S is the set of states, A is the set of actions, P the state transition probability matrix, R the reward function and γ a discounted factor [15]. In that case of study, we need sufficient knowledge of the transition probability matrix, the set of actions and states and the associated generated rewards according to each state-action pairs being considered to be able to apply DP algorithms in order to find optimal transmission policy π^*.

Concerning the case of a model free control, we assume that we don't have any prior stochastic information about the system being studied. We manage then to permit the transmitter to explore the environment behavior itself and exploit the set of information resulting from experiences by following a reinforcement learning approach. The main objective is to learn how to make right decisions to find an ultimate policy π^* that maximizes the total reward accumulated over time.

2.2   Model-Based Control and the Optimal Policy Design

In case of a model based, the transmitter care mainly about performing successful and efficient transmission of the incoming packets, so the decision made would normally take account of the energy available inside the battery resulting of the consumed capacity up to this moment, the theoretical capacity according to the performance metrics of the battery being used and the possibility of recovering additional energy units by the battery in addition of the information available about the MDP itself.

We employ algorithms derived from the dynamic programming theory (DP) to solve the MDP problem resulting of Eq. 3 [16]. Policy iteration algorithm (PI) will be experimented first and then Value Iteration algorithm (VI) will be used.

Given that our system MDP model has finite action and state spaces and bounded and stationary reward functions, both PI and VI are proven to converge to the optimal policy when the discount factor is $0 \leq \gamma < 1$. The solution considered at this stage is to combine the set of equations composed of (5, 6, 7 and 8) to obtain the optimal policy.

The key idea of value iteration algorithm is to use the value functions to structure and organize the search of the optimal policy that guarantees the maximization goal to be achieved.

We choose to exploit the value iteration algorithm which is recognized to be more faster than policy iteration in terms of calculation duration. VI operates by exploiting the Eq. (7) as follows:

$$V_l^{\pi}(S_i) = max_{I_i \in A} Q_l^{\pi}(S_i, I_i) \tag{9}$$

$$= max_{I_i \in A} \sum_{\forall S_k \in S} p_{I_i}(S_i, S_k)[R_{I_i}(S_i, S_k)+$$

$$\gamma max_{I_i \in A} Q_{l-1}^{\pi}(S_i, I_i)]$$

For all $S_i \in S$ and for arbitrary V_0^{π} initialization, the sequence $\left\langle V_0^{\pi}, V_1^{\pi'}, V_2^{\pi''}, \dots, V_k^{\pi^{(k)}}, \dots \right\rangle$ converges to V^{π^*} under the same conditions that guarantees the existence of V^{π^*} itself, that is achieved more faster than in the policy iteration algorithms case.

The algorithm that have been implemented in our system decision making according to the value iteration fashion is described as follows:

The value iteration algorithm is proven to converge to the optimal policy for the discounted finite MDP being considered [17]. In our particular model, the computation complexity of is bounded by $O(2N_S^2)$ in the value iteration case [18]. The performance of the proposed algorithms is compared with other approaches in next section.

2.3   Model-Free Reinforcement Learning Approach: Sarsa Algorithm

In the case of model free reinforcement learning, the transmitter operates in an unknown environment trying to maximize the cumulative long term discounted reward by performing actions according to the observation of current states and rewards [19,20].

In this section, we focus on the case that our system is model free and formulated as a discounted finite Markov decision process (MDP) and we adopt the reinforcement learning field to resolve the optimization problem being treated.

We use Sarsa algorithm that is one of the most used methods for solving MDP problems in the context of model free conditions. In fact, Sarsa is an on-policy algorithm with proved capacity to converge to the optimal action-state

Algorithm 1. Value Iteration

1. Initialization step:
for each state $S_i \in S$ **do**
  Initialise $V^\pi(S_i)$ arbitrarily
end for
2. Value Iteration:
$\Delta \leftarrow 1$
$\epsilon \leftarrow 0.001$
while $\Delta > \epsilon$ **do**
  $\Delta \leftarrow 0$
  $v \leftarrow V^\pi$
  for each state $S_i \in S$ **do**
    $V^\pi(S_i) \leftarrow \max\limits_{I_i \in A} \sum\limits_{\forall S_k \in S} p_{I_i}(S_i, S_k)[R_{I_i}(S_i, S_k) + \gamma V^\pi(S_k)]$
    $\pi(S_i) \leftarrow \operatorname*{argmax}\limits_{I_i \in A} \sum\limits_{\forall S_k \in S} p_{I_i}(S_i, S_k)[R_{I_i}(S_i, S_k) + \gamma V^\pi(S_k)]$
  end for
  $\Delta \leftarrow max(\Delta, \| V^\pi - v \|_\infty)$
end while

values as long as episodes are performed if some conditions [21] are verified such as: (1) S and A are finite, (2) The reward function is bounded, (3) The policy is greedy in the limit with infinite exploration, (4) And the Robins-Monro sequence of learning rate factor is verified as follows,

$$\sum_n \alpha_i(S_i, I_i) = \infty, \tag{10}$$

$$\sum_n (\alpha_i(S_i, I_i))^2 < \infty$$

$$w.p.1$$

$$\forall (S, I) \neq (S_i, I_i), \alpha_i(S, I) = 0$$

To be able to apply Sarsa algorithm, we first assume that our transmitter is able to observe the state S_n and the reward $R(S_n, S_{n+1})$ after having performing an action I_n in TS_n. The reward is represented by the transmitted data packet size d_n which is already known at the transmitter.

Equation 10 shows that $Q(S_n, I_n)$ relative to the current action-state pair can be represented in terms of the expected reward of the current action-state pair and the state value function $V(S_{n+1}) = Q(S_{n+1}, I_{n+1})$ of the next state. The on-policy aspect of the Sarsa policy comes from that the next Q-value contains all the long term rewards resulting from taking action I_{n+1} and then following policy π^*.

Thus, to make the optimal decision one should choose the action that maximize the reward and than continue following the optimal policy. By using the $\epsilon - greedy$ policy, the decision made is conditioned by a an expansion of the set of actions being considered by balancing the exploration and exploitation approaches as long as the episodes are going on. Finally, the optimal policy can easily be derived from the $Q^*(S_i, I_i)$ being obtained.

Based on this method, Sarsa is acting with an iterative manner to estimate the optimal $Q^*(S_i, I_i)$ over the whole set of available states being visited over the performed episodes. In the nth learning episode $Q_n(S_n, I_n)$ is estimated by his current value and updated by the resulting error between the expected estimation of the next Q-value $(Q(S_{n+1}, I_{N+1})$ added to the current reward and his previous estimate $Q_{n-1}*(S_n, I_n)$. In each TS, the resulting steps are [22]:

- observe the current state $S_n \in S$,
- choose and perform an action $I_n \in I$,
- observe the next state $S_{n+1} \in S$ and the immediate reward $R_{I_n}(S_n, S_{n+1})$
- updates the estimate of $Q(S_n, I_n)$ *using*

$$Q(S_n, I_n) \leftarrow Q(S_n, I_n) + \alpha[R_{n+1} + \gamma Q(S_{n+1}, I_{n+1}) - Q(S_n, I_n)] \tag{11}$$

where α is the learning rate factor. If all actions are selected and performed with a non-zero probability, $0 \leq \gamma \leq 1$, and the conditions of Sarsa-convergence respected, than the sequence of $Q_i(S_i, I_i)$ is proven to converge to $Q^*(S_i, I_i)$ with probability 1 as $i \to \infty$ according to the Robins-Monro sequence stated before.

Algorithm 2. Sarsa algorithm

---

1. Initialization stage:
for each state $S_i \in S$ and each action $I_j \in I$ **do**
    Initialize $Q(S_i, I_j)$ arbitrarily from $\Re$ such that $Q(S_{tr}, .) = 0$ for all terminal states S_{tr}
end for
2. Sarsa optimization stage:
$S_i \leftarrow$ some start state
$N_L \leftarrow$ 200000 or 1000 as the maximum number of learning iteration considered
$l = 0$
$I_j \leftarrow \pi(S_i)$, where π is an ϵ-greedy policy based on Q
while $l < N_L$ **do**
    $l = l + 1$
    Take action I_j and observe reward R_l and next state S_k
    Choose an action $I_j' = \pi(S_k)$, where π is an ϵ-greedy policy based on Q
    $Q_{l+1}(S_i, I_j) \leftarrow Q_l(S_i, I_j) + \alpha[R_l + Q_l(S_k, I_j') - Q_l(S_i, I_j)]$
    $S_i \leftarrow S_k$
    $I_j \leftarrow I_j'$
end while

---

3   Numerical Results

We provide in this section an example of a communication system with energy harvesting as it was presented in Sect. 2. We are interested in comparing the performance achieved by the value iteration algorithm policy as a model based control and those of the Sarsa algorithm representing the case of a model free control.

We operate the calculation of the expected total transmitted data achieved in both cases by generating first a sequence of 2000 realizations of 100 arbitrarily state transition in order to average all the expected total transmitted data to guarantee a sufficient level of confidence on the obtained results.

The Sarsa policies were generated for $\epsilon = 0.001$ and 0.07, and then evaluated and averaged for 100 times to assess the associated performance when applied to the considered sequence stated before.

As a numerical values of different element of computation we have choose parameters based on IEEE802.15.4e [23] for the time slot duration fixed at $\Delta TS = 10\,\text{ms}$, the transmission period is of $\Delta Tx = 5\,\text{ms}$.

We assume that the packet sizes of data are in the set $D = \{300, 600\}$ and may vary according to the probability transition matrix $P_D = \begin{bmatrix} 0.9 & 0.1 \\ 0.1 & 0.9 \end{bmatrix}$.

The fundamental energy unit of the harvester is assumed to be equal to $2.5\,\mu\text{J}$ according to the piezoelectric harvesting device in [24], and we suppose that the harvester being used either harvest 2 energy unit or does not harvest any one so the set of possible harvested energy amount is giving by $E = \{0, 2\}$ and the probability transition matrix is $P_E = \begin{bmatrix} pH_0 & 1 - pH_0 \\ 1 - pH_2 & pH_2 \end{bmatrix}$, where pH_0 represents the probability of harvesting 0 energy unit in the current time slot giving that no energy was harvested in the previous time slot as well as pH_2. The channel state is assumed to take two states as the set giving by $H = \{1.655 \cdot 10^{-13}, 3.311 \cdot 10^{-13}\}$ which may account for indoor channel model in urban scenarios cases in [25], the probability of channel state transition matrix is given by $P_E = \begin{bmatrix} 0.9 & 0.1 \\ 0.1 & 0.9 \end{bmatrix}$.

The required transmission energy elementary unit E^{Tx} to successfully transmit a data packet of size 300 bits over a channel attenuation of $3.311 \cdot 10^{-13}$ in case of a noise power density of $10^{-20.4}$ (W/Hz) is of $2.5\,\mu\text{J}$ which may be equivalent to one unit harvesting energy. We assume that the transmission energy needed to guarantee a successful data packet transmission is an integer multiple of E^{Tx} and the energy spending over each time slot may belong to the set $E^{TS} = \{1, 2, 4\}$, which corresponds to a power consumption of 0.5, 1 and $2\,\text{mW}$ respectively. The maximal capacity size of the battery is varies from 5 to 9 energy transmission units (E^{Tx}).

We set γ to 0.9 for all the algorithms being used. Especially for the learning algorithm and the simulation purpose we settle the ϵ-greedy rate first to 0.07 and than to 0.001, the learning rate α is fixed to 0.5.

In Fig. 2 we represent the evolution of the performance obtained under Sarsa algorithm vs the learning iteration elapsed time (TSs). The achieved result is compared to that of the optimal policy calculated using Value iteration algorithm. As we can see Sarsa needs to run many episodes to learn the environment behavior before elaborating a policy that lead to maximize the obtained total cumulative reward. With ϵ fixed to 0.07 the rhythm of obtaining good result is faster than with ϵ fixed to 0.001 which illustrate the importance of exploration activities for approaching the optimal policy. High ϵ values generate oscillations at the study regime due to the fact that the algorithm still trying non greedy actions. A progressive annealing of ϵ over time can resolve this problem.

The VI approach take advantage of available information of the MDP process and represent an upper bond of the performance of those related to the Sarsa algorithm. The resulting cumulative reward on Sarsa for $\epsilon = 0.07$ and $N_L = 1000$ reaches almost 89% of the VI performance and only 78% when ϵ is less important where N_L is total number of the learning iteration time slots (TSs) being conducted.

In average for $N_L = 1000$, the considered system operates by exploitation the major battery capacity charge available at the beginning to perform massive transmission and after that rely on the harvesting process to execute additive transmissions in order to improve the expected total transmitted data as depicted in Figs. 3 and 4.

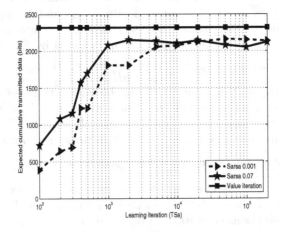

Fig. 2. Expected total transmitted data vs learning iteration with $pH_0 = pH_2 = 0.9$ and $B_{max} = 5$

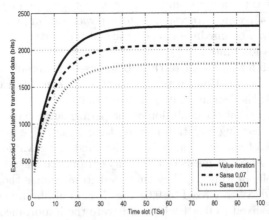

Fig. 3. Expected total transmitted data vs TSs with $pH_0 = pH_2 = 0.9$ and $B_{max} = 5$

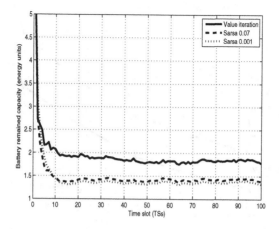

Fig. 4. Battery consumption vs TSs with $pH_0 = pH_2 = 0.9$ and $B_{max} = 5$

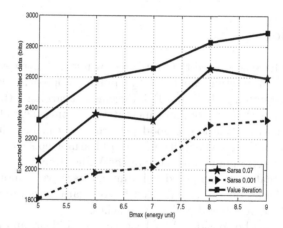

Fig. 5. Expected total transmitted data vs B_{max} with $pH_0 = pH_2 = 0.9$ and $N_L = 1000$ iterations

In Fig. 5 we illustrate the evolution of the expected total transmitted data according to the B_{max} value, so we notice that the more the battery capacity is important the more the cumulative reward obtained is significant.

The effect of pH_2 on the performance of the system is considerable, it represents how the surrounded energy is harvested by the system and use than to complete more an more transmission maximizing than the expected cumulative reward. When pH_2 starts decreasing, the impact is negative over the reward obtained by the system as illustrated in Fig. 6.

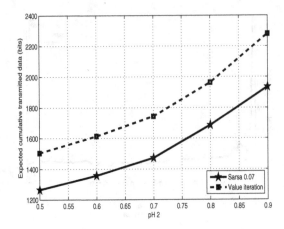

Fig. 6. Expected total transmitted data vs pH_2 with $pH_0 = 0.9$, $N_L = 1000$ iterations and $B_{max} = 5$

4   Conclusions

In our paper we have addressed the problem of wireless sensor networks battery optimization with harvesting capability by applying approaches from the fields of Dynamic Programming (DP) and Reinforcement Learning (RL) horizons.

We have proved that by the implementation of convenient algorithms into smart sensors in wireless systems, good performance can be achieved even in model free cases. With Sarsa Algorithm, only 10 learning episodes were sufficient to perform closer performances to those of the Value Iteration Algorithm.

The policies that were computed following an iterative reinforcement learning mechanism based on the experienced action-state pairs are an interesting alternative to the model based policy approaches.

Future works can be considered for large scales problems and for continuous state and action spaces. By using the value function approximation approaches, to scale up the learning methods for new prediction and control problems, we can enhance the adaptive capability of the learning algorithms for all the realistic cases of embedded system communications.

Acknowledgement. There is no word that can express our deep and sincere regret about the death of Pr. Driss Aboutajdine, the LRIT laboratory leader, that occurred on Saturday March 4th 2017. He was an extraordinary man and we are many in the community who will profoundly mourn his death as he was the model of generosity, perseverance and excellence throughout his life. May he rest in peace.

References

1. Atzori, L., Iera, A., Morabito, G.: The internet of things: a survey. Comput. Netw. **54**, 2787–2805 (2010)

2. Goldsmith, A.: Wireless Communications, 1st edn. Cambridge University Press, Cambridge (2005)
3. Estrin, D., Girod, L., Pottie, G., Srivastava, M.: Instrumenting the world with wireless sensor networks. In: Proceedings of the IEEE International Conference on Acoustics, Speech and Signal Processing (ICASSP 2001), Salt Lake City, Utah, USA, vol. 4, pp. 2033–2036, May 2001
4. Yrjola, J.: Summary of energy efficiency communication protocol for wireless micro sensor networks, 13 March 2005
5. Nguyen, L.T., Defago, X., Beuran, R., Shinoda, Y.: An energy efficient routing scheme for mobile wireless sensor networks. In: IEEE/ISWCS, pp. 568–572 (2008)
6. Vullers, R., Schaijk, R., Visser, H.J., Penders, J., Hoof, C.V.: Energy harvesting for autonomous wireless sensor networks. IEEE Solid-State Circuits Mag. 2, 29–38 (2010)
7. Devillers, B., Gunduz, D.: A general framework for the optimization of energy harvesting communication systems with battery imperfections. J. Commun. Netw. 14(2), 130–139 (2012)
8. Tutuncuoglu, K., Yener, A.: Sum-rate optimal power policies for energy harvesting transmitters in an interference channel. J. Commun. Netw. 14(2), 151–161 (2012)
9. Sutton, R.S., Barto, A.G.: Reinforcement Learning: An Introduction, A. B. Book edn. MIT Press, Cambridge (1998)
10. Prabhu, B., Antony, A.J., Balakumar, N.: A research on smart transportation using sensors and embedded systems. Int. J. Innov. Res. Comput. Sci. Technol. (IJIRCST), 5(1) (2017). ISSN: 2347-5552
11. McQueen, B., McQueen, J.: Intelligent Transportation Systems Architecture. Artech House (Intelligent Transportation Systems Library), Norwood (1999)
12. https://www.iis.fraunhofer.de/en/ff/lok/proj/daedalus.html. Accessed 4 Apr 2017
13. Blasco, P., Gunduz, D., Dohler, M.: A learning theoretic approach to energy harvesting communication system optimization. IEEE Trans. Wirel. Commun. 12(4), 1872–1882 (2013)
14. Blasco, P., Gunduz, D.: Multi-access communications with energy harvesting: a multi-armed bandit model and the optimality of the myopic policy. IEEE J. Sel. Areas Commun. 33(3), 585–597 (2015)
15. Papoulis, A.: Probability, Random Variables, and Stochastic Processes. McGraw-Hill, New York (1965)
16. Bellman, R.: Dynamic Programming. Princeton University Press, Princeton (1957)
17. Putterman, M.L.: Markov Decision Processes: Discrete Stochastic Dynamic Programming. Wiley-Interscience, Hoboken (2005)
18. Mansour, Y., Singh, S.: On the complexity of policy iteration. In: Proceedings of the 15th International Conference on Uncertainty in AI, Stockholm, SE, pp. 401–408 (1999)
19. Kaelbling, L.P., Littman, M.L., Moore, A.W.: Reinforcement learning: a survey. J. Artif. Intell. Res. 4, 237–285 (1996)
20. Szepesvari, C.: Reinforcement Learning Algorithm for MDPs. Morganand Claypool Publishers, San Rafael (2010)
21. Singh, S., Jaakkola, T., Littman, M.L., Szepesvari, C.: Convergence results for single-step on-policy reinforcement-learning algorithms. Mach. Learn. 38(3), 287–308 (2000)
22. Corazza, M., Sangalli, A.: Q-learning and SARSA: a comparison between two intelligent stochastic control approaches for financial trading. University Ca' Foscari of Venice, Department of Economics Research Paper Series No. 15/WP/2015, 10 June 2015

23. IEEE 802.15.4e Draft Standard: Wireless Medium Access Control (MAC) and Physical Layer (PHY) Specifications for Low-Rate Wireless Personal Area Networks (WPANs), IEEE Std., March 2010

24. Chalasani, S., Conrad, J.: A survey of energy harvesting sources for embedded systems. In: Southeastcon, pp. 442–447. IEEE, April 2008

25. Galindo-Serrano, A., Giupponi, L., Dohler, M.: Cognition and docition in OFDMA-based femtocell networks. In: IEEE Globecomm, Miami, Florida, USA, pp. 6–10, December 2010

Spatial Guidance [Short Papers]

Smart Screen System for Smart Buildings Made of Tablets

Michal Hodoň(✉), Martin Húdik, Štefan Tóth, and Michal Kochláň

University of Žilina, Univerzitná 8215/1, 01026 Žilina, Slovak Republic
michal.hodon@fri.uniza.sk

Abstract. Smart screen system is a system that is used for displaying information about individual rooms, which are located in the building, in which the system is implemented. The system is built on the basis of using tablet as information and recording unit of each room.

For each room, respectively for each group of rooms, the Windows tablet is used as an information unit, which can be accessible remotely through the web server by any privileged user. The user can then dynamically enter various information, which are then displayed to all those interested. According to the type of room, different data can be displayed - e.g. current room schedule (meetings, lectures, telco, …), presence of persons (business trip, lunch, consultations, …), etc.

Keywords: Tablet · Smart building · Office · Screen label

1 Problem Description

In any building, where the people are spread across different spaces, a kind of scheduling process is important, that people can meet, share rooms, performs workshops and so on. Global or local on-line calendars are used for helping the people with this process. This works really good. Until someone goes wrong, and just take the meeting room without the reservation check. Or not mentioning to anybody, where exactly within the building is the meeting located. If the only possible contact is just his phone - often forgotten in an office - meeting scenario is broken.

A web based meeting scheduler software which allows to quickly and efficiently book and arrange meetings, conferences and other real or virtual sessions within conference rooms with a very easy to use interface could provide the solution. The attendants can easily book meeting rooms by just requesting an administrator, or just through simple logging into the system under assigned account data. Then the available slots can be seen and the dedicated rooms can be booked. book the rooms using your own user account. These tasks are mostly done via a simple web user interface or through individual Calendars or E-mail Clients.

According to the report of Markets and Markets [1], the global smart building market has witnessed a significant demand with growth which is encouraged by the rising demand for smart buildings in the commercial and residential sectors. Wireless technology is expected to have a great potential to grow during the forecast period, due to increasing interest of people towards energy efficient technologies and wire free tools

© Springer International Publishing AG 2017
G. Eichler et al. (Eds.): I4CS 2017, CCIS 717, pp. 185–190, 2017.
DOI: 10.1007/978-3-319-60447-3_13

that make the communication system function smoothly. Exact numbers can be found in the quoted report but are quite encouraging.

The above mentioned facts motivated different manufacturers from around the world to come out with such solutions, which can cover all of its basic features:

- User GUI made of easy-accessible web page together with interactive screen & touch panels fasten at each meeting room location.
- Remote management for flat configuration, pushed notifications, so the screens can be continuously updated.
- Support of basic e-mail clients and servers (Microsoft® Outlook®, Lotus Notes®, Google Calendar®).

With regards to previous, some real product examples are described below:

1. RoomWizard System [2] with 7″ capacitive touch screen for the room reservation adjustment and status lights – red or green - which show the room availability. The system provides a kind of analytics console which records room occupancy and reservation patterns, then generate reports to provide insight into space utilization.
2. Meetio Room application [3] is based on a preinstalled commercial grade 10″ tabletbuilt for 24/7 screen use. The tablet connects through Wi-Fi or RJ45 and can be powered by DC power adapter or through Power over Ethernet (PoE). The application supports over 20 languages.
3. Evoko Room Manager System [4] is famous for its design with green or red background illumination visible from a distance which shows whether the room is free or occupied. Integrated statistical function allows user to optimize the use of company resources. Decision-making support allows users to optimize the scheduling scheme.
4. Many other solutions, e.g. [5], are based on the special, dedicated, wall-mount tablet computers, with integrated operating systems (Windows®, Android®, Linux), where just the software implementation makes the difference between the single solutions. Such "raw" tablets can be cheaply purchased from Asian manufacturers [6], and it is just the application, what makes the added value and differs the products from each other.

Some system examples can be seen in the figure below [2, 4] (Fig. 1).

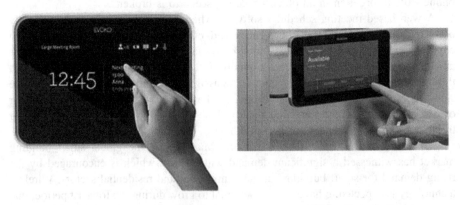

Fig. 1. Some examples of room-management-system. (Color figure online)

Taking into account the advantages named above, the system has far more practical features than described. If the room occupancy is scheduled, different management schemes can be applied defining behavior of any smart-building system. For example in [7], there was presented a smart meeting room scheduling and management system which could detect occupancy status of meeting rooms in a real time and integrate this information into the scheduling application to support ad-hoc meetings and increase room utilization. In [8], an approach to save the meeting room energy by more intelligent meetings assigning to the available rooms was presented. The authors determine the key factors affecting the building energy consumption with respect to the meeting assignment, and develop the energy savings model. Using this model, the authors show how meeting room, meeting schedule, and weather related parameters affect the energy savings potential of smart meeting scheduling.

2 Smart Screen System

With respect to previous information, our solution is almost the same - easy-to-implement solution that is used for displaying information about individual rooms and persons, which are located and working in the building, where the system is installed. For each room, not only the meeting room, the Prestigio® 10" tablet with OS Windows® installed, is used as an information unit, which can be accessible remotely through the web server by any privileged user. The user can then dynamically enter various information, which are then displayed to all those interested. According to the type of room, different data can be displayed - e.g. current room schedule (meetings, lectures, telco, ...), presence of persons (business trip, lunch, consultations, ...), etc. The tablet device can be also used as an intelligent terminal that provides the users with a variety of information with direct interaction to persons/devices belonging to the room (e.g. leaving a message for the person absent from the office, contact options,...).

The product, as hardware installation, together with the service, which runs on an installed HW infrastructure, are based on the utilization of current high-end technologies, which makes them really value added. Utilization of tablet PC for the purpose of IoT end-device is quite non-traditional solution, which due to the very good ratio between its costs and performance offers almost unlimited opportunities.

Since the system solution is based on the utilization of tablet devices, which comprise almost whole physical layer at the client site, the system hardware can be described as AAA - easily available, accessible and applicable. It is only necessary to fix up a sufficient number of supported tablets, to fix them on the wall, to set up an Internet connection as well as power feeding for tablets and to install an appropriate application. Then, all other adjustments can be made remotely, according to the single installation specifications (Fig. 2).

The tablet (Tablet Application) can be remotely accessed through the web interface (User Web Application) or via authentication on site by using RFID/NFC communication. The whole system infrastructure is created through Admin Web Application. Additional application options are related to the integration of other peripherals - alarm (PIR sensors, cameras), opening the door by card/phone (RFID, NFC), etc. For this purpose, tablet USB port is used together with communication gateway assuring the

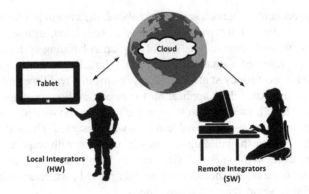

Fig. 2. Installation scheme of smart screen system.

connectivity with other sensors through dedicated communication buses (SPI, I2C, USART). A simple block diagram of the system is shown in the Fig. 3.

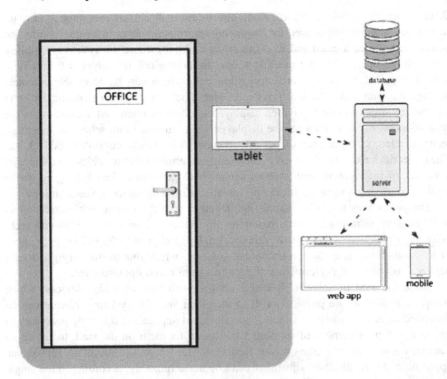

Fig. 3. Simple block diagram of the smart screen system.

The system architecture is due to the solution universality based on the usage of web applications (Java, Javascript) + HTML5. The GUI runs as a web application directly in the web browser of each system devices (tablet, desktop PC,...). This guarantees the platform independence of the solutions. Block diagram of the system architecture is shown in the Fig. 4.

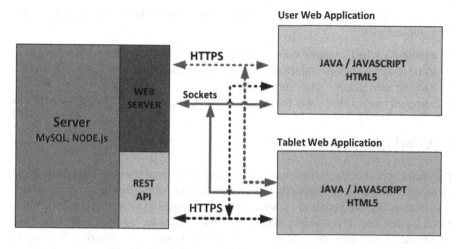

Fig. 4. Block diagram of the system architecture.

The pilot installation of the system was performed in the new building of Research Centre of the University of Žilina in Žilina, Slovakia, Slovakia, where the system consisted of 40 tablets was successfully installed (Fig. 5).

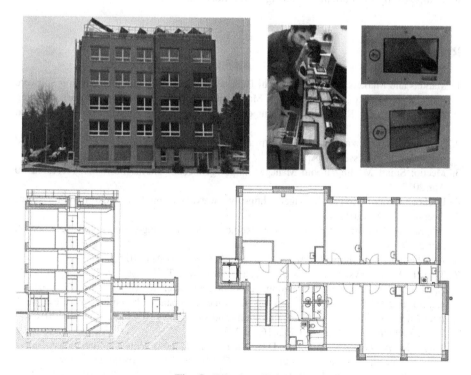

Fig. 5. Pilot installation.

In the pilot installation, different advancements opposite to similar systems, has been implemented:

- remote door bell - remote door opening through Bluetooth relay;
- VoIP communication - tablet as communication unit using Ozeki C# SIP Stack;
- building navigation - maps integrated;
- emergency navigation - after the electricity black-out, automated navigation to the exit.

3 Conclusion

The social impact of the system was evaluated on the basis of the testing application. We found out that using our system (in test scenario) make people feel more comfortable in environment that the people are working in. They seemed to be less stressed when they could see that there is possibility to use interactive system for the dedicated tasks. Other pilot installation is now discussed with the Žilina Hospital representatives. We decided to orient into the problematic of patient navigation in hospitals. In many cases, it is really tough to come into the right place, especially in such wide areas such the hospitals are. This is the problem of patients who have to come to the doctor/specialist for the first time, or for elderly people who have the orientation/navigation problems in this rush world. A kind of intuitive intelligent navigation system could bring significant behavior into their treatment since the treatment - from the viewpoint of hospital management - starts already by the patient's entering of the hospital.

References

1. Markets and Markets: The report "Smart Building Market by Building Automation Software (Intelligent Security Systems, Energy Management, Infrastructure Management), Building Type (Commercial, Residential, Government), Services (Professional and Managed) - Global Forecast to 2021"
2. Steelcase: RoomWizard Homepage. https://www.steelcase.com/products/scheduling-systems/roomwizard/. Accessed 30 Apr 2017
3. Meetio: Smart Meeting Room Manager. https://getmeetio.com/meetio-room/. Accessed 30 Apr 2017
4. Evoko: Evoko Room Manager. https://www.evoko.se/products/evoko-room-manager/. Accessed 30 Apr 2017
5. Netpractise: LBfoster. http://www.netpractise.com/room-booking-systems.php. Accessed 30 Apr 2017
6. Alibaba hqmepage. https://www.alibaba.com/. Accessed 30 Apr 2017
7. Tran, L.D., Stojcevski, A., Pham, T.C., de Souza-Daw, T., Nguyen, N.T., Nguyen, V.Q., Nguyen, C.M.: A smart meeting room scheduling and management system with utilization control and ad-hoc support based on real-time occupancy detection. In: IEEE Sixth International Conference on Communications and Electronics (ICCE), 27–29 July 2016, Ha Long, Vietnam. doi:10.1109/CCE.2016.7562634
8. Majumdar, A., Zhang, Z., Albonesi, D.H.: Characterizing the benefits and limitations of smart building meeting room scheduling. In: ACM/IEEE 7th International Conference on Cyber-Physical Systems (ICCPS), 11–14 April 2016. doi:10.1109/ICCPS.2016.7479070

A Realistic Location Service for VANETs

Tawfiq Nebbou[1], Hacène Fouchal[2]([⊠]), Mohamed Lehsaini[1],
and Marwane Ayaida[2]

[1] STIC Laboratory, Tlemcen University, Tlemcen, Algeria
tawfiq.nebbou@gmail.com, m_lehsaini@mail.univ-tlemcen.dz
[2] CReSTIC, Université de Reims Champagne-Ardenne, Reims, France
{hacene.fouchal,marwane.ayaida}@univ-reims.fr

Abstract. Position-based routing also called geographic routing is considered a more promising routing approach for highly dynamic and mobile networks like Vehicular Ad-hoc Networks (VANETs). In this kind of networks, the high-speed mobility of vehicles causes rapid changes in vehicles density and limited-time communication links. Hence, the need of location service has become extremely important to be able to find the position of a target node in a very short time.

This paper proposes a realistic location service for unicast routing over VANETs in an urban environment. The proposed approach is able to find the path with higher connectivity in urban environment by exploiting information of each vehicle in the network to reach the destination. For this reason, we used a new metric called Link Connectivity (LC) in order to find the path with higher connectivity between the source vehicle and the destination vehicle.

Keywords: VANETs · Location-based services · Geographic routing protocols · Mobility

1 Introduction

Vehicular Ad-hoc Networks (VANETs) are an emerging technology of wireless communication that allows to form self-organized networks. In VANETs, communication among vehicles can be carried out using Vehicle-to-Vehicle (V2V) communications or Vehicle-to-Infrastructure (V2I) communications. Moreover, VANETS share some common features with Mobile Ad-hoc Networks (MANETs), namely in terms of self-organization of the nodes. However, they also differs in some issues: in VANETs, the level of node's mobility is generally higher and the mobility is constrained by the roads and the nodes are not so constrained in terms of energy, computing and location since the devices are carried by vehicles. Indeed, in VANETs the high mobility of vehicles and the short-range communications result frequent network topology changes. This causes serious challenges to data dissemination since messages cannot be easily delivered to destination node.

© Springer International Publishing AG 2017
G. Eichler et al. (Eds.): I4CS 2017, CCIS 717, pp. 191–196, 2017.
DOI: 10.1007/978-3-319-60447-3_14

The features of VANETs make topology-based routing protocols designed for the MANETs unsuitable to VANETs since the nodes in this kind of networks are highly mobile which causes frequent changes in topology and consequently the probability of a successful reception of the delivered messages will be very low. Moreover, in topology-based routing protocols either in reactive or proactive mode the links between the nodes are discovered and maintained through periodical Hello packets exchange. Thereby, to overtake this limit we should minimise the sending period of Hello messages, which generates a large overhead. However, in position-based routing protocols such as GSR [10], GPSR [6], or GyTAR [5] the nodes use the location of their neighbors and the location of the destination node to determine the neighbor that forwards the packet to destination. These protocols require information about the position of the nodes, which is possible and less expensive in VANETs since most vehicles are equipped with GPS (Global Positioning System) device in order to find its own geographic position as a localization system. Most of the time, mobile nodes do not need to store any route or routing table to the destination.

This paper proposes a realistic location service for unicast routing over VANETs.

The remainder of the paper is organized as follows. Section 2 is dedicated to related works. Section 3 details our contribution. Section 4 concludes the study and gives some hints about future works.

2   Related Works

In the literature there are two ways to handle location services: A flooding-based technique which is a reactive or a proactive service or a synchronization-based technique which is based on a quorum method or a hierarchy method. The flooding proactive approach is simple to be implemented but generates a high overhead load since each node should send its position to the whole network.

The flooding reactive approach reduces the overhead but introduces a higher latency. This is due to the fact that when a node needs to send a message, it needs first to have the response to its location request sent over the network.

The synchronization-based technique aims to split the network on groups which are not disjoint as in the quorum approach or which are hierarchical with disjonction as in Grid Location Service (GLS) [9] or without disjonction as the Hierarchical Location Service (HLS) [7].

We have proposed in [2] a hybrid approach, denoted mobility-Prediction-based Hybrid Routing and Hierarchical Location Service (PHRHLS), coupling a VANET routing protocol, the Greedy Perimeter Stateless Routing (GPSR), and the Hierarchical Location Service (HLS). In [1], we have focused only on the hybrid part. Most of these approaches are difficult to be implemented in real VANETs deployment since they generate either higher overhead or higher latency. In this paper, we propose a simple approach to provide a location service in urban environments which could be implemented easily.

Routing protocols must choose some criteria to make routing decisions, for instance the number of hops, latency, transmission power, bandwidth, etc. The topology-based routing protocols suffer from heavy discovery and maintenance phases, lack of scalability and high mobility effects short links. Therefore, geographic routing protocols are suitable for large scale dynamic networks. The first routing protocol using the geographic information is the *Location-Aided Routing (LAR)* [8]. This protocol used the geographic information in the route discovery. This latter is initiated in a *Request Zone*. If the request does not succeed, it initiates another request with a larger *Request Zone* and the decision is made on a routing table. Another geographic routing protocol is the *Geographic Source Routing (GSR)* [10]. It combines geographical information and urban topology (street awareness). The sender calculates the shorter path (using Djikstra algorithm) to the destination from a map location information. Then, it selects a sequence of intersections (anchor-based) by which the data packet has to travel, thus forming the shortest path routing. To send messages from one intersection to another, it uses the greedy forwarding approach. The choice of intersections is fixed and does not consider the spatial and temporal traffic variations. Therefore, it increases the risk of choosing streets where the connectivity is not guaranteed and losing packets. Like GSR, *Anchor-based Street and Traffic Aware Routing (A-STAR)* [11] is anchor-based. However, it reflects the streets characteristics. A connectivity rate is assigned to the roads depending on the capacity and the number of bus using it. This metric is used in addition to traditional metrics (distance, hops, latency) when making routing decisions. As a consequence, the streets taken by busses are not always the main roads where connectivity is ensured and the greedy approach does not consider the speed and direction for the next hop selection. This is why *improved Greedy Traffic Aware Routing (GyTAR)* [4] was designed as a geographical routing protocol adapted to urban environments and managing the traffic conditions. A sender selects dynamically an intersection (depending on the streets connectivity) through which a packet must be forwarded to reach the destination node. Between intersections, an improved greedy approach to forward packets is used. GyTAR takes advantage from the urban roads characteristics, selects robust paths with high connectivity and minimises the number of hops to reach an intersection. We have compared in [3] three location-based services: Reactive Location Service (RLS), Grid Location Service (GLS) and Hierarchical Location Service (HLS) while coupled to the well known geographic routing protocol Greedy Perimeter Stateless Routing (GPSR).

3   Contribution

In this section, we propose a Realistic Location Service represented by RSUs (Road Side Units). This algorithm will help to establish a path between a source node and a destination node. The proposed routing algorithm enables to find the best path between two nodes based on the connectivity criterion in order to ensure a successful reception by the destination node with help of a location system (RSU). For this issue, we assume that in each intersection, a Road Side Unit (RSU) is placed, and every vehicle has a static digital map to get the position of all RSUs. Indeed, each vehicle has also the knowledge of its geographic position using its GPS receiver, speed and direction of movement. This allows the vehicle to find the closest RSU in order to send a request about the path to the destination.

3.1 Realistic Location Service

Realistic Location System is a set of RSUs connected and distributed throughout the network as shown in Fig. 1. Each RSU plays the role of a location server and maintains a part of all vehicles information. These vehicles's information will be periodically shared with the others location servers. The role of a location server is not only to maintain the vehicle's information but also to calculate the best path between a source vehicle and a destination vehicle when it receives a route request from a vehicle (the sender node).

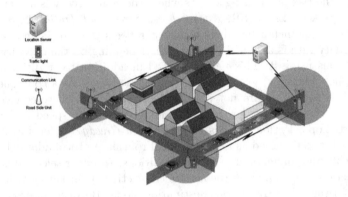

Fig. 1. Location system communication network

3.2 Proposed Algorithm

Since each location server maintains and shares its part of vehicles information, it has information about all vehicles in the network. According to all these vehicles information, the location server is able to represent the network with a graph $G = (V, E)$ comprising a set V of vertices (intersections) together with a set E of edges (roads) wherein each edge is associated with two vertices. Moreover, Link Connectivity (LC) is a function related to edge in order to calculate the value of connectivity of an edge. Formally, LC can be calculated as follows:

$$LC : E \rightarrow [0, 1[$$

$$LC_{Edge} = \frac{MLL_{Edge}}{R_{tr}} \tag{1}$$

where MLL_{edge} is the Mean Link Liaison between all vehicles in the given edge and R_{tr} represents the range of transmission, the Mean Link Liaison (MLL) can be calculated as follows:

$$MLL_{Edge} = \frac{\sum_{i=1}^{N-1}(R_{tr} - dist(vehicle_i - vehicle_{i+1}))}{N-1} \tag{2}$$

where N represents the number of vehicles in the given edge and $vehicle_i$ represents the vehicle number "i" in such edge.

3.3 Routing Algorithm

Route Request. When the source vehicle has to send some data to destination vehicle, then, initially it sends a Route-Request message to the closest RSU and this message to the other RSUs using a routing scheme based on the Greedy Forwarding approach. We assume that each vehicle knows the geographical position of all RSUs in the network, this information is obtained using the map already embedded.

Route Reply. When the RSU receives a Route-Request message from the sender vehicle, it will calculate the best path between the source vehicle and the destination vehicle. This path is composed of a sequence of intersections through which the packets will transit to reach the destination vehicle. Finally, the path found will be encapsulated in a message Route-Reply and forwarded to the sending vehicle using a routing process based on the Greedy Forwarding approach.

Update Position Table. Each RSU maintains an update of a table, which contains a list of positions, speeds and time stamps. When a RSU receives a vehicle beacon or a local table from an other RSUs, it updates the positions, speeds and the receiving times of theses vehicles. The position table will be shared with all others RSUs periodically. The objective is that each RSU knows the positions of all vehicles in the network.

Forwarding Between Two Intersections. Once the source vehicle receives the Route-Replay message, it adds it in its header packet and deduces the destination intersection. Then, it forwards the packet to the closest neighbor to the destination intersection using a routing scheme based on improved greedy forwarding approach.

4 Conclusion and Future Works

We have proposed a simple location service algorithm which could be implemented in urban environments.

   This proposed location system exploits better all the information of the network to locate a vehicle and determinate the best path. However, this solution needs an aware-infrastructure which increases the cost of the network deployment.

As future works, we intend to implement our protocol on a simulator and run it on a large network in order to handle the scalability of our algorithm approach and decreasing the number of RSUs by using a distributed location system algorithm.

References

1. Ayaida, M., Barhoumi, M., Fouchal, H., Ghamri-Doudane, Y., Afilal, L.: HHLS: a hybrid routing technique for vanets. In: 2012 IEEE Global Communications Conference, GLOBECOM 2012, Anaheim, CA, USA, 3–7 December 2012, pp. 44–48. IEEE (2012)
2. Ayaida, M., Barhoumi, M., Fouchal, H., Ghamri-Doudane, Y., Afilal, L.: PHRHLS: a movement-prediction-based joint routing and hierarchical location service for vanets. In: Proceedings of IEEE International Conference on Communications, ICC 2013, Budapest, Hungary, 9–13 June 2013, pp. 1424–1428. IEEE (2013)
3. Ayaida, M., Fouchal, H., Afilal, L., Ghamri-Doudane, Y.: A comparison of reactive, grid and hierarchical location-based services for vanets. In: Proceedings of the 76th IEEE Vehicular Technology Conference, VTC Fall 2012, Quebec City, QC, Canada, 3–6 September 2012, pp. 1–5. IEEE (2012)
4. Jerbi, M., Senouci, S.-M., Meraihi, R., Ghamri-Doudane, Y.: An improved vehicular ad hoc routing protocol for city environments. In: IEEE International Conference on Communications, ICC 2007, pp. 3972–3979, June 2007
5. Jerbi, M., Senouci, S.M., Rasheed, T., Ghamri-Doudane, Y.: Towards efficient geographic routing in urban vehicular networks. IEEE Trans. Veh. Technol. **58**(9), 5048–5059 (2009)
6. Karp, B., Kung, H.T.: GPSR: greedy perimeter stateless routing for wireless networks. In: Proceedings of the 6th Annual International Conference on Mobile Computing and Networking, MobiCom 2000, pp. 243–254. ACM, New York (2000)
7. Kiess, W., Fussler, H., Widmer, J., Mauve, M.: Hierarchical location service for mobile ad-hoc networks. SIGMOBILE Mob. Comput. Commun. Rev. **8**, 47–58 (2004)
8. Ko, Y.-B., Vaidya, N.H.: Location-aided routing (LAR) in mobile ad hoc networks. Wirel. Netw. **6**(4), 307–321 (2000)
9. Li, J., Jannotti, J., De Couto, D.S.J., Karger, D.R., Morris, R.: A scalable location service for geographic ad hoc routing. In: Proceedings of the 6th Annual International Conference on Mobile Computing and Networking (MobiCom 2000), pp. 120–130. ACM, New York (2000)
10. Lochert, C., Hartenstein, H., Tian, J., Fussler, H., Hermann, D., Mauve, M.: A routing strategy for vehicular ad hoc networks in city environments. In: IEEE IV2003 Intelligent Vehicles Symposium. Proceedings (Cat. No. 03TH8683), pp. 156–161, June 2003
11. Seet, B.-C., Liu, G., Lee, B.-S., Foh, C.-H., Wong, K.-J., Lee, K.-K.: A-STAR: a mobile ad hoc routing strategy for metropolis vehicular communications. In: Mitrou, N., Kontovasilis, K., Rouskas, G.N., Iliadis, I., Merakos, L. (eds.) NETWORKING 2004. LNCS, vol. 3042, pp. 989–999. Springer, Heidelberg (2004). doi:10.1007/978-3-540-24693-0_81

Author Index

Printed in the United States
By Bookmasters